THE BIGFOOT FILES

The Reality of Bigfoot in North America

Adventures Unlimited Press

THE BIGFOOT FILES

The Reality of Bigfoot in North America

David Hatcher Childress

Adventures Unlimited Press

The Bigfoot Files: The Reality of Bigfoot in North America

ISBN: 978-1-948803-47-2

Published by:
Adventures Unlimited Press
One Adventure Place
Kempton, Illinois 60946 USA
auphq@frontiernet.net

AdventuresUnlimitedPress.com

Cover illustration by Mister Sam Shearon
www.mistersamshearon.bigcartel.com

THE BIGFOOT FILES

The Reality of Bigfoot in North America

Thanks to all sorts of people who have made
great contributions to bigfoot research including:

Colin and Janet Bord, John Green, Christopher Murphy, Thomas
Steenburg, Loren Coleman, Robert Robinson, David Paulides, Matthew
Moneymaker, Craig Woolheater, J. Robert Alley, Chas Berlin, David
Hancock, Grover Krantz, Jeff Meldrum, Rene Dahinden, Roger
Patterson, Bob Gimlim, Peter Guttilla, and the whole host of bigfoot
researchers out there—there are many of you and I cannot possibly name
you all. Please look through the bibliography, which I tried to make as
thorough as possible, to find the many other bigfoot researchers over the
years. And to the many other researchers—old and new—keep on hiking
down those lost trails, but watch where you are going.

An early drawing of the Mayat Datat from 1889 on the Tule Reservation.

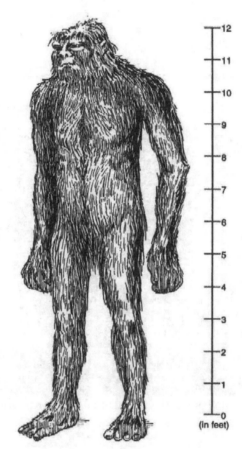

12
11
10
9
8
7
6
5
4
3
2
1
0
(in feet)

Have you seen a twelve-foot hairy giant?

TABLE OF CONTENTS

CHAPTER 1

THE EMERGENCE
OF BIGFOOT

Walk out of any doorway
Feel your way, feel your way like the day before
Maybe you'll find direction
Around some corner where it's been waiting to meet you.
—Grateful Dead, *Box of Rain*

Today the creature called sasquatch or bigfoot is known throughout the world. He is in advertisements, movies, cartoons, product names and a host of other media. Bigfoot is everywhere, it seems. Do the creatures known as sasquatch, bigfoot, yeti, and other names really exist? If so, where is the official record for this elusive animal?

[Note that the terms for bigfoot will not be capitalized in this book, since I think they are comparable to words like bears, cats, and unicorns.]

The evidence is there for the continued existence of a missing link that is similar to man, albeit a hairy man—often a large hairy man. He and his kin do not use fire. They do not have the ability to speak as we do, but they do make whistling, screaming and other sounds. They are both curious about and frightened of humans, who have been encroaching for many centuries on their territory.

This territory is astonishingly large. As I attempted to demonstrate in my book *Bigfoot Nation* the extent of bigfoot activity in the USA and Canada is astounding. While sasquatch are now officially recognized by Canada with stamps and commemorative coins, the USA has yet to officially recognize or protect this endangered animal.

The Emergence of Bigfoot

There may be several reasons for this. The first is that it is very problematic to recognize the existence of bigfoot and the threat that he may pose to humans and livestock. While the existence of bigfoot is debated—and possibly hidden—he is apparently real and exists on the fringes of society, occasionally being seen by people who then report the encounter to a news organization.

We should be thankful to all of these news organizations and their stringers. We need this reporting and it has become more common for news media to feature such phenomena. The majority of Americans and Canadians—and others around the world—have heard about bigfoot and yeti. Many Americans and Canadians believe in sasquatch and bigfoot. The belief in sasquatch and bigfoot is especially strong with Native American and First Nation tribes who often live on the edge of wilderness areas and national parks. You might say that city folk tend to not believe in bigfoot, while the country folk tend to believe in the critter, especially if they have heard local stories.

There are convenience stores in Indiana named "Bigfoot" and plenty of movies about this hairy creature, many of which portray bigfoot as a very dangerous monster—the original boogey man. Bigfoot is afraid of man but is very curious about him. It seems that bigfoot in general are not really afraid of children or women. There have been numerous stories of women and children who have disappeared while hiking on their own. If a bigfoot has been watching a child or woman for a long time he might decide to suddenly confront that person. This could mean that an abduction will occur as well as the sudden death of the victim from the powerful arms of a bigfoot. This has happened to men as well.

Early Bigfoot Reports

In the very early days of newspapers in North America there came the occasional report of a "wildman"; starting around 1869 the word "gorilla" was used. Native Americans had their own names such as "skookoom" and "sasquatch." The term "boogey man" is thought to have arisen because of bigfoot. The name "bigfoot" was coined in 1958 and terms like "skunk ape" and "swamp booger" have come into common use in the Southern United States. Curiously, bigfoot is rarely reported south of the border in Mexico or other countries.

The first bigfoot reports referred to wildmen and newspapers were springing up all over the eastern United States and Canada by the early 1800s. Probably the earliest known report of bigfoot comes from the Canadian Rockies. The incident occurred in Jasper, Alberta in 1811 when a British fur trader and explorer named David Thompson encountered giant footprints in the Athabasca River area. Said Thompson in his diary published by the *Oregon Historical Quarterly*, Number 15 (March-June 1914):

> I now recur to what I have already noticed in the early part of last winter, when proceeding up the Athabasca River ...we came to the track of a large animal, which measured fourteen inches in length by eight inches in breadth by a tape line. As the snow was about six inches in depth the track was well defined, and we could see it for a full hundred yards from us, this animal was proceeding from north to south. We did not attempt to follow it, we had not time for it, and the Hunters, eager as they are to follow and shoot every animal, made no attempt to follow this beast, for what could the balls of our fowling guns do against such an animal? Reports from old times had made the head branches of this River, and the Mountains in the vicinity the abode of one, or more, very large animals, to which I never appeared to give credence; for these reports appeared to arise from that fondness for the marvelous so common to mankind: but the sight of the track of that large a beast staggered me, and I often thought of it, yet never could bring myself to believe such an animal existed, but thought it might be the track of some Monster Bear.

1818 Report of a Wild Man of the Woods

The earliest newspaper report of a bigfoot seems to be an 1818 report from the *Exeter Watchman* dated September 22, 1818. It concerns a bigfoot being seen around the town of Ellisburgh near Sacket's Harbor which is on Lake Ontario in the very northwest section of Upstate New York. The story is from Sacket's Harbor and had the headline: "ANOTHER WONDER." The article went on to say:

Report says, that in the vicinity of Ellisburgh, was seen on the 30th, by a gentleman of unquestionable veracity, an animal resembling the Wild Man of the Woods. It is stated that he came from the woods within a few rods of this gentleman—that he stood and looked at him and then took his flight in a direction which gave a perfect view of him for some time. He is described as bending forward when running—hairy, and the heel of the foot narrow, spreading at the toes. Hundreds of persons have been in pursuit for several days, but nothing further is heard or seen of him.

The frequent and positive manner in which this story comes, induces us believe it. We wish not to impeach the veracity of this highly favored gentleman—yet, it is proper that such naturally improbable accounts should be established by the mouth, of at least two direct eyewitnesses to entitle them to credit.[3]

1839 Reports about Bigfoot in Indiana and Wisconsin

Some 20 years later we get a report from December 1839 in La Porte County, Indiana. There a "wild child" was seen repeatedly around Fish Lake and was reported in the *Michigan City Gazette* that said, "It is reported to be about four feet high and covered with a coat of light chestnut-colored hair. It runs with great velocity, and when pursued, as has often been the case, it sets up the most frightening and hideous yells, and seems to make efforts at speaking."[11]

Another early report comes from 1839 concerning an event in Wisconsin. The highly detailed story was reported in the *Boston Daily Times* on April 1, 1839. The article was sent to Cryptomundo by Scott McClean, who wondered if it was just a coincidence that the bizarre story was published on April Fool's Day. Still, the story has a ring of authenticity to it. The story is of a lumber steamship that goes up the Mississippi to Prairie Du Chien in Wisconsin and then continues north to what is now known as the Minnesota River, but was called the Saint Peters River back then. While spending time at this northerly timber camp the lumbermen encounter—and capture—a bigfoot. The article was entitled, "When Will Wonders Cease?"

The article describes the capture of a bigfoot which is called a "monster" and described as about 8 feet tall, hairy with powerful arms. At one point it is called an orangutan. Driving it out into a field, the group of men are able subdue the creature and tie him up. He is taken back to the camp in a litter dragged by a horse where it howls all night. Two small "cubs" then show up as the creature howls from the camp. They are easily captured and fed. The bigfoot, possibly a female bigfoot and mother of the young ones, refuses to eat for some days but eventually become docile and begins eating. The article speaks of the adult as a male but it is probably a female.

Eventually, the adult bigfoot and the two small "cubs" are placed on a steamer headed for St. Louis and other ports on the Mississippi. They are never heard of again and we do not know whether they appeared in some circus or travelling show around 1840. Perhaps there was an opportunity for the bigfoot and cubs to escape or something else happened shortly after their capture and departure on the steamer. We simply do not know what happened.

1847: Mount St. Helens a Forbidden Area

An explorer in the Pacific Northwest, the artist Paul Kane, comments on a strange creature in his book *The Wanderings of an Artist.* His entry for March 26, 1847 reads:

> When we arrived at the mouth of the Kattlepoutal River, 36 miles from Vancouver [Washington], I stopped to make a sketch of the volcano, Mt. St. Helens, distant, I suppose, about 30 or 40 miles. This mountain has never been visited by either whites or Indians; the latter assert that it is inhabited by a race of beings of a different species, who are cannibals, whom they hold in great dread …these superstitions are taken from a man, who they say, went into the mountain with another, and escaped the fate of his companion, who was eaten by the "skoocooms," or "evil genii." I offered a considerable bribe to any Indian who would accompany me in its exploration but could not find one hardy enough to venture there.[21]

It would seem that this mysterious and feared race of skoocooms are in fact bigfoot. Mount St. Helens is an area where many bigfoot have been reported.

1851: Two Hunters See Bigfoot in Arkansas

Colin and Janet Bord report in their book *Bigfoot Casebook* that two hunters in Greene County, Arkansas saw a herd of cattle that was being chased by a bigfoot. They watched the creature for some time which was "an animal bearing the unmistakable likeness of humanity. He was of gigantic stature, the body being covered with hair and head with long locks that fairly enveloped the neck and shoulders."[3]

A man named John Weeks recalled how his grandfather told him about being a gold prospector in California's Mount Shasta area in the 1850s. The Mount Shasta area is known to be an area of many bigfoot sightings—this seems to be the earliest. Said Weeks:

> My grandfather prospected for gold in the eighteen fifties throughout the region described as being the home of the Snowman. Upon grandfather's return from to the East he told stories of seeing hairy giants in the vicinity of Mount Shasta. These monsters had long arms but short legs. One of them picked up a 20-foot section of a sluiceway and smashed it to bits against a tree.
>
> When grandfather told us these stories, we didn't believe him at all. Now, after reading your article, it turns out he wasn't as big a liar as we youngsters thought he was.[3]

1868 Report of an Ape Man in Alabama

An early bigfoot/skunk ape report came from Alabama in 1868. Chad Arment, author of *Historical Bigfoot*, reproduces a fascinating story about a giant wild apeman that was seen near Meadville, in Franklin County, Alabama where men with hunting dogs:

> ...discovered the tracks of the game in some miry places, which appeared similar to the track of a human foot; and they observed, also, that the toes of one foot turned backward. On coming up with the dogs, who were now baying, they beheld a frightful looking creature, of about the average height of man, but with far greater muscular development, standing menacingly a few yards in front of

16

the dogs. It had long, coarse hair flowing from its head and reaching near its knees; its entire body, also, seemed to be covered with hair of two or three inches' length, which was of a dark brown color. From its upper jaw projected two very large tusks, several inches long. ...it fled toward the Mississippi River, and was not overtaken again until within a few yards of the bank. When the party came up with the dogs the second time, the monster was standing erect before them, none of them having yet dared to clinch with it. But when the dogs were urged by their masters, they endeavored to seize it, when it reached forward and grabbed one of them, and taking it in its hands, pressed it against its trunk, which pierced it through and killed it instantly. Becoming alarmed at this display of strength, the hunters fired several shots at the creature, which caused it to leap into the river... after sinking and rising several times, it swam to the Louisiana shore and disappeared.[44]

Arment says that this story came from the *Daily Herald* of Dubuque, Iowa for June 27, 1868, and we see that we might conclude from this account that bigfoot is a good swimmer! Indeed, the common southern terms of grassman and swamp ape indicate that these creatures are semi-aquatic apemen who are good swimmers and can live in swamps and remote river valleys that contain dense forests and brush. The large tusks on this bigfoot, from the upper jaw, are unexplained and this is not something that is typically reported. They would seem to be describing large canine teeth and perhaps the bigfoot was missing other teeth.

1869: A Gorilla in Ohio

Another early bigfoot incident occurred in Ohio and was reported in the *Minnesota Weekly Record* on Saturday, January 23, 1869. The title of the story was "A Gorilla in Ohio." The first gorilla was captured in Liberia, Africa in 1847 and the word came into the English language at that time. Said the 1869 article:

Gallipolis [Ohio] is excited over a wild man, who is reported to haunt the woods near that city. He goes naked, is covered with hair, is gigantic in height, and "his eyes start from their sockets." A carriage, containing a man and daughter, was attacked by him a few days ago. He is said to have bounded at the father, catching him in a grip like that of a vice, hurling him to the earth, falling on him and endeavoring to bite and to scratch like a wild animal. The struggle was long and fearful, rolling and wallowing in the deep mud, [half] suffocated, sometimes beneath his adversary, whose burning and maniac eyes glared into his own with murderous and savage intensity. Just as he was about to become exhausted from his exertions, his daughter, taking courage at the imminent danger of her parent, snatched up a rock and hurling it at the head of her father's would be murderer, was fortunate enough to put an end to the struggle by striking him somewhere about the ear. The creature was not stunned, but feeling unequal to further exertion, slowly got up and retired into the neighboring copse that skirted the road.[44]

It is interesting to note that this incident took place in Ohio but the newspaper clipping that we have of the story comes from a Minnesota newspaper. This shows us how newspapers were cropping up all over the place after the Civil War and that there were almost certainly newspapers in Ohio at this time that also carried this story. Many old newspapers no longer exist and often records of old issues are lost in fires and floods.

We also see with this story that until the name "bigfoot" came along in 1958, people struggled for a name for the creature they encountered. Gorilla is still used to occasionally describe bigfoot sightings (such as, "I took this picture of a gorilla in our back yard...").

Also in 1869, according to Janet and Colin Bord, in the Arcadia Valley of northwest Arkansas a bigfoot was seen repeatedly and it approached cabins, especially when the men were gone and only women and children were around. It was described as a "wild man, gorilla, or 'what is it?'" At one point over sixty of the local citizens got together to hunt the animal, which they called Old Sheff, and it disappeared for some days but then returned.

18

The Bords also chronicle another incident in 1869. A letter written by a man from Grayson, California to the Antioch *Ledger* says he witnessed a bigfoot playing with the sticks in his campfire. He was in an area called Orestimba Creek, about 20 miles north of Grayson, and had seen large footprints around his campsite. He was determined to see who or what it was that was visiting his camp while he was gone. He hid in some bushes nearby and waited. Said the man in his letter to the newspaper:

> Suddenly I was surprised by a shrill whistle such as boys produce with two fingers under their tongues, and turning quickly, I ejaculated, "Good God!" as I saw the object of my solicitude standing beside the fire, erect, and looking suspiciously around. It was the image of a man, but it could not have been human.
>
> I was never so benumbed with astonishment before. The creature, whatever it was, stood fully five feet high, and disproportionately broad and square at the fore shoulders, with arms of great length. The legs were very short and body long. The head was small compared with the rest of the creature, and appeared to be set upon his shoulders without a neck. The whole was covered with dark brown and cinnamon colored hair, quite long on some parts, that on the head standing in a shock and growing close down to the eyes, like a Digger Indian's.
>
> As I looked he threw his head back and whistled again, and then stopped and grabbed a stick from the fire. This he swung around, until the fire on the end had gone out, when he repeated the maneuver. I was dumb, almost and could only look. Fifteen minutes I sat and watched him as he whistled and scattered my fire about. I could easily have put a bullet through this head, but why should I kill him? Having amused himself, apparently, as he desired, with my fire, he started to go, and having gone a short distance he returned, and was joined by another—a female, unmistakably—when both turned and walked past me, within twenty yards of where I sat, and disappeared in the brush.[3]

It is unusual for bigfoot to play with a campfire and hold a burning torch. In this case the bigfoot was curious about the fire, but had no use for it. In another incident, also from 1869, a bigfoot—or wild man—was seen carrying a club by cowboys in northern Nevada near the Idaho border:

> ...A large party, armed and equipped, lately started in pursuit of "it," and one night a splendid view was obtained of the object which, it was concluded, had once been a white man, but was now covered with a coat of fine, long, hair, carried a club in the right hand and in the left a rabbit. The moment it caught sight of the party, as the moon shone out, it dashed past the camp "with the scream like the roar of a lion," brandished the huge club and attacked the horses in a perfect frenzy of madness.
>
> The savage bloodhounds which the party had brought along refused to pursue the object; and so the party hastily raised a log rampart for self-defense; but instead of making attack, the object merely uttered the most terrible cries through the night, and in the morning disappeared. It was evident, however, from the footprints, that the object would require a "pair of No. 9 shoes," and this is all we know. The party could have shot it on first seeing it, but failed to do so.[3]

It is interesting that the bigfoot carried a club. This is seen in other bigfoot reports, such as a sighting in Dover, New Jersey in 1894; an incident in Chesterfield, Idaho in 1902; and a sighting from Labrador, Canada in 1913. Also, it commonly believed that uses a club or tree branch to make loud knocks against a tree.[71] That the bloodhounds refused to follow or attack the creature is very standard in bigfoot reports, though there are incidents when dogs have engaged a bigfoot. There are also the occasional report of a bigfoot with a pet animal such as a dog, wolf, or even a big cat. We will explore all of this in the chapters to come.

It is also interesting to note the whistling sound that the man heard. Bigfoot are said to communicate in different ways and a strange whistling is often associated with bigfoot. They are said to make chattering sounds, similar to children, and to make loud, piercing screams. They are said to take tree limbs or other wooden clubs and bang them against a tree making a loud knocking sound. This tree knocking may be in the distance or very close and it seems to be a way of bigfoot communicating with each other over distances—perhaps to warn other bigfoot that invasive humans are in the area.

1871: Woman Kidnapped by Sasquatch

One of the early abduction stories involving sasquatch happened in 1871 on the Chehalis Reservation in northern British Columbia, an area of many bigfoot reports. In that year Stephanie Long was abducted while collecting cedar roots in the forest and was returned one year later in 1872. She said that one of the hairy giants that inhabited the region grabbed her and smeared tree sap on her eyes so she could not see where he was taking her. He took her to a cave somewhere where the sasquatch forced her to live with him and his elderly parents. "They fed me well," she reportedly said.

She convinced the bigfoot to take her back to her village and the bigfoot again took tree sap and put it on her eyelids so she could not see and took her to the vicinity of the village. She finally arrived back after one year missing and collapsed of exhaustion. She was put in a bed and that same night gave birth, but the infant died a few hours later. Interviewed in 1925 she said that she was glad the baby had died and she hoped she would never see the hairy giant again.[7]

This is an important story as the woman was still alive and photographed in 1925. It also foreshadows the many frightening stories of women and children being kidnapped by a bigfoot. Why would a bigfoot want to kidnap a woman or child? Perhaps out of curiosity,

Stephanie Long in 1941.

loneliness, or sexual desire. In the case of Stephanie Long in Canada, she was apparently abducted for sexual desire. She survived a year in captivity with a bigfoot and had his child—which died shortly afterwards. Many women or children abducted by a bigfoot may have not been so lucky.

1877: A Wild Man at the Smithsonian Institution

A newspaper report from the Washington, D.C. newspaper *The Daily Telegram* had an astonishing report on April 9, 1877 on its first page about a live "wild man" who was on display at the Smithsonian Institution. This newspaper report was dug up by bigfoot researcher Joe Fex and carried several headlines. The headlines started with "EXTRA: THE WILD MAN AT THE SMITHSONIAN." The second headline read, "HIS SAVAGE ATTACK UPON A YOUNG LADY," and finally, "HER CLOTHING IN RIBBONS," "HE WILL BE INCARCERATED IN AN IRON CAGE TO-DAY." The brief story went on to say:

> Among the curiosities from the Centennial, received by, and now on exhibition at the Smithsonian Institution, is a specimen of "Wild Man" who, although perfectly tame and subdued at Philadelphia, now has become unmanageable to such an extent that an iron cage had to be procured to prevent him from injuring people. The savage attack he made upon a young lady, some several days ago tearing her clothing in ribbons and bruising her severely before she could be rescued, was the principal reason a cage was ordered for him, and since the assault on the young lady eight men have alternately kept watch over him, night and day. The cage arrived at the Smithsonian on Saturday, and workmen were engaged yesterday (Sunday), in placing it into position. The creature will be incarcerated in it some time to-day.

So, here we have some pretty startling facts that can be identified directly from the article and by inference. These facts would be:

1. This would seem to be the first documented attack on a

The 1877 story of a bigfoot in Washington D.C. Courtesy of Joe Fex.

woman by a bigfoot. Bigfoot is attracted to human females and is generally not afraid of women or small children.

    2. He had been "subdued" in Philadelphia but was apparently from somewhere else.

    3. He had been brought to Washington, D.C. to be exhibited for the 1877 centennial celebrations.

    4. In April of 1877 the Smithsonian Institution was in

possession of a bigfoot and it was being exhibited in an iron cage.

5. This story of a captured bigfoot—in our nation's capital no less—is now part of a cover-up and conspiracy to keep the existence of bigfoot a secret. If bigfoot doesn't exist, then it would be impossible for him to have been on display in an iron cage in April of 1877.

Indeed, we have the first stark evidence with this story that—at least at one time—the various authorities in Washington were aware that rural America contained "wild men," what we would call bigfoot today.

What happened to this wild man in possession of the Smithsonian? One has to imagine that there would be another article or two out there a few days later on the subject. However, it would appear that talk of the wild man in an iron cage ceased and this creature disappeared from history. No scientific papers were written about this curious subject, despite the fact that he was being held at a prestigious museum. Is it possible that somewhere in the depths of the Smithsonian there is a whole file on this wild man? Perhaps his skeleton is preserved and on display, for the special eyes of only a few.

That is probably the most disturbing part of this news story, that some sort of cover-up is involved and like some post-Civil War *X-Files*, we have the government (or elements within) withholding information from the public at large. Is it because the reality of bigfoot is just too frightening?

1894: Man-Beast Stealing Chickens in Kentucky

A newspaper report from Dover, New Jersey on January 8, 1894 said that there was a wild man in the woods near Mine Hill. The wild man was hairy and naked, nearly six feet tall and had tried to get into some of the homes, apparently in search of food. A hunting party was organized to find the creature but nothing was found.[3]

In May of 1894 there were reports coming out of Deep Creek, Kentucky that a "man-beast" had been seen in the area and that chickens, eggs, young pigs and lambs had been missing from farms. A man named Joseph Ewalt had seen the creature and described it

24

as having "great long white hair hanging down from his head and face that was coarse as a horse's mane. His legs were covered with hair and the only article of clothing he wore was a piece of sheepskin over the lower portion of his body, reaching nearly for his knees. He said a light came from his eyes and mouth similar to fire."

Men in the area decided to try to catch the creature and started keeping an eye out for it. Then, one morning Eph Boston and his sons saw it making for their barn. They said it was a man-beast with clawed feet and cat-like hands. Soon it came rushing out of the barn grasping three chickens. Tom Boston shot at the creature but it continued to run and went into a nearby cave. They got their neighbors and entered the first part of the cave where they saw bones, feathers and such. Then they heard an "unearthly yell" and quickly retreated. All efforts to catch the beast failed, including smoking it out of the cave.

The Astonishing 1894 Bigfoot Photo

There is an astonishing photo from Canada taken in 1894 which would seem to be the oldest known photograph of bigfoot. Craig Woolheater posted the photo on his blog at Cryptomundo. com on November 16, 2006. The photo had originally been sent to Tom Biscardi by Lyle Billett of Victoria, Canada.

Fellow Cryptomundo blogger Loren Coleman found the photo on Woolheater's website and posted it again, where I saw it. The photo also appears in the updated version of the 1982 book *The Bigfoot Casebook* by Colin and Janet Bord.[4]

It is said that a picture tells a thousand words, and this photo says a lot. It does not seem to be a fake. The photo is cracked from a fold in the upper quarter. A sasquatch is lying on snow with its arms in front so the hairy hands can be seen. The face is hairy but not very detailed. Snowshoes can be seen at the left edge of the photo. There seems to be a fence and a building on the right side, just beneath the crack. The feet of the dead sasquatch are not seen, cropped out of the right side of the photo.

The story that this photo tells us is that in 1894 in the wilds of western Canada some trappers and mountain men encountered a bigfoot and shot him. It may have happened near their cabin. They took a photograph of it. But there is more: the photo had some

25

The complete bigfoot photo from 1894 showing a dead creature in Canada.

writing on the back of it, maybe in the hand of Lyle Billett.

The back of the photo bore this text:

Year 1894
Yalikom River Around Lilliott B.C.
Forestry-Hudsonbay Co.
They took the picture and the Guy that was in the picture went
& stole them back from the forestry records (hudsonbay co.) I
believe his last name was Holiday (Don't know the first name)
Never took all pictures (only one) and took pictures of the rest.
(Glass Plate Photography)

This is very interesting information and confirms what some have suspected for many years: there is something of a cover-up going on concerning evidence of bigfoot. We now get a more complete story: There was more than one photo and someone named Holiday apparently took the photos, or was pictured in one or more of them. He went to the forestry records of the Hudson's Bay Company where he "stole back" one of the photos—the number of photos taken of the bigfoot is not known. We might guess that there were four or five original, glass plate photos.

So, some trappers shot and killed a bigfoot in 1894, and they worked for the Hudson's Bay Company, Canada's earliest trading company, founded in 1670. The Hudson's Bay Company is no ordinary company; it was the de facto government in large parts of

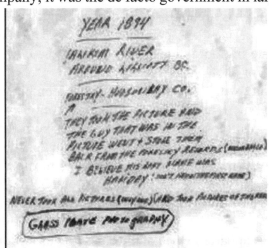

The backside of the bigfoot pboto from 1894.

North America before European states or the United States were able to lay claim to areas in this vast domain. Today it is one of the oldest operating companies in the world. Begun as a fur trading company on the Hudson Bay, it now has its headquarters in the Simpson Tower in Toronto. At one point the Hudson's Bay Company had its own country of a sort, called Rupert's Land. At that time, the Hudson's Bay Company was one of the largest landowners of the world, with approximately 15% of the land mass of North America. Rupert's Land consisted of lands that were in the Hudson Bay drainage system—basically the land surrounding any rivers that drained into the Hudson Bay. It was named after the first governor of the company, Prince Rupert of the Rhine, who was a nephew of Britain's King Charles I. The governor and the Company of Adventurers of England Trading comprised the original group that chartered the Hudson's Bay Company.

Rupert's Land and the Hudson's Bay Company had their headquarters at the York Factory, a town and fort along the Hayes River leading into Hudson Bay. Once the capital of Rupert's Land, it was closed down by the company in 1957.

The Hudson's Bay Company nominally owned Rupert's Land for 200 years, until about 1870, some 24 years before this photo was allegedly taken—and suppressed. Still, the Hudson's Bay Company was very powerful in 1894 and remains a major fixture in the Canadian economy today as the owner of many of Canada's retail chains such as The Bay, Zellers, Fields and Home Outfitters. The company has archives, located in Winnipeg, Manitoba, said to be a collection of the company's records and maps—does it include some bigfoot photos? That is what the writing scribbled on this bigfoot photo suggests.

And what of this location in British Columbia? I found that if I searched the Internet for the Yalikom River, as written on the back of the photo, what I found was the Yalakom River which is a tributary to the Bridge River which is a principal tributary to the Fraser River, a major part of Rupert's Land territory. Plus, I was able to find out that the Yalakom River enters the Bridge River near the town of Lilooet, which is apparently the town mentioned as Lilliott.

Lilooet is apparently one of the oldest towns in North America.

It is so old that its age is not known. It is considered to be one of the oldest continuously inhabited locations in North America, reckoned by archaeologists to have been inhabited for several thousand years. The town attracted large seasonal and permanent

A 1934 article about sasquatch from the Lincoln, Nebraska *Sunday Journal and Star.*

populations of native peoples because of the confluence of several main streams with the Fraser, and also because of a rock shelf just above the confluence of the Bridge River that is an obstacle to the annual migration of salmon—an abundant food source.

Did this salmon-shelf cause the downfall of our unfortunate sasquatch, shot by a trapper in the employ of the Hudson's Bay Company? According to the information on Lilooet this natural shelf along the riverbed is an important salmon station on the Fraser-Bridge-Yalakom River:

> This rock shelf, known in gold rush times as the Lower Fountain, was reputedly made by the trickster Coyote, leaping back and forth across the river to create platforms for people to catch and dry fish on. This location, named Sat' or Setl in the native language and known as the Bridge River Rapids or Six Mile in English, is the busiest fishing site on the Fraser above its mouth and there are numerous drying racks scattered around the banks of the river canyon around it.

We now have the final scene of the tragic bigfoot in our photograph: he had come to Lilooet (Lilliott as spelled on the backside of the photo) to get some salmon which was known to be plentiful at this spot. While Native Americans who had lived in the area for thousands of years knew not to bother the sasquatch that came to this area of plenty, this poor beast was shot and killed by the Europeans now penetrating the area for the Hudson's Bay Company. What they found shocked them. They shot and killed it. Then they took a photograph of it. Then someone in the company ordered the photo suppressed.

1897: Gorilla-like Creature in Ohio

In late April 1897 a man near Sailor, Indiana shot a bigfoot. Two farmers, Adam Gardner and Ed Swinehart, saw a hair-covered, man-sized "beast" walking on its hind legs. When it saw them approaching, it made for thick woods and they shot at it. It dropped onto all fours and bounded away.[11]

Also in late April 1897 a "wild man" was seen in the woods

near Stout, Ohio. After it was alleged that the wild man had attacked a boy, a party of thirty men went searching for the creature. One witness said it was very tall, nearly naked and could run like a deer. Another witness said that it wore a pair of tattered pants.[3] It is likely that these witnesses were not expecting the "wild man" to be completely covered in hair, they mistook the matted hair for tattered pants. On the other hand, maybe it was a pair of tattered pants as there have been other reports of bigfoot "wearing" something like pants or a belt.

Christopher Murphy, Joedy Cook and George Clappison record a number of early incidents in the Midwest in their book *Bigfoot Encounters in Ohio: Quest for the Grassman.*[66] They report that on May 26, 1897 near Rome, Ohio in the very south of the state, Charles Lukins and Bob Forner claimed that they encountered a wild man while cutting timber out of town. After struggling with the "gorilla-like creature" they were able to drive it into retreat among the cliffs. They called the creature a "terror" and said it was about six feet tall. This report came from the *Cleveland Plain Dealer*, May 27, 1897.

The authors also chronicle several other events in 1897, such as farmers around Logan, Ohio reporting in May that a strange animal had appeared in the vicinity and numerous sheep had disappeared. Several old pioneers who heard the beast crying at night thought it

The Rat Portage Saw Mill on Harrison Bay, British Columbia, circa 1910.

was a panther. They hunted for the strange animal but failed to kill or capture it.[66]

In the summer of 1897 a Native American from Tulelake, in northeastern Siskiyou County, California, nearly on the border with Oregon, became friends with a bigfoot. The witness said that on a summer evening he saw what at first looked like a tall bush ahead of him on the trail. Then he caught a strong, musky odor and realized the bush was alive and that it was a creature with eyes and thick, coarse hair. The creature made a noise and the man laid down his line of fish as a gesture of friendship. The creature took the fish and went into the trees where it made a long, low call. A few weeks later the man heard the strange noise outside his cabin and found a pile of fresh deerskins left by the door. Then he heard the strange bigfoot call in the trees. Sometimes other things were left as well, like wild fruits and berries.[3]

As the year 1900 was coming up the world was changing fast. There was now electricity in many cities and motorcars were starting to ply the roads along with buggies and carriages. The train network had expanded considerably throughout the West and Midwest. Settlers were clearing more land and moving into even the most isolated areas of the mountain west. Newspapers cropped up in new towns and they were thirsty for stories to print. Some of these stories were about sasquatch or wildmen.

Sasquatch Gets Publicity in British Columbia

As a new century began the name sasquatch began to sink into the English language. The word "sasquatch" was basically developed in 1926 by John W. Burns, a teacher at Harrison Mills on the Chehalis Reservation in British Columbia. Burns anglicised the Chehalis word "Saskehavis" which essentially means "wild man." He was fascinated by the local culture and went on to write some of the earliest articles on sasquatch. He said that the locals knew he was a teacher at the school and would not be skeptical of their stories, so many told him things that they would not tell other outsiders. Burns worked on the reservation from 1925 to 1946. Eventually, sasquatch became a household word.[7]

The Chehalis Reservation is located near the town of Harrison Mills. Harrison Mills, formerly known as Carnarvon

Chehalis First Nation Tribe of British Columbia, circa 1910.

and also Harrison River, is an agricultural farming and tourism-based community in the District of Kent west of Agassiz, British Columbia. The community is a part of the Fraser Valley Regional District. Harrison Mills is home to the British Columbia Heritage Kilby Museum and Campground.

Harrison Bay is a lake-like expansion of the Harrison River, located west of its main course and has the communities of Chehalis and Harrison Mills. Extremely shallow, the bay outlets to the Fraser at Harrison Mills, where in pre-gold rush times there had been a "riffle," which was dredged to enable easier steamer traffic to Harrison Lake and Port Douglas. Says Wikipedia which mentions a slightly different word, sesqac:

> Harrison Bay is the home of the Scowlitz (Scaulits) people, whose main reserve is on the bay's western shore, across from Harrison Mills, and also of the Sts'Ailes or Chehalis people, whose reserve is located on the north side of the bay along the lower Harrison River and around that river's confluence with its tributary, the Chehalis. The Scowlitz and Chehalis peoples once had large and famously-carved longhouse villages, long since destroyed by the encouragement of missionaries .
>
> The dialect spoken by the Sts'Ailes, whose name means "beating heart," includes the word sesqac, which

33

is the source of the English word sasquatch. The vicinity of Harrison Bay, Harrison Mills and the lower Harrison River is reputed to have the greatest number and density of sasquatch sightings worldwide. The sasquatch is the emblem of the Chehalis First Nation and is sacred in Sts'Ailes culture.

The whole Chehalis-Harrison Bay area is teaming with large salmon during certain parts of the year. This yearly salmon feast was enjoyed by the Chehalis people, as well as the local bears and eagles, and, of course, by the local sasquatch.

The Chehalis River is a subsidiary of the Harrison River, which is the de facto continuation of the Lillooet River, which is where the famous dead bigfoot photo was taken. This is also the area where the Chehalis woman Stephanie Long was kidnapped for a year by a sasquatch.

In May of 1909 on the Chehalis Reservation, a local named Peter Williams encountered a sasquatch near Harrison Mills. Williams was chased back to his house by a sasquatch in a rage. The amazing ordeal was described by Williams himself:

> I was walking along the foot of the mountain about a mile from the Chehalis Reserve. I thought I heard a noise—something like a grunt nearby. Looking in the direction in which it came, I was startled to see what I took at first sight to be a huge bear crouched upon a boulder twenty or thirty feet away. I raised my rifle to shoot it, but, as I did, the creature stood up and let out a piercing yell. It was a man—a giant, no less than six and one-half feet in height, and covered with hair. He was in a rage and jumped from the boulder to the ground. I fled, but not before I felt his breath upon my cheek. I never ran so fast before or since—through brush and undergrowth toward the Staloo, or Chehalis River, where my dugout was moored. From time to time I looked back over my shoulder. The giant was fast overtaking me—a hundred feet separated us; another look and the distance measured less than fifty—the Chehalis [came in view] and in a moment I [was in] the dugout and

shot across the stream to the opposite bank.

The swift river, however, did not in the least daunt the giant, for he began to wade in immediately. I arrived home almost worn out from running and I felt sick. Taking an anxious look around the house, I was relieved to find the wife and children inside. I bolted the door and barricaded it with everything at hand. Then with my rifle ready, I stood near the door and awaited his coming.

If I had not been so excited, I could have easily shot the giant when he began to wade the river. After an anxious waiting of twenty minutes, I heard a noise approaching like the trampling of a horse. I looked though a crack in the old wall. It was the giant. Darkness had not yet set in and I had a good look at him. Except that he was covered with hair and twice the bulk of the average man, there was nothing to distinguish him from the rest of us.

He pushed against the wall of the old house with such force that it shook back and forth. The old cedar shook and the timbers creaked and groaned so much under the strain that I was afraid it would fall down and kill us. I whispered to the old woman to take the children under the bed. After prowling and grunting like an animal around the house, he went. We were glad, for the children and the wife were uncomfortable under the bedstead. Next morning I found his tracks in the mud around the house, the biggest either man or beast I had ever seen. The tracks measured twenty-two inches in length, but were narrow in proportion to their length.[29]

1915: Sasquatch Eating Huckleberries

In the summer of 1915 near Hope, British Columbia, Charles Flood, a prospector, was with two friends—Donald McRae and Green Hicks—when he saw a sasquatch. The group had crossed an unknown divide in a wilderness area near the Holy Cross Mountains. Said Flood:

...A mile further up was Cougar Lake. Several years ago a fire swept over many square miles of mountains

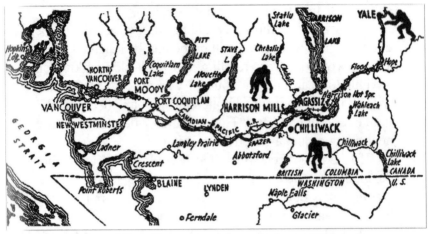

An early map of Canadian sasquatch hotspots from a 1934 newspaper.

which resulted in large areas of mountain huckleberry growth. Hicks suddenly stopped us and drew our attention to a large, light brown creature about eight feet high, standing on its hind legs pulling the berry bushes with one hand or paw toward him and putting berries in his mouth with the other hand, or paw. I stood still wondering while McRae and Hicks were arguing. Hicks said, "It's a wild man" and McRae said, "It's a bear." The creature heard us and suddenly disappeared in the brush around 200 yards away. As far as I am concerned the strange creature looked more like a human being, we seen several black and brown bears on the trip, that 'thing' looked altogether different.[7]

1919: A Huge Nude Hairy Man

Charlie Victor, who lived near Hatzic, British Columbia, on the Fraser River, said that in the summer of 1919 he had been bathing with friends in a lake and while dressing a "huge nude hairy man" stepped out from a rock where he had apparently been watching Charlie. Victor stated, "He looked at me for a moment, his eyes were so kind looking that I was about to speak to him, when he turned about and walked into the forest."[29]

1927: Sasquatch Shows Up at a Picnic

In September of 1927, William Point and Adaline August were at a hop-pickers picnic near Agassiz, just north of Chilliwack in

36

southern British Columbia when they encountered a bigfoot. Said Point of the incident:

> Adaline August and myself walked to her father's orchard which is about four miles from the hop fields. We were walking on the railroad track and within a short distance of the orchard, when the girl noticed something walking along the track coming toward us. I looked up but paid no attention to it as I thought it was some person on his way to Agassiz. But as he came closer we noticed that his appearance was very odd, and on coming still closer we stood still and were astonished—seeing that the creature was naked and covered in hair like an animal. We were almost paralyzed from fear. I picked up two stones with which I intended to hit him if he attempted to molest us, but within 50 feet or so he stood still and looked at us. He was twice as big as the average man, with arms so long that its hands almost touched the ground.
>
> It seemed to me that the eyes were very large and the lower part of his face, gave the creature such a frightful appearance that I ran away as fast as I could. After a minute or two I looked back and saw that he resumed his journey. The girl had fled before I left, and she ran so fast that I did not overtake her until I was close to Agassiz, where we told the story of our adventure to the Indians who were still enjoying themselves. Old Indians who were present said: the wild man was no doubt a sasquatch, a tribe of hairy people who they claim have always lived in the mountains—in tunnels and caves.[3]

1928: Ape is Seen and Shot at Bella Coola

Several things happened around southern British Columbia in 1928. A woman outside of Lavington was ill in bed and asked her daughter to send away the man standing by the fence of their property. The daughter looked out and saw a tall, bulky and furry creature standing behind a fence post, with its hands resting at the top of the post. The creature left shortly after that and the woman told her daughter that she had seen it farther up the fence line earlier, watching the house.

Then near Bella Coola, BC, a man named George Talleo said he shot at an ape. He said he saw the creature stand up from behind a fallen tree and took a shot at with a small caliber rifle. The creature fell to the ground and Talleo ran from the scene. He said that he had noticed a pile of moss stripped from a rock face that was used to cover a pile of excrement.[7]

A work crew cutting a trail to a lake near Windermere, BC were reported to have uncovered four extremely large skeletons of what appeared to be men—or sasquatch—in 1928. The skeletons ranged from 6-foot-9-inches tall to an incredible (but not for bigfoot) nine feet tall. Such skeletons are normally given by the Canadian authorities to the local First Nations tribe who then

A Maclean's (Canada) magazine article from 1934.

dispose of the remains.[7]

1934: Sasquatch Throws Rocks off of Cliff

In March of 1934 it was reported that Tom Cedar of Harrison Mills on the Chehalis Reservation had a frightening encounter with a bigfoot. Cedar was fishing in the Harrison River when his boat was bombarded with huge rocks from the cliffs above the river. He narrowly escaped after one large rock almost hit the boat. He looked up to the cliffs above and saw a huge, hairy man-like creature waving its arms wildly and stamping its feet, clearly agitated by the appearance of Cedar and his boat. The frightened Cedar cut his fishing line and paddled away as fast as he could. Cedar also suspected that the sasquatch had been stealing salmon that he had hung outside to dry, well above where his dogs could reach.

A few nights later Frank Dan reported that he met a sasquatch at Harrison Mills when he went outside to see why his dog wouldn't stop barking. He saw a "hairy giant" standing there with hair covering it from head to feet except for a small hairless area around the eyes. It was extremely tall with a muscular build and the terrified Dan ran back into the house and bolted the door. The sasquatch walked back into the forest and though Dan was teased about his sighting and fear, bigfoot sightings continued in the area, seemingly a focal point for sasquatch activity.

On April 9, 1934, the *Fresno Bee* (Fresno, CA) ran a story entitled "Californians Out to Bag Legendary Sasquatch." The story was about two brothers and medical students at the University of California, J.F. Blakeney and C.K. Blakeney, who were headed to Canada to find sasquatch, probably after seeing the popular feature that appeared on sasquatch in the April 1929 issue of the long-time Canadian magazine *MacLean's*. There appears to be no follow-up article. This seems to be the first official bigfoot expedition.[7]

1937: Face to Face with Sasquatch at Abandoned House

In the summer of 1937, Mrs. Jane Patterson, who lived with her husband on a ranch near Osoyoos, BC in the Anarchist Mountain area, encountered a bigfoot. She had wandered over to an old abandoned house on the ranch property to look for rhubarb that she had been told was growing in the garden. As she came up to the house she had to duck under a tree branch and then came face to face with a sasquatch about ten feet away.

Patterson inadvertently said to the creature, "Oh there you are." The sasquatch just blinked its eyes. She backed away and headed for home, hastening her pace when she got away from the house. When she told her husband about the incident he refused to go to the abandoned house with her, stating he did not wish to see a monkey, as Jane had said, "it looked just like a monkey to me!" Three days later he agreed to visit the abandoned house but found nothing.

Also in 1937 Floyd Dillon claimed that he uncovered a nearly 8-foot skeleton with a skull twice the size of a man's skull while digging a trench behind his house along the Fraser River near Lillooet, BC. He left the bones where they were and reburied them. Later they were dug up and the fragments that were left were sent to the Provincial Museum in Victoria. Dillon also said that the giant seemed to have an 8-inch tail as well, though researchers like Christopher Murphy think that Dillon probably mistook something else for a tail.[29]

Note that this happened in Lillooet, the same location where the astonishing 1894 photograph was taken.

1941: Sasquatch Chases Mom and Kids

In October of 1941 George and Jeannie Chapman and their family had a frightening experience with bigfoot. They lived in a small, isolated house on the banks of the Fraser River near Agassiz in southern British Columbia. George was a railroad maintenance worker at a small town called Ruby Creek.

One afternoon the three children, ages 5, 7 and 8, were playing in the front yard when one of the children ran into the house shouting that a "big cow is coming out the woods." A dark-haired bigfoot that was nearly eight feet tall was approaching the house

as the other children came inside. Jeannie gathered the children and they ran terrified down the railroad tracks in the direction that George would typically walk home. They soon approached him and shouted that a sasquatch was after them.

Bigfoot used to be in the news.

George gathered other men and they went to the house where they found 16-inch-long footprints leading to a shed where a heavy barrel of smoked fish had been dumped out. The prints led across a field and into the mountains. The huge creature had apparently easily stepped over a fence that was nearly five feet high.

The Chapmans returned to their home but they were continually bothered by howling noises and serious agitation of their dogs, and left again after a week. Another family moved in briefly and left, and ultimately the property was abandoned. A cast was made of one of the footprints.[29]

Later that year, in November 1941 near Harrison Hot Springs, it was reported that three canoes full of First Nations people were reported to be fleeing a giant sasquatch terrorizing the village of Port Douglas at the head of Harrison Lake. The occupants said that the sasquatch walked on two legs and was 14 feet tall.[7] This is tall, even for a sasquatch!

Harrison Hot Springs has now dedicated a 1,217-hectare Sasquatch Provincial Park that touches on four lakes, including the massive Harrison Lake, which is surrounded by magnificent mountains covered in second-growth deciduous forests.

In the summer of 1943 it was reported that an unnamed man from Hope, BC was out berry picking with his wife and others when he strayed from the group. They were about a mile from the small community of Katz when the man was attacked by a sasquatch that came running at him from behind some rocks. The bigfoot hit the man—"hit him in the head, and side, and arms."

The man yelled and others came to his assistance. The sasquatch

41

ran off to pick berries elsewhere. The man's wife reasoned that since the sasquatch was small by sasquatch standards, he had been treated badly as a runt and so was taking out his frustrations on First Nations people. The man was said to have a "crooked arm" until his death in 1955.[7]

1947: A Skin-Clad Sasquatch?

A strange occurred on Canada's Vancouver Island in 1947 when a Mr. and Mrs. Werner were driving on Grouse Mountain. While they were travelling on an old logging road they said they saw two creatures that were naked except had "a skin wrapped around them." Both had shoulder-length hair, but there is no mention of body hair.

Both of the creatures were barefoot and had "huge feet." The leading bigfoot was about 8 feet tall while the other was about 6 feet tall. They had very bushy eyebrows over very small eyes and wide, flat noses. The taller creature was carrying a stick over its shoulder with what may have been a bag tied to the end. It appeared to be leading the smaller creature, which possibly had its hands tied together. The taller sasquatch was very thin while the smaller one was very broad.[7] Perhaps it was a pregnant bride being led to her new home in a cave. Sightings of bigfoot that are partly dressed, or carrying a club or stick are especially interesting. Would a bigfoot be able to tie the hands of another bigfoot?

1948: A Bicycle Race

A strange report of a sasquatch racing a bicycle was reported in 1948 on the Chehalis Reservation. Henry Charlie said that he was cycling toward Harrison Mills when saw two unusual creatures come off the hill opposite the Fenn Pretty property. One of the creatures chased him for a distance of more than a mile down Morris Valley Road. He described it as between 7 and 8 feet tall and covered in dark hair, except the face.[29]

Charlie said that the sasquatch had no problem keeping up with him as he pedaled as fast as he could down the road. He saw the creature only when he glanced behind himself as he pedaled madly. Eventually it was gone, probably having had some fun— bigfoot style!

1949: Horse Stops Because of Bigfoot

In July of 1949 Mrs. G. Mason reported seeing a strange animal near Harrison Hot Springs in south central British Columbia, an area that we have seen is a hotbed of bigfoot activity. She was on horseback riding on a bridal trail when her horse balked at going any further. She dismounted and tried to lead the horse forward but it balked again. She then tied the horse up and walked up the trail where she came upon a creature that she thought was a bear.

She approached it and it ran off on all fours and then suddenly stood up and walked into the bush. She said that it had unkempt brown hair and was 7 to 8 feet tall. It was heavily built with medium length arms and did not have a snout like a bear. She returned to her horse which would not continue down the bridal trail until it sensed that the creature was completely out of the area.

Then in the autumn of 1949 a Mr. Hentges reported that he saw what he thought was a gorilla while he was driving down Cluculz Lake near Vanderhoof, northern British Columbia, west of the major town of Prince George. Hentges was driving down a highway under construction when he saw what he thought was a gorilla walk across the road in the distance. The creature was walking on two legs with its arms hanging down. When he got to the area where he had seen the giant figure he could not see it and

43

assumed that it was hiding from him in the piles of brush nearby. Alarmed that some gorilla was on the loose, he decided to report it to the police.[29]

So, we can see that bigfoot and sasquatch sightings go back hundreds of years and that the First Nation tribes of Canada already had various names for the animal. The sightings of "wild men" who were covered with hair, and sometimes carried a club, were becoming more common as civilization intruded on the more remote parts of the West. Sightings and newspaper reports continued in the Midwest and rural parts of the Eastern States as well.

Yet, bigfoot remained on the very periphery of popular culture until the 1950s when bigfoot really made the news.

CHAPTER 2

BIGFOOT:
A NATIONAL CELEBRITY

Tumbled down shack in Bigfoot County,
Rained so hard that the roof caved in
And Delilah Jones went to meet her god
And the old man never was the same again.
—Grateful Dead, *Brown Eyed Women*

As the 1950s came upon the denizens of rural America and Canada the creature known as the "wildman," "monster," "rock ape," or "gorilla," began to have a new identity, one that shaped his image for many decades to come. He got the moniker "bigfoot."

It all began on the morning of August 27, 1958 when a road construction worker named Jerry Crew walked up to his bulldozer in the wilderness of northern California and found a circle of enormous footprints around the vehicle. He looked at them in amazement. No man could have feet that big, he told himself. Besides, no one lived in this rugged mountain forest of northern California. This area was 17,000 square miles of mountain forest that had never been explored or settled in the past. Except for this road gang, the area was completely uninhabited and the roads they were creating were the first sign of civilization in the huge area. What could have made these footprints?

At first Crew thought that someone was playing a prank on him. But he soon discarded this idea as could not fathom any of his fellow crewmembers taking the time to create such a hoax. He decided that it must be an animal of some kind, but what was it? He had never heard of sasquatch before and was unfamiliar with any early reports.

45

Crew followed the tracks as they left his bulldozer. He found that the strides were twice as long as his own. The unexplained tracks were pressed deeply into the ground. His own tracks barely made an impression and he surmised that the creature must be very heavy.

He was able to clearly see how the tracks came down a steep incline of 70 degrees to the bulldozer. After circling the bulldozer several times the tracks then led down the newly cut road and then suddenly turned off the road and went down a very steep incline into the forest. Crew could see that the creature had no difficulty in crashing through thick bush and trees in the heavily forested area.

Having looked in wonder at the tracks for some time he drove back to the Bluff Creek workers camp and asked some of the other men to come and have a look. Naturally, they were as amazed as Crew was and one of them had a tape measure and they measured the prints finding them to be 16 inches long and 7 inches wide. The man said, "No wonder the guy has to run around in his bare feet. There's not a place in the world where they sell shoes big enough to fit feet that size."[5]

They all agreed that the tracks must have been made by a "giant wild man." It had five foot strides and must have been very heavy, perhaps 700 or 800 pounds. The men continued their work and about a month later footprints were again seen around the bulldozer, now a few miles from where it had been before. A small forward camp had been made near the bulldozer, now some distance from the Bluff Creek camp.

This time the footprints showed that the creature came up to the bulldozer and walked around it and then it walked down the road where it took a drink from a nearby spring and then disappeared into the forest.

On October 2, Crew found more large footprints around his bulldozer and over the next three days the tracks were found on the road and around the machinery. On two occasions they heard a high pitched whistling wail in the middle of the night. The men began to get a bit scared and realized that they could get cut off from the outside world by a landslide for several days.

One man said, "I don't like it one bit. We've got this giant wild man hanging around up here and there's nothing we can do about it. How do we know that the thing isn't going to come into camp and tear the whole place apart?"

"It gives me the creeps," said another. "I've always got the feeling that something was watching me when I'm out there in the bush. I spend half my time looking over my shoulder."

Several wives also lived in the Bluff Creek camp. They were usually alone during the day and they began keeping loaded rifles close to them. If the giant wild man gave them a visit, "we'll give him a belly full of lead," said one young wife.[5]

One of the wives, Mrs. Jesse Bemis, became quite interested in the footprints of the giant wild man and wrote a letter to *The Humboldt Times* in Eureka, California. In her letter she reported what had been happening around the equipment and asked, "Have you ever heard of anything like this before?"

The editor of *The Humboldt Times*, Andrew Genzoli, found the letter intriguing and decided to publish it in his newspaper. To his astonishment, instead of ridicule, he got a number of letters in support of her, including stories of footprints others had seen. This included a reported footprint that was 22 inches long.

There were also reports from people who had seen the tall, hair-covered giants and noted that they were 7 to 9 feet tall, weighed 700 to 1000 pounds and always walked upright. Meanwhile, Jerry Crew came into town with plaster casts that he had made of two of the footprints to show to a friend. Genzoli heard about this and rushed over to interview Crew and get photographs.

During the interview Genzoli asked Crew what he thought the name of the creature was. Crew's reply was, "Bigfoot. That's what we call him."

The story with photographs was published the next day, October 14, 1958, in *The Humboldt Times*. This story was then picked up by the news

Jerry Crew with a bigfoot print.

47

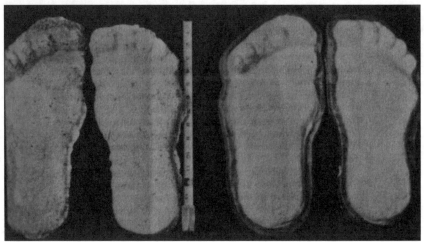

A photo of four of Jerry Crew's plaster casts of the prints around his bulldozer.

wire services and the name "bigfoot" was broadcast around the world. It was such an interesting story with fascinating photos that it was picked up by nearly every major newspaper in the United States and the name bigfoot spread like wildfire.

There were all sorts of letters pouring into the newspaper now, some asking if Hollywood had let King Kong loose, while others were grateful for such a detailed and interesting story. Ivan T. Sanderson read about the Bluff Creek bigfoot and headed to California to investigate the incidents himself.

What he learned made a very deep impression on him and he could not doubt the sincerity of the witnesses he interviewed. The evidence presented to him fit in with his research into the abominable snowman during the 1940s and 50s. Sanderson surmised that Giganthropithicus, a huge, 12-foot-tall apelike creature that was a missing link between humans and apes. If mastodons, great rhinos, and other animals had crossed from Asia into North America during the last ice age, then Sanderson surmised these giant apes could have done so as well.

Sanderson also surmised that these giant apes would also live in remote areas where modern man did not live. The rugged, uninhabited mountains of northern California were an obvious place for such animals to live with plenty of food, water, and isolation.

Meanwhile, back in Bluff Creek the contractor to build the

road for the public works department, Ray Wallace, was wondering what was going on at his work site. What was all this talk about "bigfoot"? Why did his workers keep quitting their jobs?

Ray's brother, Wilbur Wallace, was one of the foremen on the crew and he confirmed the strange goings on. He told Ray that a week before, his men reported to him one morning that a 55-gallon drum of diesel fuel that had been standing by the side of the road had disappeared. Wilbur investigated and found footprints that went to the edge of a steep ravine. At the bottom of the ravine they found the oil drum.

Ray Wallace was astonished. The drum must have weighed about 400 pounds. But that wasn't all of it. Wilbur told him that the bigfoot came back the following night and dragged off some steel culvert from the dump and tossed it off a cliff. Then a night later he took one of the huge tires that go on an earthmover and weigh 250 pounds, and threw it into a ravine.

Ray Wallace had found an enemy. It was a bigfoot. The original bigfoot, back when bigfoot was spelled with a capital B. Ray Wallace told his brother, "I'll fix that rascal. I'll fix him for once and always. You just see if I don't."

Ray Wallace then hired two hunters to track and kill the bigfoot. "Get bigfoot," he ordered them. "I don't care who he is or what he is, but he's ruining my business and I want him shot."

Wallace hired Ray Kerr and Bob Breazele. Breazele had hunted professionally in Mexico and owned an enormous British-made rifle that impressed all the locals. He also owned four well-trained dogs. "These dogs ain't afraid of nothing," he told Wallace. "If they see a rhinoceros out there in the brush, they'll go straight for him."[5]

A bigfoot was sighted the day before by an excited worker who saw him drinking from a creek. The bigfoot stood up and ran into the forest. He described it as ten feet tall with brown shaggy hair. The man quit his job that day and left the camp.

Kerr and Breazele found that the terrain was very mountainous and difficult and it was difficult to actually leave the road. After some days of fruitless hunting for bigfoot they were driving slowly back to the camp one night when they suddenly came upon a gigantic creature covered in hair squatting by the side of the road. He leapt up and in two strides crossed the road. The hunters measured the stride and tracks, but were not going to pursue the bigfoot into the forest. The bigfoot had covered 20 feet in two strides, they calculated.

Back at the camp Kerr and Breazele excitedly told the same story about the bigfoot, which they thought was 8 to 10 feet tall with long swinging arms. Breazele said that, "It wasn't a man. I don't what it was, but it wasn't a man and that's definite."

At first light Kerr and Breazele were at the spot where they had seen the bigfoot. They turned their four dogs loose and they quickly found the scent of the bigfoot and took off into the forest. Kerr and Breazele tried to follow the dogs through the forest but after a while they realized that the dogs had simply vanished. There was only silence when the men called for the dogs.

The men searched for a few more hours and then returned to the camp in confusion. The next day a tribesman named Curtis Mitchell arrived at the Bluff Creek camp and told a strange story. He had been working on a bridge a few miles from the camp when he wandered into the forest for a few minutes and found the bodies of four dogs that had been torn to pieces.

They asked him if he had seen any tracks. "I didn't stick around to look," the man said. "I got out of there as fast as I could."[5]

With their dogs dead, Kerr and Breazele decided to pack it in but Wallace continued to build his road. It was eventually completed and new roads were beginning to be cut in the area.

Letters continued to come into *The Humboldt Times* and Andrew Genzoli would read them, sometimes publishing the stories told in the newspaper.

One story that Genzoli published was about Benjamin Wilder who was on a newly created California road near Arcata and had pulled over to sleep in his car for a bit. Shortly after falling asleep he was awakened by his car shaking violently. When he turned on his flashlight he thought that he saw a bear standing next to the driver's side window.

"Beat it," yelled Wilder at the animal. "Get out of here!"

The creature screamed and shook the car again. Frightened now Wilder yelled and honked his car horn. The creature suddenly ran into the forest.

"I never saw his face," said Wilder, "and I'm glad I didn't. The part of it I did see was bad enough."

Other interested people came to Arcata to look into the mater themselves. One was a geologist named Dr. Maurice Tripp who discovered a footprint that was 17 inches long; another was the famous Canadian sasquatch researcher John Green. Green had already written three books on sasquatch and had come to compare footprint casts that he had made in Canada to those around Bluff Creek. Green declared, "There can be no doubt at all about it, bigfoot and sasquatch are one and the same fellow."[5]

The next group to show up in Arcata and Bluff Creek was the brief Pacific Northwest Expedition which was sponsored by the Texas millionaires Tom Slick and Kirk Johnson. This expedition also included Rene Dahinden, Bob Titmus, Gerri Walsh and Ed Patrick. Oil millionaire Tom Slick had been on some yeti expeditions in Nepal and Sikkim and wondered if bigfoot was related to the yeti.

Slick told the local media, "It's our intention to photograph and definitely prove the existence and identification of the creature. If we can do that, it could be one of the most important scientific events of all time."

Ivan T. Sanderson even joined the expedition and at one point he is said to have told the group that he preferred the name bigfoot to that of "abominable snowman" and told them, "In the first place, we have no right to call these creatures 'abominable.' In the second place, they do not live in the snow. In the third place, we don't even know for sure that these creatures are actually men."

Not much came of the expedition and sadly Tom Slick died in a private plane crash in Montana in 1962.[57]

Bigfoot was now a national celebrity. Soon there would be Bigfoot Convenience Stores and Jack Link's beef jerky ads, bigfoot would become a dynamic marketing engine. Some people would even devote their entire lives to studying and searching for bigfoot. One of these people was Roger Patterson. When Patterson learned of Jerry Crew's footprints and the creature called bigfoot, he began a quest to discover bigfoot that would ultimately include his friends Rene Dahinden and Bob Gimlin as well as Bob Titmus and others.´

Patterson began collecting stories and searching for bigfoot. In 1966 he self published his book *Do Abominable Snowmen of North America Really Exist?*[16]

Patterson went on a lecture circuit about bigfoot that included high schools and civic groups like the Elks Club and such. He showed photos of footprints and casts of footprints and toward the end he played a tape recording of a bigfoot screaming in the night. I attended one of these lectures myself as a junior high school student in 1968. Patterson had not gotten his famous film footage yet, that was to come a year or two later. Patterson sold copies of his book after the lecture and I bought one. The price was one dollar.

In the book Patterson interviewed Fred Beck who told Patterson about shooting a sasquatch in the Pacific Northwest decades before:

> So we seen him running down this ridge then, and then he took a couple more shots at him. Marion, when he first shot I rushed over there, it was hard going, he said: "Don't run, don't run, Fred, don't run," he said, "he won't go far," he said, "I put three shots through that fool's head, he won't go far."
>
> So we got up the ridge and looked down there he was goin', just jumpin', looked like it'd be twelve, fourteen feet a jump, runnin'. The old man took a couple more shots at him and the old man said, "My God, I don't understand it, I don't understand it, how that fella can get away with them slugs in his head," he says, "I hit him with the other two shots, too."[16]

Regarding that night in their sturdy cabin of pine logs, Beck told Patterson:

> When we seen 'em, you know, why we heard that noise—pounding and whistling, at night they come in there

and we had a pile of shakes piled up there, big shakes. Our cabin was built out of logs. We didn't have rafters on it, we had good-sized pine logs, you know, for rafters, two-inch shakes, pine shakes. We had them rafters close apart, they was about a foot apart, 'cause he said he wanted to make a roof what'd hold the snow. We made one to hold the snow. Them buggers attacked us, knocked the chinking out on my dad's, on my father-in-law's chest, and had an ax there, he grabbed the ax.

And the old man grabbed the ax and the logs and then he shot on it, right along the ax handle, and he let go of it. And then the fun started! Well, I wanta tell you, pretty near all night long they were on that house, trying to get in, you know. We kept a shootin'. Get up on the house we'd shoot up through the ceiling at them. My God, they made a noise. Sounded like a bunch of horses were running around there. Next day, we'd find tracks, anywhere there was any sand on the rocks, we found tracks of them.[16, 29]

Prior to Jerry Crew's announcement of bigfoot, there were a number of bigfoot incidents, particularly in Canada, where bigfoot was already well known as sasquatch. In the summer of 1952 a motorist driving near Terrace, in northern British Columbia (on the Skeena River where the Kitselas people, a tribe of the Tsimshian Nation, have lived for thousands of years), saw an odd creature standing erect beside the main road to the town. The man slowed down and then stopped his car. The sasquatch watched him quietly for a while and then turned and walked into the bush. It turned in the underbrush to look at him again. It was dusk and the man could not see the facial features clearly but he believed it to be a sasquatch. Several other sightings had been made in the area during that same year.[29]

A year later, Canadian Jack Twist was on a camping trip with friends near the Oyster River about 20 miles northwest of Courtenay, British Columbia in September 1953 when, as he walked alone down a logging road, he saw a dark figure several hundred yards away. He thought it was one of his friends and he called out to the figure but did not get an answer. The figure was in front of him and he continued to walk toward it and as he got closer he could see that it was an 8-foot creature covered in dark hair. The bigfoot turned and faced Twist and then turned and walked into the forest.[7]

Another famous bigfoot encounter occurred in British Columbia in October of 1955. William Roe provided a sworn statement about his encounter with a female sasquatch. Roe, who had worked as a hunter, trapper, and a road worker, was doing a job in British Columbia during 1955 and one day he hiked five miles up Mica Mountain to explore a deserted mine.

As he was stepping out of a clearing, he saw what he thought was a grizzly bear. When the animal stood up, he realized this was no grizzly bear! The animal, a female sasquatch, was six feet tall, three feet wide, and weighed approximately 300 pounds. Her arms reached almost to her knees, and when she walked she put the heel of her foot down first.

Roe was hiding in some brush and was able to observe the creature from a distance of some 20 feet. He said that he watched, fascinated, as she used her white, even teeth to eat leaves from a nearby bush. Her head was "higher at the back than at the front"; her nose was flat. Only the area around her mouth was bare—the rest of her body was covered in hair, none of which was longer than an inch. The ears looked very much like a human's. The eyes were small and dark, similar to a bear's.

At this point, the animal caught Roe's scent and walked back the way she had come, looking over her shoulder as she went. As she disappeared into the bush, Roe

The female bigfoot as drawn by Roe.

heard her make a sound he described as "a kind of a whinny."

Roe said he wanted to find out whether the animal was a vegetarian or whether she consumed meat as well. He searched for and found feces in several places. Upon examination, no hair or insect shells were found. Roe concluded this animal lived solely on vegetation. Most researchers agree however, that these animals probably eat a variety of foods, including fish, fowl, frogs and even deer, plus all kinds of berries, pine cones, wild onions, cattails, and everything else edible, much like bears.[7]

In May of 1956 near Marshall, Michigan, three friends were sleeping out in the woods when a "huge, hair-covered creature" with green eyes "as big as light bulbs" and smelling "like something rotten" picked up Otto Collins and Philip Williams in their sleeping bags, holding one under each arm. Their companion, Herman Williams, grabbed his rifle which scared the bigfoot who then dropped the men and ran into the woods.[3]

We don't know if bigfoot was trying to abduct the young men or just trying to scare them, but the encounter certainly terrified the men. The term "bigfoot" had yet to come into the vocabulary so it was a "huge, hair-covered creature." Like a gorilla?

In the Autumn of 1957 Gary Joanis and Jim Newall were hunting in the area of Wanoga Butte near Bend, Oregon, and Joanis had just shot a deer. However, before the two could walk over to the dead deer a 9-foot hairy creature came into the clearing, picked the entire deer up and began to carry it back into the woods under one arm. Joanis was angry that his deer was being stolen and fired repeatedly into the back of the bigfoot with his 30.06 rifle. The bigfoot did not stop walking but made a "strange whistling scream." Joanis and Newall had no choice but to let the bigfoot abscond with their deer.[3]

Bigfoot is known to have been shot on a number of occasions but his thick skin, bones and bulky body make it almost impossible to bring the massive critter down with shots to the upper body. It has been suggested that the best way to kill a bigfoot is to shoot him through one of his eye sockets—a shot that would take some timing and skill.

In October of 1959, a year after the term "bigfoot" had been coined, at a place called Ten Mile, west of Roseburg, Oregon, two boys decided to hunt bigfoot at an abandoned sawmill. Wayne Johnson, 12 years old, had seen a bigfoot near the abandoned sawmill and after telling his friend, 17-year-old Walter Stork, the two decided to go back with rifles and shoot the bigfoot.

When they got to the abandoned sawmill bigfoot was there waiting for them. The two both fired shots at the bigfoot, Stork with his 30.06 rifle. The bigfoot kept coming at them, but dropped down on his knuckles each time he was shot. The bigfoot had his arms outstretched as if he were herding the boys away. The boys ran and even though the bigfoot could have caught up to them, he did not and they later felt that he was essentially shooing them away from the area.

Suddenly the bigfoot stopped following them and they did not see where he went. The boys estimated that the bigfoot was almost 14 feet tall, perhaps an exaggeration. Bigfoot has been reported to reach a height of 15 feet or more, though any 10- to 12-foot-tall bigfoot would seem gigantically huge to any normal person.

The famous bigfoot investigator named Bob Titmus came to the scene within two days and found some unusual tracks. They were less than 12 inches long but 12 inches wide at the toes, which did not seem very long for a 14-foot bigfoot, though extremely wide. There were no apparent claws on the footprints and in wet ground the prints were an astonishing 13 inches deep. When Titmus tried to make his own footprint in the wet soil he could only make his heel sink as deep as 2 or 3 inches.[3]

Also, sometime in late 1959 a road crew working in the Armstrong area of British Columbia discovered a skeleton of a "man" that was nearly 7 feet tall. The coroner of Lillooet (yes, the place in the 1894 bigfoot photo story), Arthur Phair, was informed of the find and he notified a government official in Victoria. Apparently the skeleton was turned over to the First Nations people of the area for burial. Some speculation is that it was the skeleton of a dead sasquatch.[7] This is an interesting story since a common question that is asked is, "Why don't they ever find any bigfoot skeletons?"

Bigfoot in the Rearview Mirror

Sometimes encounters with bigfoot are like a scene out of a

monster movie. Its like having some hairy monster coming up on your car and you can see him in the rearview mirror but you can't start your car and you're in a panic… help! Yea, sometimes bigfoot is reaching in your car and grabbing you and you just cannot believe that this is happening. This only happens in the movies!

Sometime in the fall of 1961 Larry Martin and some friends from Alpine, Oregon went into the forest one evening to retrieve a deer that one of them had shot while hunting earlier in the day. When they arrived at the place where the deer had been left, they found that it had been dragged away, plus they heard thrashing noises in the nearby brush. As it was dark, they cautiously looked around with flashlights and were startled when Martin's light illuminated a tall bigfoot only a few feet away. Said Martin, "I knew it wasn't a bear 'cause it had human-like features, you know, it looked like an ape or gorilla or something like that, and it was coming at me."

Martin, nearly six-feet tall, had to shine his flashlight upward into the face of the bigfoot and as he did so his group immediately turned and ran back to the car in fright. The car would not start immediately and Martin could see bigfoot in the rearview mirror walking up to the car. Suddenly, the car started and the group tore down the road; Martin later said, "We got out of there."[3]

The *Oregon Journal* reported in 1962, in a story entitled "Monster Sightings Rekindle Interest in Mt. St. Helens Hairy Giant Saga," that three persons driving along a remote mountain road east of the Cascade wilderness area said that they saw a 10-foot, white, hairy figure moving rapidly along the roadside. The white-haired sasquatch was caught in the headlights as their car passed, but they were too frightened to turn around to investigate. They apparently reported their sighting to the police.

The *Oregon Journal* also said that a Portland woman and her husband fishing on the Lewis River south of Mt. St. Helens saw a huge beige figure, "bigger than any human," along the bank of the river. As they watched the tall creature, it "moved into a thicket with a lumbering gait."

The article also mentioned that the Clallam Indian tribe of Washington State had traditions of hairy giants on Mt. St. Helens.

These hairy giants are called the Selahtik, and are believed to be a tribe of "renegade marauder-like people, who lived like animals in the caves and lava tunnels in the high Cascades."[3]

In another encounter that seems straight out of a monster movie, in June of 1962 Robert Hatfield was awakened in the middle of the night by the barking of his dogs at his house just outside of Fort Bragg in northern California. He went outside the front door to investigate and thought he saw the largest bear that he had ever seen: a dark form looking at his barking dogs from the other side of a 6-foot fence.

He ran back into the house to wake his brother-in-law Bud Jenkins to show him this gigantic bear. Outside, neither of them could see the gigantic animal so Jenkins returned to the house to fetch a flashlight and a gun. Hatfield decided to check around the back of the house and as he rounded the corner he suddenly came "face to chest" with an 8-foot bigfoot. At that point Jenkins said that Hatfield:

> ...let out a scream and stepped backwards and as he stepped backwards he fell, so he came into the house on his hands and knees going like mad.
>
> My wife was at this time holding the screen door open for him to come in. I heard the commotion and I ran to the inside door we have here before you step onto the porch, and as he came through the door I saw this large creature going by the window, but I could see neither its lower body nor its head, all I could see was the upper part of its body through the window there.
>
> When he came in my wife tried to close the door and they got it within about two to for inches of closing and couldn't close it. Something was holding it open. My wife hollered at me and said, "Hurry and get the gun, it's coming through the door!"
>
> Of course by that time I was standing right behind her here in this door leading to the porch, and I said, "Well, let it through and I'll get it."
>
> At that time the pressure went off the door and I shut the door and threw the lock on it. And I walked to the

window and put my hand up to the window and looked out, so that I could see out into the yard, because it was still dark, and it was raining, and this creature was standing upright, and I would judge it to be about 8-feet tall and it walked away from the house, back out to this little fence we have, and stepped over the little fence and walked past my car and out towards the main road.[3]

Jenkins judged that the bigfoot must have weighed about 500 pounds, and it always walked upright and had a terrible odor which lingered in the air after the creature had gone. In daylight they searched the yard for footprints and found some four-toed prints that were 16 inches long. On the wall by the house door was found a handprint 11-and-a-half inches long. The two men later said that, while they had been very frightened at the time, the attitude of the creature was one of curiosity rather than aggression.

During the summer of 1963 a lone Canadian camper named Harry Squiness was preparing to get in to his sleeping bag when suddenly his tent flap was opened and a hairy monkey face with human eyes peered in at him. He was camped near a lake in British Columbia called Anahim Lake at a place called Goose Point. Squiness grabbed his flashlight—which failed to work—and he then ran outside the tent and quickly flung some petrol onto his dying campfire which suddenly burst into a big blaze.

In the light of the big flames he could see four bigfoot about 14 feet away, all lying down in the tall grass as if trying to hide. As the firelight revealed them they stood up and walked away into the darkness. Squiness called out, "Hey, what are you doing here? Come back!"

The four bigfoot ignored his calls and silently withdrew to the dark forest. In the morning Squiness searched for footprints in the grass but could only find a huge handprint on a tree trunk. He later showed it to Clayton Mack, a respected Indian hunting guide from Anahim Lake, who confirmed the creatures were probably sasquatch.[7]

It has been noted that bigfoot are often seen around wild berry fields when the berries are ripe. It has been noted that occasionally people who are out picking berries disappear. Is bigfoot kidnapping these people? In some parts of the United States and Canada picking berries can be a dangerous pastime.

The berry fields around Sister Lakes, Michigan saw the odd bigfoot report, but in June, 1964 there were a series of encounters with a 9-foot bigfoot that was said to lurk in the adjoining swamps. This was a commercial berry operation that hired out-of-state berry pickers at picking time, but this year many were quitting the job because of bigfoot.

Then on June 9, Gordon Brown, a fruit picker from Georgia, was driving near the berry patches at night with his brother when they suddenly saw a bigfoot in the headlights. They stopped the car as the bigfoot disappeared into the woods. They decided to follow its tracks and when they caught up with it they found a 9-foot-tall monster that was a cross between a gorilla and a bear. The two mean hastily retreated to their car and made a quick getaway. Brown later said that he had seen the bigfoot the year before but had been afraid to tell anyone.

The berry farm was part of a farm owned by Evelyn Utrup and her husband John. In the past they had some encounters with bigfoot as it frequently prowled their property. Berries are an important food to bigfoot and, as previously mentioned, berry patches are a spot where bigfoot has been frequently spotted.

Evelyn had seen the bigfoot standing in their yard with the car's headlights on him. She said it had "big bright shining eyes" and that it chased her back into her house with "great thundering feet." She also reported that one of her Alsatian dogs had chased the creature one night and had returned with one eye changed to blue. After a few weeks it changed back to its normal color, brown. What might have caused this? Could a swipe at the dog's face have caused one of its eyes to change color—or does bigfoot have some other occult power that we are unaware of?

On June 10 some locals glimpsed the bigfoot and heard some "baby crying" noises. Then on June 11, three 13-year-old girls were walking on a lonely road in nearby Silver Creek Township— in daylight—when they were suddenly confronted by the smelly creature. He stood in front of them on the road and one of the girls, Joyce Smith, immediately fainted. The other girls, Gail and Patsy Clayton, were frozen with fear. After a few terrifying moments the bigfoot lumbered off into the bushes.[3]

This report in the local news turned the quiet community of Sister Lakes in southwest Michigan near Benton Harbor into a veritable circus. Hundreds of monster hunters and sensation seekers descended on Sister Lakes where the local café started selling "monster burgers" and every store in town had a monster sale of some sort with even monster hunting kits being sold for $7.95. It was monster-mania for a while in this part of Michigan but bigfoot wasn't having any part of it and apparently took off for another berry patch with a swamp next to it.

On September 13, 1964 a camper named Benjamin Wilder was sleeping in his car on a forest road near remote Blue Lake in the northwest corner of California. Wilder was awoken at one a.m. by his car moving. At first he thought it was an earthquake and a rockslide but when he heard no rocks falling he switched on his car's dome light to take a look.

He was shocked to see a large shaggy creature with 3-inch hairs on its chest standing by the driver's door with its two arms on top of the car—shaking it. Wilder shouted at the bigfoot, but it only made "pig-like" noises back. He then sounded the car's horn which scared the bigfoot off and it walked away on two feet over a nearby hill. Wilder never saw the bigfoot's face.

Having a tall bigfoot shaking your car seems pretty scary, but how about a bigfoot reaching inside the car window and grabbing you? In a curious encounter on August 17, 1965, 17-year-old Christine van Acker was driving, with her mother in the passenger's seat, through a wooded area near Monroe in very southeast Michigan, about halfway between Detroit and Toledo, Ohio. The windows of the car were rolled down on that hot August night and as they rounded a bend a large, dark bigfoot stepped out of the forest onto the road.

As in some grade-B horror movie, in her startled terror, Christine meant to accelerate past the creature, but instead stepped on the brake and the car came to a halt and stalled with the motor shutting off. Christine frantically tried to start the car again and suddenly the bigfoot put his huge, hairy hand through the driver's window and grabbed her by the top of her head. Both women were now screaming and bigfoot banged Christine's head against the inside of the car as he suddenly left.

Christine began honking her car horn. Some nearby workmen heard the screams and car horn and came running to the road where they caught a quick glimpse of the 7-foot-tall creature. Christine suffered a black eye and said the creature must have weighed 300 or 400 pounds and had a strong odor about it. [3]

Bigfoot reaching through the car window happened again, but this time in southern California, on the outskirts of Los Angeles and Hollywood! In August of 1966 near the town of Fontana, near Anaheim and the Cleveland National Forest, some boys reported encountering a small bigfoot; one boy said he had been scratched by the creature and had his clothes torn.

Then on August 27 a couple of teenage girls from the area were driving around looking for the monster when they had a shocking encounter with the "man" himself. The driver, 16-year-old Jerri Mendenhall, had driven up a rough dirt track and was backing the car back to the main road when bigfoot suddenly stepped out of the bushes and grabbed her through the window, which was open on the August evening. Jerri screamed and hit the accelerator back to the main road and bigfoot walked back into the bushes. She described it as having very slimy and matted hair and smelling like "a dead animal."

The ordeal was reported to the police who went to the location and found an unexplained footprint that was 17-inches long and had only two toes. Later Jerri Mendenhall went through a hypnotic session about the incident in which she exhibited "extreme fright."[3]

This is pretty normal with any encounter with bigfoot. Except for small children and autistic adults, most people when they encounter bigfoot go into extreme fright and shock. Even those people who have briefly spotted bigfoot before—say in the headlights of

The cover of *Argosy*, 1969.

their car—are still very frightened when they come on the powerful creature again, often in a much closer setting. There is a sudden adrenaline rush when you find bigfoot on the side of the road—with him even reaching into your car—as you drive around in search of the very monster who is now grabbing you. Hollywood can't make this stuff up (but they will be inspired by it) and it is only normal that a teenage girl would need some counseling concerning the traumatic incident, including hypnotism.

The late 1960s were good years for bigfoot. In October of 1967 Bob Gimlin and Roger Patterson filmed the famous bigfoot—a female—at Bluff Creek, California. This 16mm footage would become famous and would earn the men thousands of dollars. More on Patterson and Gimlin in the chapter on bigfoot photographs.

Janet and Colin Bord tell an interesting tale which happened at the end of October 1967. A forest worker named Glenn Thomas had been operating a saw at nearly 6,000 feet on a mountainside near Estacada, Oregon. Thomas took a break from his work and walked down a trail into the woods. He came to a clearing where he saw three bigfoot digging among the rocks. Thomas took them to be a bigfoot family of mother, father and child who were busy foraging for food.

The group was sniffing at the various piles of rocks and suddenly the male began digging furiously and throwing up large rocks, some that would weigh 100 pounds or more. He then brought out some sort of nest of rodents, Thomas thought. The trio chomped the rodents down in several bites each and Thomas said he watched them for about 15 minutes. They then became aware of him and moved off into the forest. He described their faces as more cat-like than human.[3]

Two teenage girls reported that they came face to face with a bigfoot on September 28, 1967 on Vancouver Island, British Columbia. They were near Comox in the Comox Valley area when they heard the loud sound of the slapping of water. They walked around a point and came upon a 7-foot sasquatch with long, dripping reddish-brown hair. The creature held four ducks in one hand and a four-foot-long stick in the other. The girls and the sasquatch stared at each other for several seconds and then both parties ran in different directions. The girls assumed that the stick had been used to slap the water and possibly to kill the ducks.[7]

Another curious encounter which included a mysterious dog happened during the summer of 1969, wherein several bigfoot were seen around a sawmill situated about 20 miles north of Orofino, Idaho. The watchman was a Mr. Moore who had seen three different sizes of footprints in the sawdust, ranging from child-size to very large. He also claimed he heard jabbering and timber being thrown about. Moore said he watched a large, black-haired female bigfoot with large breasts and red eyes for five minutes. The nipple area, face and breasts were not covered with hair. An unpleasant odor was associated with the bigfoot, as is typically indicated, but Moore also said that he saw an enormous dog (black?) with the bigfoot at times.

Reports of bigfoot with pet dogs—or perhaps a pet wolf—are extremely rare but they have been filed occasionally, as well as a bigfoot with two large cats, like cougars.

The cats feature in the Cayton family sightings near Paris Township, near Minerva, Ohio on August 21, 1978. The family of nine witnesses were sitting on their porch at 10:30 in the evening when they heard noises near a demolished chicken coop. Several in the family shone flashlights in the direction, some distance away, and saw two pairs of large yellow eyes reflecting the light of their beams. Eighteen-year-old friend Scott Patterson then drove to the area in his car to see the animals more clearly. He was astonished to see that the two pairs of eyes belonged to two cougar-like animals. As he watched the cougars, suddenly a large bigfoot strode out of the darkness between the two cougars, as if protecting them.

The large bigfoot then lurched at Patterson in his car and the teenager drove back to the house where they phoned the police. The family all sat in the kitchen in a frightened commotion waiting for the police when the bigfoot looked in the kitchen window and then was clearly seen in the outdoor lighting for ten minutes while it stood there in the backyard. The bigfoot—and accompanying pumas—suddenly left and when the local sheriff arrived, deputy

James Shannon, he could find nothing, except for the putrid smell which was lingering.

The next day Mrs. Cayton and a Mrs. Ackerman saw bigfoot around the house, and this time there were two of them. The authorities told them that they thought they had seen a mother bear with two bear cubs. Mrs. Cayton rejected that analysis.[3] In the summer of 2015 a film was released of the incident called *Minerva Monster*.

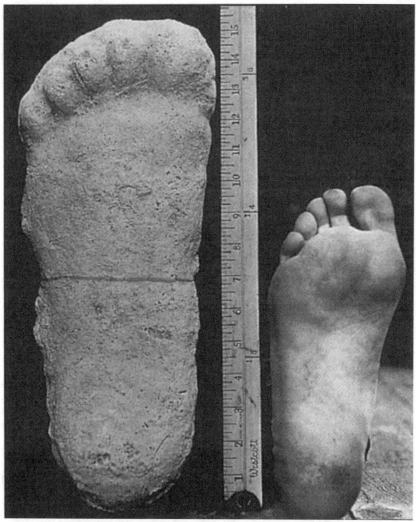

One of the Bluff Creek footprints by Patterson and Gimlin in 1968.

Roachdale, Indiana Meets Bigfoot and some UFOs

The total weirdness came home to middle America in 1972 when bigfoot was seen at the same time as some UFO phenomena occured. During August of 1972 people in the rural areas around Roachdale, Indiana had a number of bigfoot encounters. Roachdale is in central-western Indiana, near the Illinois border, and is famous for its Fourth of July cockroach races, a gimmick started by the town mayor in 1981. During 1972, husband and wife Randy and Lou Rogers were living in a farmhouse outside of the town when, for several nights in a row, a loud banging on the walls and windows of the house occurred. Randy ran out of the house one night with a shotgun in his hands to catch the culprit and saw a 6-foot-tall bigfoot running into a nearby cornfield.

The nighttime visits continued for nearly three weeks, with the smelly creature arriving between 10 and 11:30 every night to pound on the walls of the farmhouse. Lou Rogers became curious about the bigfoot and reasoned that if it had meant to harm them it would have already done so, therefore she began leaving scraps of food out in the evening. The bigfoot began taking the food and would occasionally pop his head up to a window and look inside at Mrs. Rogers. Both Randy and Lou said that the bigfoot would stand on two legs but it ran on all four limbs. A curious illuminated object, like a UFO, was seen hovering above the cornfield where the bigfoot would often disappear.

Then on August 22 at least 60 chickens were found dead on the Roachdale farm owned by Carter Burdine and his uncle Bill Burdine. The chickens had been dismembered and drained of blood, but their bodies not eaten. They were strewn for 200 feet around the chicken house; when they brought the local marshal out to survey the scene, he, together with the Burdines, saw a large animal dash across a nearby road and smash part of a fence down. It left a deep trail through the weeds.

The next day the two men took Carter Burdine's wife into town to stay with relatives until the strange episode was over, and when they returned to the farm they saw a massive bigfoot standing in the 8-foot-high doorway to the chicken house. It completely filled the doorway with its head about a foot higher than the opening, giving the bigfoot a massive appearance. The two men were joined by Carter's father, Herman, and the three of them grabbed their shotguns and cornered the bigfoot in the nearby hay barn. It broke out and ran into the night with the men firing their shotguns at the creature. The men then discovered that another 110 chickens, out of an original flock of 200, had been dismembered and drained of blood. It appears the bigfoot had so much available food in the chicken house

Bigfoot was famous once.

that he gorged himself on chicken blood. He did not return to the farm and things quieted down in rural Roachdale.[3]

In March of 1979 Tom Goff and his wife were in their home at Flower Lake near Tunica, Mississippi, when they heard a ruckus outside. Investigating, they smelled a strong, foul odor and the next evening they spotted a 7- or 8-foot bigfoot in the woods near the house. The next evening, March 9, Tom and his son Rodney armed themselves and waited for bigfoot. When he showed up again they fired a volley of .22 bullets from their rifles and the bigfoot ran away. He came back later that night, however, and pushed on the front door, breaking the frame. The next day the terrified family found blood spots on the door and footprints 16 to 18 inches long.[3] Yes, bigfoot does bleed, but it is hard to bring these creatures down.

Bullets were flying again in late April of 1979 at Dunn Lake outside of Barriére, British Columbia. On April 28 Tim Meissner, age 16, with three of his friends, saw a sasquatch at the lake. After the bigfoot disappeared the boys went to investigate and discovered a dead deer that was concealed under branches and moss. Its neck had been broken and the hind legs were missing.

Then on April 30 the boys returned to the site at Dunn Lake and separated in their search for the bigfoot. Meissner, now alone, suddenly encountered the bigfoot and shot at him. Said Meissner:

He was about 9 feet tall, black and hairy. He had a human-like face with great big glaring bright eyes and shoulders 4 feet wide. He stood there glaring at me for at least three seconds. He was 50 feet away—so close I could smell him. I don't even know why I shot. I was just scared, really scared. I was aiming for right between the eyes and he went down on one knee and one hand. At first I thought he was dead, but I guess I only grazed him, because he got up and ran away at about 30 miles an hour. It couldn't have been any other animal, and it wasn't a human because no human can run that fast, especially straight up an embankment.

Meissner ran back to get his friends, one of whom had a camera, and they searched for evidence of the creature. They found a five-toed footprint with no evidence of claws that was 16 inches long and 9 inches wide at the ball of the foot.[7]

Yes, bigfoot around the country were creating a commotion. They were well known as bigfoot now, stealing chickens, chasing cars, hanging out on the edge of town. Bigfoot was now everywhere and there was no stopping this creature or his publicity campaign. Still, he would have to live a life in the shadows.

Chapter 3

A LIFE IN THE SHADOWS

If you can abide it
Let the hurdy gurdy play
Stranger ones have come by here
Before they flew away
—Grateful Dead, *China Doll*

Despite his newfound fame, bigfoot has remained in the shadows. He crops up from time to time; sometimes he is seen crossing the road, or at the edge of a parking lot late at night. Bigfoot may be standing there, watching you from the shadows.

One story out of the shadows is on the night of April 24, 2021 when a 20-year-old woman walked out of the Warehouse 24-Hour Gym in Richland, Oregon around midnight, her workout complete. She turned to the right and headed to her car in the well-lit parking lot. There were no other vehicles in the lot on that side of the building, which had been constructed and opened in 2018. Said the *Richland Source News* on May 20, 2021:

> The woman heard a twig snap. She looked and saw a creature, seven or eight feet tall and covered in gray fur, racing back into the woods about 30 yards away. It was far too large, likely several hundred pounds, and moved too quickly to be a man, she believed. Shaken and in tears, she called her parents from a nearby restaurant, asking them to come and drive her home.
>
> She had likely encountered a sasquatch, according to nationally acclaimed bigfoot investigator Matthew Moneymaker, who has devoted much of his life to the pursuit of the mysterious creature, including the national

cable TV show, "Finding Bigfoot."

Moneymaker, a California resident who founded the Bigfoot Field Researchers Organization in 1995, spoke to the woman and to her father before posting Report #69065 on his website. There were plans to visit her in person to gain more information and research the location of the sighting, outside the gym at 1151 Commerce Parkway on the city's east side. Unfortunately, Moneymaker said, some of the woman's friends and co-workers learned of her experience through the website and made light of her claim.

She and her father asked her name be removed from the website report, a request with which Moneymaker complied. She isn't interested in further participation.

"She isn't backing off what she claimed she saw. She stands by what she saw and so do her parents," he said. "She is a young woman and doesn't want people who may be ignorant making fun of her. I believe her and I do think it happened."

This woman was so shaken by her experience that she phoned for her parents to come and get her at a restaurant, leaving her car in the parking lot. A meeting with a bigfoot is usually a very frightening encounter. It is quite possible that this encounter could have ended up tragically different and she might have been abducted by a bigfoot.

Richland is in the Snake River area of eastern Oregon and this town is also surrounded by national parks and wilderness areas. To the north of Richland is the Umatilla National Forest and the Wallowa-Whitman National Forest, while to the east is the Payette National Forest. This grey bigfoot was obviously coming from one of these national forests, the same national forests surrounding Fruitland, Idaho, which we will discuss shortly.

Matthew Moneymaker.

Peeping Tom Bigfoot in East Texas

A couple described several bigfoot incidents in a March 5, 2022 report submitted to the BFRO website. These incidents happened around their home in rural Rusk County near Henderson, Texas. This is an area of hilly pine forests and farms near the Louisiana border. Said the report:

> My wife and I live in a rural area in East Texas about 10-15 minutes from a town of about 13-14K people [Henderson]. My wife and I have heard howls on 2 different occasions. Once together about a year and a half ago. ... The first sighting that she had, which was about 2 1/2 years ago, happened at night while she was letting our dogs back in from using the restroom. The dogs were unusually on high alert while she was trying to call them in. She saw and then heard a very large, dark bipedal "thing" running through the pasture behind us. From the sound she knew it was extremely heavy, and it was too quick for a person. I examined the area that night and the next day but the ground was too firm for tracks. I firmly believe she saw and heard a bigfoot that evening.
>
> That brings me to her most recent encounter. On 3-4-22, about 9:20 P.M., I get a text from her while sitting in my recliner while she was in the bathtub that she sees red eyes outside the bathroom window looking at her! I wait for her to finish getting out of the bath to talk to her. She explains to me that while she was standing up to get out of the tub, she had the feeling of being watched. She looked over to the window and saw the red eyes looking at her about mid way up the window.
>
> After she saw them, she immediately looked away due to being startled. The motion light on that end of the house came on when she looked away, and when she looked back, whatever was there was gone. I asked her if she noticed the light coming on and off before she exited the tub and she said that she didn't recall it coming on, but wasn't really paying attention. She said she wouldn't have

noticed the light due to her being on her phone while in the tub, and most of, if not nearly all of the window in her line of sight is blocked by a large plant that's by the window. The motion light is very sensitive and responds well to the slightest movement. After she saw nothing was there, she immediately closed the window and curtains.

She told me that she didn't feel threatened by whatever it was looking at her, just startled to see red eyes and something right outside the window. She did not see the outline of a body, just the eyes. I asked how far apart the eyes were, and from what she showed me, it came out to be about 6 inches apart. Further apart than our eyes are for sure. She said that she did not hear it run away, and did not smell anything unpleasant, except the coil cleaner.

After hearing this, I grabbed my .45 and walked outside to the window to examine the area. I had her go to the window on the inside so that I could get a little more information out of her. Understandably she was pretty shaken up at this point. When I get to the window she showed me approximately how high the eyes were off the ground and where they were positioned. Now keep in mind our house sits off the ground and isn't on a slab. She said the eyes were just below the bottom sash bar of the window. When I opened the window earlier, I opened it up as far as it would go up. I'm 6 feet tall and going off where she said the eyes were, I estimated them to be around 6 foot 8, to 7 feet off the ground.

Yes, bigfoot is a Peeping Tom, looking in bathroom windows and even bedroom windows. A 2005 police report from the White Mountain Apache Reservation was about a bigfoot that was peeking a couple in their bedroom around midnight one night and they called the police. When a female police officer arrived at their house only minutes after they called the police, she filed a report saying that she had seen a bigfoot standing in the driveway as she pulled up to the house. It immediately ran away, but the officer was not afraid to file an official police report of the incident. I tell this tale in my book *Bigfoot Nation*.

Unfortunately, it may be the case that a woman or child that is alone may find that a bigfoot looking in a window or tent flap is determined to kidnap them. Sadly, this may be the case with some missing people in rural areas.

Police Look into Michigan Bigfoot Sighting

Meanwhile, according to the *Oakland Press* (Michigan) on June 22, 2022, local police said that they had responded to a bigfoot sighting in Shelby Township in Macomb County in the Upper Peninsula of Michigan. The police responded to a call from a local resident the night of June 17 reporting she had captured an image on her home surveillance camera that resembled a bigfoot. The woman was apparently afraid that a bigfoot was hanging around her house and called the police. According to the Macomb County Scanner Facebook page, officers searched the area but did not find a sasquatch or anything resembling the fabled large, apelike creature.

The possible bigfoot sighting in Shelby Township is now being downplayed by police and described as a "suspicious incident" and a "shadow or silhouette" captured on a resident's surveillance camera. A release from Shelby Township Police on June 23 confirms that officers searched the area but "after a thorough investigation, there was no bigfoot sighting in Shelby Township."

Michigan Bigfoot researchers Gabe Heiss, of Southeast Michigan Bigfoot Research Organization, and Josh Parsons, who produces the Hide and Seek Archives Bigfoot podcast, say that kind of response from law enforcement or government officials is not uncommon. In particular, reported urban bigfoot sightings tend to make some people uncomfortable.

"A lot of times police want to keep bigfoot reports quiet," said Parsons. "Part of it may be that they don't want to alarm people."

Heiss notes that a well-known sasquatch sighting in Monroe in 1965 was downplayed by local officials. "The police went as far as taking a caveman statue from the Prehistoric Forest in Irish Hills and placing it in a field near the reported encounter as a cover-up," said Heiss.

Indeed, for many decades the local police in many states have sought to downplay reports of bigfoot or sasquatch, as well as reports of missing people in areas known for bigfoot sightings. This would seem to be a sensible practice as alarming residents to a nocturnal boogeyman may not be a very good policy.

A Missing Boy in Idaho

Children are often part of the story when a bigfoot is seen around a farm, ranch or rural property. It has been suspected that some young children are kidnapped by a bigfoot purely out of curiosity. Sometimes these children are found alive, sometimes they are found dead, and sometimes they are never found at all.

On July 27, 2021 a five-year-old boy named Michael Joseph Vaughan went missing in a small town in western Idaho called Fruitland. A search for him began immediately but no trace of him has ever been found. Fruitland, near the Oregon border, is known for its many orchards. The town is also surrounded by national parks and wilderness areas. A number of forest fires were burning in the vast forests of Idaho just north of Fruitland at the time of the boy's disappearance. This is an area that is known for bigfoot sightings.

An August 5, 2021 article on kivitv.com entitled "Fruitland Police detail latest search efforts to locate missing 5-year-old boy" said:

> The Fruitland Police Department said search crews have scoured 3,000 acres of farmland, 29 miles of the riverbank, and about 200 residential homes hoping to find five-year-old Michael Vaughan. Vaughan disappeared near his home in Fruitland on July 27. "I have to tell you that I spent my entire childhood in the neighborhood where Michael went missing," said JD Huff, Fruitland Chief of Police. "My children are growing up here. My law enforcement partners are mothers, fathers, uncles, or friends of children just like Michael. We are all in and we are committed to finding Michael."
>
> On Wednesday, Fruitland held another press conference to share the latest on the search.
>
> "We have gathered 60 different video files from residential and business security cameras and are combing

through the data as we speak. To date, we have received 163 tips, all have been assigned to investigators for follow-up. Many have already been cleared, others are being worked on as we speak," Huff said.

Huff says about 13 law enforcement agencies have helped and their next plan is to bring in a dive team.

"The reason why we're doing that is because we have lots of resources available. We're not too sure what happened. They're going to be at the end of Southwest 8th street down by the Snake River and slough area," he said. Police continue to ask residents to search their properties thoroughly and people outside the Fruitland area can still provide support by passing out flyers.

"Our primary goal, the number one goal, is to find Michael and bring him home," he said.

As of the 2010 census, Fruitland had a total population of 4,684. The Snake River runs through Fruitland and the town is virtually surrounded by national forests and wilderness areas. These include the Payette National Forest to the north and the Boise National Forest to the east.

The Snake River is the largest tributary of the Columbia River,

IDAHO MISSING PERSONS CLEARINGHOUSE
ENDANGERED MISSING

VAUGHAN, MICHAEL JOSEPH

Last Contact: 07/27/2021 (age 05)

Age: 05
Gender: MALE
Race: WHITE
Height: 3'07"
Weight: 60 LBS
Hair Color: BLONDE
Eye Color: BLUE

LAST SEEN WEARING A LIGHT BLUE MINECRAFT SHIRT AND BLACK BOXER BRIEFS WITH LIME GREEN STITCHING, WITH SIZE 11 FLIP FLOP SANDALS. LAST SEEN AROUND SOUTHWEST 9TH STREET IN FRUITLAND, IDAHO. THIS PHOTO WAS TAKEN 1 MONTH PRIOR TO LAST SEEN DATE

IF YOU HAVE ANY INFORMATION CONCERNING MICHAEL PLEASE CONTACT FRUITLAND POLICE DEPARTMENT DISPATCH @ (208) 642-6006 or email tips and leads to findmichael@fruitland.org

https://www.facebook.com/IDMPC Twitter: @ISP_Alerts https://isp.idaho.gov/bci/missing-persons/

A poster for the missing Idaho boy Michael Vaughn.

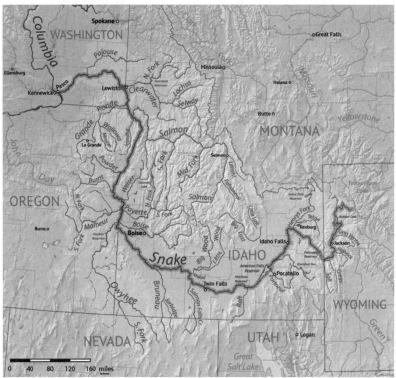

The Snake River drainage area of Wyoming, Idaho, Oregon and Washington.

which in turn is the largest North American river that empties into the Pacific Ocean. The Snake River rises in western Wyoming, then flows through the Snake River Plain of southern Idaho, the rugged Hells Canyon on the Oregon–Idaho border and the rolling Palouse Hills of Washington. It empties into the Columbia River at Tri-Cities, Washington.

The Snake River drainage basin encompasses parts of six U.S. states—Idaho, Washington, Oregon, Utah, Nevada, and Wyoming. Gigantic glacial-retreat flooding episodes that occurred during the previous Ice Age carved out canyons, cliffs and waterfalls along the lower and middle sections of the river. Two of these catastrophic flooding events, the Missoula Flood and Bonneville Flood, significantly affected the river and its surroundings.

It is thought that Native Americans have lived along the Snake River for more than 11,000 years. Salmon from the Pacific Ocean spawn by the millions in the river every year, and were a vital source of food for people living on the river. The area around the town of Fruitland is a wild area full of salmon, bears, elk, and, dare I say, bigfoot. In Fruitland the police updated the press every few weeks through October of 2021 on the progress of the search for Michael Vaughan. On September 27, 2021, the CBS2 website, under the title "5-year-old Michael Vaughan missing now for two months," said:

> The exhaustive search for a missing Fruitland boy has been underway now for a staggering two months.
>
> Last week, Fruitland Police shared with the community another update on the ongoing search for Michael Joseph Vaughan, who disappeared July 27. To date, the department's tipline has received 446 tips.
>
> "We are committed to scrutinizing every detail in this investigation and it is going to take time," Fruitland PD said. "This remains a very active investigation at all levels and will continue."
>
> Police also said in its update that many folks have shared concerns about the cornfields, but "those fields have been harvested and cleared leaving no trace of Michael."
>
> The reward for information leading to the safe return of Michael is up to $26,000.
>
> Tips can be sent to findmichael@fruitland.org or to Crime Stoppers, 343COPS.com. Tips may remain anonymous.

In a final update by the police on October 8, 2021, the reward for Michael's safe return was increased to $60,000. Vaughan has never been found. None of the 446 tips came to anything. This 5-year-old boy had vanished from the rural edge of town. What happened to Michael Joseph Vaughan? Apparently the police believe he was abducted—but by whom? Was he abducted by someone with a car who then drove away with the young boy? Or is it possible that Michael was one of the many children who go missing in or near wilderness areas—abducted by a bigfoot?

While we do not have evidence that a bigfoot was involved in this boy's kidnapping, it is an example of children who do indeed go missing even playing in their own backyards near a wilderness area. I mention this case because it is one of the most recent. In my book *Bigfoot Nation* I describe a number of cases where a bigfoot is seen on the edge of a town, or even dumpster diving near a supermarket.

Skinwalker Caught on Camera in Texas?

Speaking of strange creatures hanging around the edge of town or dumpster diving, something strange was seen lurking outside a Texas zoo on the night of May 21, 2022 and a photo was taken of the curious entity by a security camera. The dark figure in the photo, seen here, looks to be something of a wolfman.

The Fort Worth Star Telegram (and other newspapers) reported on June 8, 2022, that the security cameras at the Amarillo Zoo captured the mysterious creature "in the dark and early morning hours" of Saturday, May 21, according to a June 8 news release from the city of Amarillo. A still photo from the recording shows the life form outside the zoo's perimeter fence at 1:25 a.m. Said the newspaper article, quoting the city of Amarillo:

> "Was it a person with a strange hat who likes to walk at night?" the city asked. "A large coyote on its hind legs? A Chupacabra? It is a mystery–for Amarillo to help solve."
>
> As the visitor's identity remains unknown, the Texas Panhandle city has declared it an "Unidentified Amarillo Object"—or UAO, for short. But city officials hope someone may be able to offer a better explanation.
>
> "We just want to let the Amarillo community have some fun with this," Director of Parks and Recreation Michael Kashuba said in the news release. "... It is definitely a strange and interesting image. Maybe Amarillo can help solve the mystery of our UAO."
>
> The city said it does not have video footage of the encounter to share, so eager UAO detectives will have to use the still image to crack the case. Is it a curious skinwalker, wolfman, or someone in a costume?
>
> "It is important to note that this entity was outside the Amarillo Zoo," Kashuba said. "There were no signs of attempted entry into the zoo. No animals or individuals were harmed. There were no signs of criminal activity or vandalism."

05/21/2022 01:25 AM   51°F

The photo of a skinwalker or bigfoot from the Fort Worth Zoo.

The photograph is fascinating. One can see the ears standing up like a coyote or wolf's ears. Is it possibly a bigfoot? There have been stories and sketches of bigfoot that have tufted or pointed ears. There have also been reports of so-called "dogmen" or werewolf-type skinwalkers. These are shamans who have the ability to shapeshift into a coyote or wolf. Can bigfoot be mistaken for other animals?

Is Bigfoot a Bear?

As a young man in the 1970s I spent portions of several years trekking and climbing in the Himalayas of Nepal. I became fascinated by the lore of the Himalayas which include stories of the yeti and the abominable snowman. In the last 20 years or so, a number of books have been written by Europeans, but not by Nepalese or Indians, that have suggested very strongly that sightings of the yeti are simply mistaken viewing of a bear, usually thought to be the Himalayan Black Bear. This bear is only about 5 feet in height but there is an Asian Brown which also ranges in the Himalayas and is larger, reaching about 9 feet in height for the largest of these animals.

What has been suggested by the Austrian mountain climber Reinhold Messner, an accomplished climber and the author of a number of books, including *My   Quest for the Yeti,*[42] is that all of the yeti sightings in Nepal, Bhutan, India, Pakistan, Tibet, Mongolia and elsewhere are simply the misidentification of bears, either Asian Black Bears or Asian Brown Bears.

The main argument that these authors make is that bears will sometimes stand up on two legs and walk forward. Their front paws are up and they standing as tall as they can so as to frighten the intruder, who is a human. This human then mistakes the bear standing on two legs as a yeti, or shall we say, a bigfoot.

Even though Messner gives us some pretty interesting yeti accounts that he has been privy to, he ultimately concludes that they are encounters with bears. A similar approach is the Oxford Press of New Delhi's publication of the book *Yeti: The Ecology of a Mystery* by Daniel Taylor.[53] Taylor is a British biologist who has taken an interest in the ecology of eastern Nepal, near the Sikkim border and the area of Kanchenjunga, the third highest mountain in the world.

As I explain in my book *Yetis, Sasquatch and Hairy Giants*[28] the Kanchenjunga area is an area of many yeti stories. In fact, a term for yetis in the area is Kanchenjunga Demons. It was in this area that the sighting occurred that created the term "abominable

A Himalayan brown bear standing on its back legs.

snowman." It is also in this area that the famous yeti footprints were photographed by the British mountain climber Eric Shipton. Yeti stories are numerous in Nepal and Bhutan and they specifically refer to an intelligent apelike man.

What Taylor ultimately concludes in his 2017 book is that the yeti sightings in eastern Nepal and elsewhere, including Bhutan, are simply encounters with bears who are standing on their hind legs. It is that simple. Bears stand on their hind legs and people mistake them for yetis because they are startled and afraid.

This may sound like a sound argument to researchers who are coming from Austria and Britain where few stories of bigfoot animals exist. There are no bears in Britain. But when this argument that "bigfoot is a bear" is brought to researchers in Canada and the USA it completely falls apart. While the occasional forest service employee might suggest to a witness that they had "seen a bear," most witnesses know what a bear looks like and what they saw was definitely not a bear.

Essentially these authors on the yeti are simply unaware of the amount of evidence for bigfoot in North America and choose to ignore it. I can tell you as a collector of books on bigfoot, yetis and sasquatch that no book has ever been written in North America that asserts that all of the bigfoot sightings are mistaken encounters with bears. The few books that are openly skeptical about bigfoot claim that the animal is completely mythical and the sightings and photographs are hoaxes. There is no real suggestion that these hundreds of stories are about bears in any book, but skeptics must acknowledge that some of these people have seen something, and that that something was maybe a bear.

Yet, this "bigfoot is a bear" view of yetis and such is still promulgated by these European yeti experts who push their bear theory in their yeti books. One recent story was of one of these authors being in the United States promoting their yeti book. When a woman who believed she had encountered a bigfoot asked the visiting author about it he told her that she had only seen a bear. The woman then burst into tears in disbelief of his statement.

Bears are familiar to most Canadians and Americans and while a bear standing up on two legs might induce a frightened person to believe they had seen a bigfoot the overwhelming evidence in

The famous 1951 photo of a yeti footprint near Mount Everest.

the form of testimony and photographs indeed shows that there is a form of giant ape in North America that is as yet unrecognized.

Despite the notion that yetis are being exposed as bears in Bhutan, Sikkim and Nepal, there is prominent product placement in the form of Yeti Airlines, the Yak and Yeti Hotel, and plenty of yeti burgers and drinks being sold in Kathmandu. Yes, marketing for the yeti is strong in Nepal but the big marketing is in the USA and Canada where bigfoot and sasquatch are serious advertising icons selling everything from gasoline to lawn ornaments and key chains.

The New York artist Andy Warhol said that everyone will be

famous for fifteen minutes in their lifetime. Well, bigfoot has had his fifteen minutes and his time is not up. He will not fade. He will not back down.

The FBI Releases Its Bigfoot Files

Yes, the FBI has a file on bigfoot. Yetis and bigfoot were back in the news in early June of 2019 when the FBI decided to release its files on bigfoot. The FBI usually doesn't make such documents public until after the subject of the investigation dies, which makes the latest release from the FBI something special as it seems that bigfoot is not dead and is probably very much alive. The FBI did not say that he was a wanted man, however.

The "FBI Bigfoot Files" were only 22 pages and one has to assume, I think, that this in not the full extent of bigfoot in the FBI database. In fact, there may be thousands of pages of FBI files that concern bigfoot—we will never know.

The 22 pages that were released were essentially about avid British-American yeti and bigfoot researcher Peter Byrne. Byrne had visited India and Nepal while in the British Air Force and had taken a keen interest in yetis and bigfoot. He eventually moved to The Dalles, Oregon where he became the founder and director of the Bigfoot Information Center and Exhibition.

All 22 of the pages concerned the origin of 15 unidentified hairs and tissue sent to the agency by Byrne. The documents, which date back to the 1970s, include a letter from Peter Byrne asking if the FBI would analyze some mysterious samples—"the first that we have obtained in six years which we feel may be of importance"—that he suspected of belonging to a sasquatch.

An NBC news story by Dan Mangan was published on June 6, 2019 entitled "FBI releases 'Bigfoot' documents from 1970s" The subtitle said: "A man intent on proving the existence of the mythical creature got the agency to test samples, which turned out to be deer hair." Said the story:

Yeti persisted.
An Oregon man intent on proving the existence of

the mythical creatures known as Bigfoot, Sasquatch, the Abominable Snowman and Yeti in 1976 managed to get the FBI to test hair and tissue samples that he believed might help his case, according to newly released records.

"The FBI has analyzed hair in connection with the search for Sasquatch, aka 'Bigfoot,'" an internal FBI memo noted in February 1977.

On Wednesday, the same man who spurred that analysis, 93-year-old Peter Byrne, told CNBC that he still hasn't given up hope of proving that Bigfoot is a real—if exceedingly rare—creature.

"It's a great challenge," Byrne said, when asked to explain his interest over nine decades in finding creatures widely believed to be figments of imagination, or the inventions of con men. Byrne's web page says that he "has always had an interest in the unknown and the mysterious" since his father used to tell him bedtime stories about the Yeti of the Himalayas.

The page says his "first opportunity to go looking for the Yeti occurred in 1946, when he was still in the British Royal Air Force in Bombay, India."

A photo on that page shows him "with the famous Yeti scalp" at a temple in the Himalayas in Nepal in 1958. Another photo shows a very big footprint of a possible Bigfoot.

His desire to see a Yeti for himself led him to launch three extensive expeditions searching for the Yeti in Nepal in the late 1950s. Byrne said that in the past 50 years he had found two or three sets of possible Yeti footprints, with five toes on each foot, left in tracks in the Himalayas, at altitudes of 15,000 feet.

But he conceded Wednesday that those prints could have been left by Hindu holy men, or sadhus, whom he has seen walking barefoot in the snows at such heights. After moving to the U.S. in the 1960s, Byrne went on to direct "The Bigfoot Information Center and Exhibition" in Oregon.

With the backing of what he said were wealthy men, he

1 – [   ] (Information)
1 – Mr. Cochran
1 – [   ] (Attn: [   ]   b6
1 – [   ]   b7C

December 15, 1976

OUTSIDE SOURCES
LABORATORY EXAMINATIONS AND
INQUIRIES CONCERNING THE BIGFOOT
INFORMATION CENTER AND EXHIBITION
THE DALLES OREGON
(SAS QUATCH)

Mr. Peter Byrne
Director
The Bigfoot Information Center
and Exhibition
West Sixth Street and Hostetler
The Dalles, Oregon 97058

Dear Mr. Byrne:

I have received your letter of November 24th
requesting an FBI Laboratory analysis of 15 unidentified
hairs and tissue.

The FBI Laboratory conducts examinations primarily
of physical evidence for law enforcement agencies in connection
with criminal investigations. Occasionally, on a case-by-case
basis, in the interest of research and scientific inquiry,
we make exceptions to this general policy. With this
understanding, we will examine the hairs and tissue mentioned
in your letter.

They should be submitted to the FBI Laboratory,
Scientific Analysis Section, J. Edgar Hoover Building,
Washington, D.C. 20535, Attention: Special Agent [   ]
In your reply please include available background information
concerning the source of the specimen.

Sincerely yours,

(S) Jay Cochran, Jr.

Jay Cochran, Jr.
Assistant Director FBI
Scientific and Technical
Services Division

1 – SAC, Portland (Enclosures)
(For information)

One of the pages of the FBI bigfoot files.

tried to find conclusive evidence of Bigfoot, also known as Sasquatch in America's Pacific Northwest.

"I was in it full time, seven days a week," Byrne said of his earlier Bigfoot hunts, which last were funded in the 1990s.

"Right now, I'm still active," Byrne said.

"We have motion-sensitive cameras out in the mountains" of Oregon, he said.

But, he added, "it's a hobby for me now."

When told about the FBI documents showing his correspondence with the agency in the 1970s asking it to test hair samples, Byrne chuckled.

But he also said, "I don't remember this."

"It's out of my memory," he added, while noting that he does recall asking the FBI in the 1970s about an incident at a campground in Washington state where a Bigfoot was suspected.

However, FBI records disclosed by the agency on its public documents page show that in 1976, Byrne repeatedly wrote the FBI asking for the tests to be conducted on both hair his group had obtained, and on other samples that he had heard might be in the agency's possession.

"We do not often come across hair which we are unable to identify and the hair that we have now, about 15 hairs attached to a tiny piece of skin, is the first that we have obtained in six years which we feel may be of importance," Byrne wrote in a Nov. 24, 1976, letter to FBI Assistant Director Jay Cochran Jr.

In an earlier letter, in August of that year, Byrne had asked if hair, "supposedly of a Bigfoot," that he believed had been sent to the FBI by others had been examined.

"Will you kindly set the record straight, once and for all, inform us if the FBI has examined hair which might be that of a Bigfoot, when this took place, and if it did take place what the results of the analysis were," he wrote.

"Please understand that our research here is serious," Byrne wrote.

"That this is a serious question that needs answering."

In a response finally sent to Byrne on Dec. 15, 1976, Cochran, of the bureau's scientific and technical services division, noted that the FBI laboratory normally conducts examinations "of physical evidence for law enforcement agencies in connection with criminal investigations."

But Cochran added, "occasionally, on a case-by-case basis, in the interest of research and scientific inquiry, we make exceptions to the general policy."

"We will examine the hairs and tissue mentioned in your letter," Cochran wrote to Byrne.

It was the first time that the FBI apparently tested a sample of hair to see if it was a Bigfoot, according to the records, which contain photocopied images of the hairs. The FBI acted relatively quickly after Cochran told Byrne the tests would be done.

In February 1977, Cochran wrote Howard Curtis, executive vice president of the Academy of Applied Science in Boston, which had a relationship with Byrne's Bigfoot group. The academy had been the chief sponsor of a search for the Loch Ness monster in Scotland. Cochran's letter noted that the results were being sent to Curtis, at his request, because "Mr. Byrne will be out of the country for several months."

Byrne, according to Curtis, was in Nepal at the time.

Cochran said the examination of the hair "included a study of morphological characteristics such as root structure, medullary structure and cuticle thickness in addition to scale casts."

"Also, the hairs were compared directly with hairs of known origin under a comparison microscope," he added.

At the end of all that: "It was concluded as a result of these examinations that the hairs are of a deer family origin," Cochran wrote.

"The hair sample you submitted is being returned as an enclosure in this letter."

Even though he does not recall that test being performed, or the FBI's conclusion, more than 40 years later Byrne still dreams of finding a Bigfoot.

OFFICIAL FORM NO. 10
MAY 1962 EDITION
GSA GEN. REG. NO. 27

UNITED STATES GOVERNMENT

Memorandum

TO : Mr. Cochran

FROM :

SUBJECT: REQUESTED EXAMINATION OF
UNIDENTIFIED HAIR FROM THE
BIGFOOT INFORMATION CENTER
AND EXHIBITION
THE DALLES, OREGON

1 - Mr. Cochran
1 -
1 -

DATE: 2/22/77

b6
b7C

Assoc. Dir. _____
Dep. AD Adm. _____
Dep. AD Inv. _____
Asst. Dir.:
Adm. Serv. _____
Ext. Affairs _____
Fin. & Pers. _____
Gen. Inv. _____
Ident. _____
Inspection _____
Intell. _____
Laboratory _____
Legal Coun. _____
Plan. & Eval. _____
Rec. Mgnt. _____
Spec. Inv. _____
Training _____
Telephone Rm. _____
Director Sec'y _____

PURPOSE:

To report the results of the examination of hairs from the
captioned organization.

DETAILS:

By memorandum, Cochran to McDermott, dated 12/13/76, we
agreed to examine a hair sample on behalf of the captioned organization.
A letter to this effect dated 12/15/76, was sent to Mr. Peter Byrne,
Director of captioned organization.

Recently, the hair sample (photograph attached) was delivered
to the Laboratory by Mr. Howard S. Curtis, Executive Vice President,
Academy of Applied Science, Boston, Massachusetts. This Academy
sponsors the captioned organization.

The hairs were determined to be from a member of the deer
family.

ST-126   REC 61   95-213013-6

Mr. Curtis requested that a letter setting forth the results of
the examination be furnished to him since Mr. Byrne will be out of the
country for several months. He also requested that the hairs be
returned to him.

ENCLOSURE ATTACHED

Enclosure

22 MAR 1 1977

MSC/pjm* (4)

(CONTINUED – OVER)

One of the pages of the FBI bigfoot files.

"No, no," Byrne answered ruefully, when asked if he had ever actually seen a Yeti or Bigfoot. "I'd love to see one."

"There's been sightings," he said.

He noted that he once found in the Pacific Northwest a "huge footprint" of what would have been an upright mammal with five toes on each foot and a "46-inch stride." And, "We had a sighting 10 days ago [of a Bigfoot] from a very reliable, very good friend of mine," Byrne said.

Last year, he said, there was a sighting of a suspected Sasquatch by seven loggers, who were surprised to see a huge creature ambling their way. When it came to believing in Bigfoot, Byrne noted, those men were "all totally skeptical right until then."

Byrne pleaded guilty in August 2013 to defrauding the Social Security Administration, the Oregon Department of Human Services and Medicaid out of more than $78,000 by concealing his travels outside of the United States from 1992 through 2012. Byrne, who was sentenced to three years of probation and full restitution, had been receiving Supplemental Social Security Income, and had been required to report to Social Security certain travel outside of the U.S. at times he was getting that need-based benefit.

"Between 1992 and 2012, Byrne traveled outside the U.S. for more than 30 days at least 15 times, on some occasions remaining outside the U.S. for more than four months," prosecutors said at the time. He also had more than $85,000 in bank accounts at one time when he was getting SSI and food stamps, authorities said.

According to federal prosecutors in 2013, investigators found a copy of a letter Byrne had sent his publisher, Safari Press, "directing that any future royalties for his published books be sent to his girlfriend."

"Byrne had previously been questioned by investigators whether he was receiving royalties for the books he had written on topics such as his search for Bigfoot and game-hunting in Nepal," the U.S. Attorney's Office for Oregon said in a press release at the time. "

"Byrne denied receiving royalties."

The FBI decided that the hair samples were from the deer family and you could say, "case closed." Peter Byrne didn't even remember sending the samples or writing the letters to the FBI. He was away in Nepal during much of the correspondence. When the FBI bigfoot files were released in 2019 Byrne was 93 years old. He is definitely getting up there in age.

In a July 23, 2019 article about Byrne for Portland, Oregon's NBC Channel KGW8 (kgw.com) they said:

> A 93-year-old man who lives in Oregon's coast range has a pastime most of us wouldn't expect. He may be in his 90s, but that's not stopping his hunt for Bigfoot.
>
> Peter Byrne has spent much of his life searching for Sasquatch.
>
> In fact, back in the 1970s Byrne ran The Bigfoot Information Center headquartered in The Dalles. We decided to track him down after seeing his name in recently released FBI documents that show that at least for a little while, the Bureau was actually looking into Bigfoot thanks to Byrne, who sent the agency a hair sample he thought was suspicious.
>
> In 1971, KGW interviewed people in Skamania County who said they had experiences with Bigfoot or heard about someone who did.

Peter Byrne in Oregon at the age of 93.

"Suddenly turn around and I'm face to face with him," said one woman who spoke with former KGW News reporter Jon Tuttle.

She said the creature she saw had wide shoulders, no neck, and stood 12 feet tall. The woman, referred to as Mrs. Baxter, also said its hair was dark brown, had "terrible glowing eyes" with a receded forehead, big teeth and long hair. Tuttle reported that her story was similar to dozens of others told every year in the area.

"It seems to me that there's a preponderance of evidence, and I'm, let's say 95-98%, that there is such an animal," another man said.

Call it lore, call it legend, stories say the infamous Sasquatch supposedly lives in the woods of the Pacific Northwest. Byrne said there was a credible sighting in the 70s. "We got there quickly and we searched for hair and we found hair snagged on some thorn bushes," he said. At the time, Byrne was the founder of The Bigfoot Information Center headquartered in The Dalles.

He sent the samples into the FBI for testing in 1976. The agency decided to take on the task of determining the origin of the hair. For more than 40 years, Byrne waited for a response from the FBI. Although documents indicate the agency tried to get back to him, word never reached Byrne.

That is until last month when the bureau publicly released documents related to Bigfoot. In those pages were their findings regarding the hair samples Byrne had sent in.

"They say the hair is deer hair," Byrne said.

… What's clear is that Byrne's search for Sasquatch is still on.

"I believe in it. I think there's something there," he said. These days at 93 years old, the search for Bigfoot has become more of a hobby for Byrne.

He said he's never personally seen Bigfoot, but has heard strange noises in the woods and fielded many reports.

"I've interviewed far too many people, you know state policemen, engineers, loggers, people who will look you straight in the eye and give you a straight story," he said.

We should also mention that the science of identifying hair samples has evolved considerably since the 1970s and a reexamination of that hair sample could yield a different result.

One has to wonder if this is the totality of files on bigfoot that the FBI has accumulated. Because of the number of strange disappearances and deaths in various wilderness areas around the United States, one has to wonder if the FBI has ever investigated any of these cases and whether the term "bigfoot" is ever used? Is it possible that bigfoot appears in other FBI and police files as a "suspect"? I guess you could at least call him a "person of interest."

Bigfoot Saves a Toddler and a "Walking Tree"

Prior to the FBI releasing their bigfoot files, in late January of 2019 a toddler went missing in North Carolina and mysteriously turned up alive a few days later. This three-year-old boy told his family that he "hung out with a bear for two days."

According to a January 25, 2019 story in *The Charlotte Observer*, Casey Lynn Hathaway, 3, disappeared on January 22, 2019 from his grandmother's backyard while playing with other children, the Craven County Sheriff's Office said.

The FBI, state investigators, and the U.S. Marine Corps from nearby bases at Camp Lejeune and Cherry Point joined the effort to find the boy. On January 25, Hathaway was found. He was located by professional search and rescue teams, the FBI said. "Casey is healthy, smiling and talking," Breanna Hathaway wrote. "He said he hung out with a bear for two days. God sent him a friend to keep him safe. God is a good God. Miracles do happen."

Craven County Sheriff Chip Hughes told reporters on Thursday that authorities were able to find the boy after hearing someone call out for their mother. They then found the boy stuck in "a tangle of vines and thorns" about a half-mile from the place where he disappeared. The boy was discovered "wet, cold and scratched up" but he could talk.

Was he with a bear or with a bigfoot?

Another newspaper story concerning came out of Kentucky in late October of 2018 when a bigfoot was seen by a woman driving with her husband at dusk. A report from the *Lexington Herald Reader* on October 24, 2018 said that a woman reported seeing a frightening "creature" on a road outside the eastern Kentucky town of Sandy Hook, prompting an investigation by the Bigfoot Field Researchers Organization (BFRO). The group recently released a "follow-up report" that concludes the woman saw something that wasn't human. Sandy Hook is about 100 miles east of Lexington.

The woman is reported to have seen "a creature" while she was a passenger in her husband's vehicle, about 7:45 p.m. on October 18. She told the local newspaper, "At some point, I started screaming... 'There is something in the road!'"

She described the creature as a "walking tree." The entire encounter lasted only three to five seconds and the animal was nearly 100 feet away, she said. "I'm looking at this thing which is... at least 7 feet tall. It was the color of a tree... It turned its head and looked straight at our car."

The woman's husband saw only "a strange shadow, but not the creature," says the BFRO report. BFRO called the incident a "possible sasquatch was observed at a great distance or in poor lighting."

Attacked By a Bigfoot?

Meanwhile, in Klamath County, Oregon, in early May of 2019, as reported by NBC station KOBI-5 News, a man called the police and told them that a bigfoot had tried to kill him with an axe. The call came into Klamath County 911 dispatch in the afternoon of May 9. The caller appeared intoxicated.

"The caller was not providing a lot of information," said Klamath County Deputy District Attorney Cole Chase. "And was threatening,

Bigfoot making the headlines.

93

rude, and abusive to 911 dispatchers, but the officers still responded quickly."

Officers responded at high speed to the Chiloquin area. Deputies say Timothy Drennen told them that it was a sasquatch who attacked him. "The defendant Mr. Drennen was combative, made some threats, but ultimately was taken into custody without any physical incident," Chase said.

The deputy D.A. says he can't comment on any evidence that may be presented in court, though he added an important observation: "Upon a subsequent investigation, there were no signs that Sasquatch was present." Drennen is charged with misuse of 911 and initiating a false report.

"It doesn't appear as though there's any issue of mental health concern here," Chase said. "This was strictly intoxication."

It seems unfortunate that someone might blame bigfoot for attacking them, however bigfoot has been known to attack people. Though bigfoot has been seen carrying a club it seems unlikely that he would have an axe—but it is not out of the question.

Meanwhile, during the summer of 2019 a strange humanoid creature began terrorizing a town in Texas. *The Galveston Daily News* on September 10 reported that "an unidentified humanoid has been repeatedly spotted in the city of Santa Fe, a community just southwest of metropolitan Houston, with one witness claiming they saw the beast attempt to snatch a cat. Described as a monkey, by others as a chimpanzee and as 'anything's possible' by police, a sense of apprehension is spreading."

The story said that the creature was first reported by Patricia de la Mora. She had apparently been woken up after midnight by thunder and lightning, and after urging her husband to look out of the window when she heard "strange noises," he eventually got out of bed herself, opened the curtains and was "paralyzed by fear." "I look out the window and I see it was in there. It was a monkey, a big one," she later told the news service.

She then closed the curtains before the animal saw her and called the police and reported that she had seen some kind of primate causing pandemonium. When police arrived the creature had vanished, and despite an hour-long search, all trace of the supposed animal had evaporated.

However, the enigmatic agitator soon struck again and police received a similar report the following day. The incident occurred in the same part of town, reported by a woman who claimed she spent 20 minutes hiding in her car.

Police again launched a futile search for any physical manifestation of the supposed monkey's existence. Several residents in the area came forward and reported on social media that they too had seen a monkey. One witness claimed that the creature had tried to kidnap their cat, and another witness reported that a child had been attacked by this mysterious animal.

Bayou Animal Services, which deals with animal control in the area, was unable to provide any further insight into the veracity of the claims, said the story. Eventually the sightings stopped and we may presume that the animal moved on to another area, probably away from the city. We might assume that this was a young bigfoot who was a bit too curious about civilization—coming very close to the city of Houston.

It was also reported that there was a bigfoot sighting in Argentina in March of 2019. The local police in the community of Quines, located in northern San Luis province, were seeking a "gorilla" in the Banda Este region, a rather rural location full of chacras (small ranches).

According to *El Diario de La República* newspaper, the animal appeared March 18 prowling around the chacras. The paper said that they do not know if it is some kind of ape or where it comes from.

The policeman remarked that the initial appearance took place at around ten o'clock at night ion a small tambo (cattle farm). The paper said that a man stepped out to his yard when he saw a shape measuring about 1.80 meters (six feet) that was black in color and leaped over two wire fences without touching them.

Something similar happened a few nights later. A witness claimed to have seen the creature some 200 meters distant at a chacra. "He described it as a black shape heading toward the wilderness, calmly. It walked and stopped now and then," the policeman explained. The officer in charge of the operation, Marcelo Diaz, said that they had found some footprints that were similar to those earlier seen.

It seems that not much happened after that and the creature moved on to another area. That it was a bigfoot that was seen, although a fairly small one, would be remarkable. There have been a few reports of bigfoot in South America but not many.

Bigfoot Hunting Season Proposed and More

Bigfoot helped a realtor sell homes in California during the summer of 2020. An enterprising realtor Daniel Oster in Felton, California listed his client's beautiful million-dollar home with the help of a local bigfoot. When one views the beautiful photos in the listing there is a surprise. In various scattered photos a bigfoot shows up: reading in the living room, cooking in the kitchen, exercising, gardening, and taking a walk in the woods where it may or may not live. It is not known how much bigfoot was paid to pose at various places in the home or whether he had an agent. He was probably underpaid.

Meanwhile the sasquatch were active in British Columbia, as usual. The *Toronto Star* (thestar.com) reported on January 14, 2021 that four friends were heading to their home on Highway 6 just south of Silverton, in south central British Columbia, on the evening of December 25, 2020 when the people in the front of the vehicle saw what looked like a "huge, man-like figure" on the side of the road. Said the *Toronto Star* article:

> "I didn't see the creature myself, I saw the prints," says Erica Spink-D'Souza, who was in the back seat. She's become the informal spokesperson for her companions. "But the person on the front seat cried out 'Oh my gosh look at that! They said it looked like a huge grizzly, or it was a large man, standing up."
>
> But before Spink-D'Souza could catch a glimpse, the figure turned, went on all fours, and headed deep into the bush. "We tried to turn around and look again, but it was

gone," she says.

After arriving home and putting her kids to bed, they returned to the scene to look for signs of the mysterious creature. "We saw all these different tracks, and then we saw these tracks that were really alarming," she recalls. "They were bipedal tracks in a straight line into the woods… I got a little spooked, it was alarming to see such big prints. But there were no bear tracks."

Spink-D'Souza and the others examined and photographed the tracks, and then she filed a report with a Bigfoot organization online.

The head of the Bigfoot Field Research Group, Matt Moneymaker (who also co-hosted a long-running Animal Planet TV show called *Finding Bigfoot*), described the tracks as "un-hoax-able."

"The surrounding pristine snow proves the tracks were not fabricated by humans," he says. "The stride length is beyond the ability of a human trying to leap through knee-deep snow. The drag marks and depth of the tracks prove they are not from a leaping rabbit. The linear pattern shows that it was not a bear."

Things took a turn for the worse for bigfoot when an Oklahoma Republican House member Justin Humphrey introduced a bill that would create a bigfoot hunting season. The Associated Press reported on January 22, 2021, that Representative Humphrey's district includes the heavily forested Ouachita Mountains in southeast Oklahoma, where a Bigfoot Festival is held each year

Oklahoma Republican House member Justin Humphrey.

97

near the Arkansas border. Said the article:

> Humphrey says issuing a state hunting license and tag could help boost tourism. "Establishing an actual hunting season and issuing licenses for people who want to hunt Bigfoot will just draw more people to our already beautiful part of the state," Humphrey said in a statement.
>
> Humphrey says his bill would only allow trapping and that he also hopes to secure $25,000 to be offered as a bounty. Micah Holmes, a spokesman for the Oklahoma Department of Wildlife Conservation, which oversees hunting in Oklahoma, told television station KOCO that the "agency uses science-driven research and doesn't recognize bigfoot."

If passed, the Wildlife Conservation Commission shall promulgate rules establishing a Bigfoot hunting season with annual season dates and create any necessary specific hunting licenses and fees. Genuine bigfoot hunting licenses could be a real problem. One has to think that bigfoot in general would be opposed to such a measure.

On the other hand, one has to think that bigfoot pretty much assumes that it is open season on his hairy ass and he is completely unaware that he may be protected by laws in some states.

Bigfoot may be protected in Illinois, a state in which he was seen on November 29, 2021. On December 13, 2021 the oldest newspaper in Illinois, the *Jacksonville Journal-Courier*, published the story about a bigfoot that was seen by a motorist near Chandlerville, Illinois. Chandlerville is a small town of only about 200 people near the Sangamon River south of Peoria in central Illinois.

The *My Journal* website is the website for the city's daily newspaper, the *Jacksonville Journal-Courier*—the oldest continuously published newspaper in Illinois (since 1830) (myjournalcourier.com),. Said the article:

> The witness reporting the story was Patrick Garver who said the encounter along Illinois Route 78 near Chandler-ville lasted just seconds.
>
> But it left a lasting impression on the driver going from Cass County to Tazewell County that night. "When it hit the shoulder, it looked back at me," Garver said. "I said to myself out loud, 'F_ing Bigfoot!'."
>
> Garver was driving the stretch of road about 10:30 p.m. heading north. "I saw a large animal jump into the road about 40 yards ahead. When it hit the road, I could see very large legs spread wide in a dead run with large, swinging, hairy arms. The arms switched back and forth close to the ground as its body was leaning forward. It leaped across the road in two jumps," he told investigators for the Bigfoot Field Researchers Organization, a scientific research group.
>
> Garver said it was about two seconds before the creature vanished into the darkness. "I could see it clearly," he said. "It was very large and, even though it was hunched over nearly horizontal, it still was close to being wider than my car and nearly to the top of my windshield. It blocked out the lights of [a] car ahead." He recalled it having shiny black hair and a huge stride. "It was running and leaping very fast," he said. "Nearly as fast as a white-tail deer." He continued driving until he reached Havana, where he stopped to send a text to his wife and children about what he experienced.

This area of central Illinois has had stories of bigfoot for decades and the hairy critters were known to hang out around a spot called "Monk's Grove" to the west of Bloomington-Normal. Then there is the DuPont Monster that is seen from time to time around Seneca, Illinois, to the north of Peoria.

The DuPont Monster made headlines in 2005 when he peeped into a car on Lover's Lane near Seneca. The startled teenagers went straight to the police department like in a 60s movie. The police took their story, noted that the DuPont Monster was a fixture in the town and country nearby. Eventually the story was picked up by the *Chicago Tribune* and bigfoot investigators flooded the town for a few weeks.

But that is how it is when you live a life in the shadows. You never know who might be gunning for you—hunters with a permit even. But then, you still have to check out the women coming out of the gym at one in the morning, or maybe you need to attack someone with an axe or even help them sell a house. Perhaps you will abduct some little kid for a few days and then send him home. It is a life in the shadows that will not change for some time, as things are going.

Chapter 4

BIGFOOT IN THE SOUTHWEST

Said Jack to Running Elk, I'll gamble all my precious stones
Before I leave my body here among these bleaching bones
But now my time is drawing near and I'm filled with dark regret
My spirit longs to journey as the sun begins to set
—Peter Rowan, *Land of the Navajo*

Having grown up in southwestern Colorado, I have always been interested in bigfoot in the Southwest. I have hiked in the San Juan Wilderness of southwest Colorado a number of times, even climbing some of the 14,000 footers in the area. This was in the late 1960s and early 1970s. I am glad to say that we did not encounter a bigfoot on any of these early wilderness trips.

I went to high school in the Pacific Northwest and it was this area that was known for bigfoot sightings. One thinks of British Columbia, Washington, Oregon, Idaho and Northern California as the prime sasquatch/bigfoot sites. It wasn't until I was older and living in Illinois that I realized that bigfoot could be found from the Midwest to the Northeast. That bigfoot was in Ohio, Kentucky, New England, the Carolinas and the Gulf states like Florida, Alabama and Mississippi. Yep, bigfoot was pretty much all over the place. In Indiana they have a large chain of gas stations named Bigfoot; how about that?

And bigfoot was in the Southwest, not just in the mountains of Colorado, but in New Mexico and Arizona as well. He has been known to visit a desert oasis or two in Southern California. We think of bigfoot inhabiting mountain forests but he has also been seen in thick brush and even relatively barren areas, such as lava fields.

Despite its reputation as a desert, Arizona has a lot of remote mountain forests in the north and east of the state. New Mexico has plenty of mountain forests and has many stories of bigfoot. This area, including Utah, Nevada, and Southern California, have all had their share of bigfoot reports. The local tribes typically have stories about bigfoot and Native Americans in general tend to be believers in the shaggy creature.

The Hairy Man of the Tule Indians

The Tule River Indians of central California have a strong tradition, as well as petroglyphs, of a bigfoot creature that they call Mayak Datat. A paper written on the subject by Kathy Moskowitz Strain working for the U.S. Forest Service details the petroglyph called the Hairy Man in a cave on the Tule River Indian Reservation and some of the tales associated with him. Says Strain in her 2012 paper entitled "Mayak Datat: The Hairy Man Pictographs" she states:

> The purpose of this article is to examine the association of prehistoric pictographs with contemporary stories told by the Tule River Indians about Hairy Man. Located on the Tule River Indian Reservation, the Painted Rock Pictographs are approximately 1000 years old. According to members of the tribe, the pictographs depict how various animals, including Hairy Man, created People. Other stories tell why Hairy Man lives in the mountains, steals food, and still occupies parts of the reservation. Since the Tule River Indians equate Hairy Man to Bigfoot, the pictograph and stories are valuable to our understanding of the modern idea of a hair-covered giant.
>
> Painted Rock is located on the Tule River Indian Reservation, east of Porterville, California. Connected today with the Tule River Indian Tribe, the pictographs are said to represent Hairy Man, an important cultural character for the residents of the reservation. Although the tribe prefers to be called "Tule River Indians," their traditional language and history are associated with the larger ethnographic group known as the Yokuts.
>
> At contact, the Yokuts occupied the entire San Joaquin

Valley of California, from the Sacramento River to the Kern River, and from the Sierra foothills to the Coast Ranges. A minimum population of 35,000 people was broken into 40 individual tribes, each having a distinct name, dialect, and territory. For ease of discussion, most ethnographers refer to the three main tribes named for their geographical location: Northern, Southern, and Foothill.

After California became part of the United States, settlers and miners came by the thousands. The Northern Valley Yokuts were annihilated by disease, and continual pressure caused the remaining Foothill and Southern Valley Yokuts to be moved under federal protection. The Tule River Indian Reservation was established in 1873 on 54,116 acres and currently boasts a population of approximately 500 people. Today, although there are three

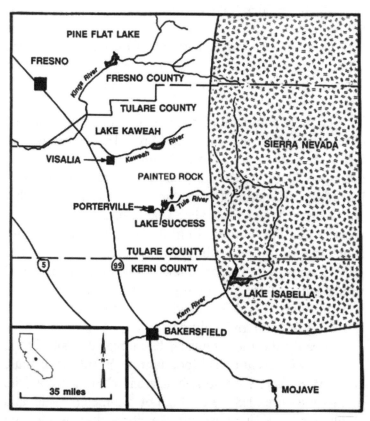

A drawing of the Tule Reservation and Painted Rock.

A drawing of the Mayat Datat on the Tule Reservation Painted Rock.

federally recognized Yokuts tribes with associated trust lands, most descendants live off-reservation in various local communities and are part of non-federally recognized tribes. This article focuses on the Tule River Reservation and the beliefs and stories of Hairy Man held by the Tule River Indian Tribe.

The most dominant pictograph at Painted Rock is that of the Hairy Man, also known as Mayak Datat or Sunsunut. Hairy Man measures 2.6 meters high by 1.9 meters wide, and is red, black, and white. The painting represents a two-legged creature with its arms spread wide. He has what appears to be long hair and large haunting eyes. The Yokuts identify the lines coming from the eyes as tears (because Hairy Man is sad according to their creation story). The pictograph is in very poor condition due to weathering and vandalism. A Hairy Man petroglyph is present at the site as well, but since this rock art style is very rare in the Sierras, it is likely a "modern" addition.

Probably the most unusual feature of this site is the presence of an entire Bigfoot family. Besides the male Hairy Man, there are also a female and child Bigfoot. The mother measures 1.8 meters high by 1.2 meters wide, and is solely red. Like her husband, she represents a two-legged creature with her arms open. She has five fingers and little other detail. Immediately adjacent to her, and directly under her right hand, is her child. The child measures 1.2 meters high by one meter wide.

Strain says that the figure of Hairy Man is essentially a classic bigfoot. She does not say one way or another whether bigfoot must be real. Strain ends her paper by telling us a few stories concerning Hairy Man, whom the Indian storytellers are also calling Big Foot. The first story tells a creation story that includes a fight between Coyote and Hairy Man:

How People Were Made

All the birds and animals of the mountains went to Hocheu to make People. Eagle, chief of all the animals, asked each animal how they wanted People to be. Each animal took a turn and said what they had to say.

Fish said, "People should know how to swim, like me, so let them be able to hold their breath and swim very deep."

Hummingbird said, "People should be fast, like me, so let them have good feet and endurance."

Eagle said, "People should be wise, wiser than me, so People will help animals and take care of the Earth."

Turtle said, "People should be able to protect themselves, like me, so lets give them courage and strength."

Lizard said, "People should have fingers, like me, so that People can make baskets, bows and arrows."

Owl said, "People should be good hunters, like me, so give them knowledge and cunning."

Condor said, "People should be different from us, so give them hair, not feathers or fur to keep warm."

Then Coyote said, "People should be just like me, because I am smart and tricky, so have them walk on all fours."

Hairy Man, who had not said anything yet, shook his head and said, "No, People should walk on two legs, like me."

All the other animals agreed with Hairy Man, and Coyote became very angry. He challenged Hairy Man to a race, and they agreed whoever won could decide how People should walk.

They gathered at the waterfall, below Hocheu, to begin the race. Coyote started and took a shortcut. Hairy Man was wiser than Coyote and knew that Coyote would cheat to win and People would have to walk on all fours, so Hairy Man stayed behind and helped Eagle, Condor, and the others to make People. They went back to the rock and drew People, on two legs, on the ground. The animals breathed on them, and People came out of the ground. Hairy Man was very pleased and went to People, but when they saw Hairy Man, they were scared and ran away. That made Hairy Man sad.

When Coyote came back and saw what they had done, he was very angry and drew himself on the rock eating the moon (he is called Su! Su! Na). All the other animals drew their pictures on the rock as well, so People would remember them. Hairy Man was sad because People were

An early drawing of the Mayat Datat from 1889 on the Tule Reservation.

afraid of him, so he drew himself sad. That is why Hairy Man's picture is crying to this day. That is how people were made.

Strain then tells the story about "When People Took Over." In this story each animal takes on a certain role. For the Mayak Datat the story relates:

Hairy Man said, "I will go live among the big trees (Giant Sequoias) and hunt only at night when people are asleep."

Strain then tells the brief tale of food stealing by Hairy Man. Food snatching is common in bigfoot stories such as food being snatched from a campsite or open window of a camper:

In the old days, women learned never to leave their acorn meal unattended. They would spend all day pounding on the big rocks near the river, making the acorn meal, and then take it down to the river to leech it. They would then leave it in the sun to dry, but they would come back and it would be gone. They would find big footprints in the sand where they left the meal and they would know that Hairy Man took it. He likes Indian food and knows to wait until the acorn is leeched of its bitterness before taking it. We always wondered if he liked the sound of women pounding acorn and knew when to come and get food.

In the last story Hairy Man, called Big Foot in the tales that Strain is quoting from, is described in some detail. This creature is apparently the equivalent of the folk creature known as the Boogey Man. Among other things, he munches down on anything, bones and all, much as bigfoot has been reported to do. He also kidnaps children. Says the story in full:

Big Foot was a creature that was like a great big giant with long, shaggy hair. His long shaggy hair made him look like a big animal. He was good in a way, because he

107

ate the animals that might harm people. He kept the Grizzly Bear, Mountain Lion, Wolf, and other larger animals away.

During hot summer nights all the animals would come out together down from the hills to drink out of the Tule River. Big Foot liked to catch animals down by the river. He would eat them up bones and all.

It was pleasant and cool down by the river on hot summer nights. That is when grown ups liked to take a swim. Even though people feared that Big Foot, the hairy man, might come to the river, people still liked to take a swim at night.

Parents always warned their children, "Don't go near the river at night. You may run into Big Foot."

Now Big Foot usually eats animals, but parents said, "If he can't find any animals and he is very hungry, he will eat you. Big Foot, the hairy man, doesn't leave a speck or trace. He eats you up bones and all. We won't know where you have gone or what has happened to you."

Some people say Big Foot, the hairy man, still roams around the hills near Tule River. He comes along the trail at night and scares a lot of people. When you hear him you know it is something very big because he makes a big sound, not a little sound. Children are cautioned not to make fun of his picture on the painted rock or play around that place because he would hear you and come after you. Parents warned their children, "You are going to meet him on the road if you stay out too late at night." The children have learned always to come home early.

So here we see how Big Foot—the Hairy Man—is the boogey man of classic folklore. He is skulking around at night and will grab unwary children who are "down by the river at night." This aspect of bigfoot and sasquatch is scary but important. They do skulk around at night and apparently they do abduct people— especially children.

Strain concludes her paper by saying, "Many questions about the pictographs and stories cannot be resolved here. Although the pictographs are thought to be approximately 1000 years old and were first documented in 1889, they were not identified, at least in print, as Hairy Man or Bigfoot until 1975. Previous to that year, the only Yokuts "giant" story recorded by an ethnographer occurred in 1936."

She also notes, "The stories and pictograph detail a large, bipedal, hair-covered human-like being. He has large feet and steals food when he can. His home is the mountains and he roams freely at night, eating animals that might cause harm to humans. The stories also suggest that Hairy Man can talk and outsmart Coyote."

This seems to show that the early inhabitants of California were aware of bigfoot and that he was part of their cosmology. He, like other animals, has been driven into the backwoods. Territory that he was used to roaming a hundred and fifty years ago was now too built up with the modern edifices of civilization. It is interesting to note here that a Forest Service employee wrote this paper and apparently believes that bigfoot is real, as described by the Yokuts.

Recent Bigfoot Sightings in Utah and Colorado

A video that was purported to show a bigfoot taken in the morning of March 23, 2019 appeared on YouTube a few days later. Tanner Hargis of Provo, Utah took the video near Lone Peak in the Wasatch Mountains just outside of Provo.

Hargis and friends were using a portable spotting scope to observe areas around Lone Peak when they noticed the figure slogging up the mountain. Pointing a video camera through the lens of his scope, he captured the entity on film and quickly submitted it to the Rocky Mountain Sasquatch Organization, a website that gathers extensive videos and photographic evidence of bigfoot sightings, as well as research conducted by their own team. The video is shaky and brief, showing a tall dark figure lumbering up a mountainside.

Hargis says in the video, "I think I have captured a video of a Sasquatch [date stamp] 03/23/19. At around 10:30 a.m. Up on Wasatch Range. Near Lone Peak. It was high up to where I don't think any man will hike up it. I think it's something to check into."

The video shows a figure appearing to be somewhere in the range of 8 feet tall, seen through the lens of the spotting scope—a high-powered portable telescope with an 80mm lens capable of extending up to 60x zoom. Such spotting scopes are often used by birdwatchers and nature enthusiasts. The creature in the video can be seen trudging up the crest of the mountain top, in the midst of a snowstorm, to an elevation of nearly 9,000 feet. The slope of the mountain is very steep. Hargis says that it would be rare to see a human hiking at that altitude, in those conditions, by themselves.

While skeptics pointed out that snowboarders and hikers with snowshoes did use the mountain in the winter, the video does not appear to depict such an athletic activity. It would seem, after viewing the video, that it is indeed a bigfoot. Either that, or Hargis was trying to pull off a hoax with a man in a gorilla suit.

You can see the fascinating video yourself at: www.youtube.com/watch?v=i-ZoBnj6ZVw&t=33s

Reports of bigfoot in the Southwest come in sparsely. The October 2021 issue of the newsletter "Bigfoot Times," published by Daniel Perez, relates the story of Nebraskan Janice Magnuson who was in the Baily, Colorado area from August 14 to 17, 2018. Baily is something of a bigfoot hotspot and has the Bigfoot Museum. She was with a group of about 20 bigfoot enthusiasts who were camped at the Meadows Group Use Campground. She slept alone in a tent on the edge of the campground, but near other campers who were often alone in their tents.

Janice Magnuson told Daniel Perez:

> I saw the silhouette of two bigfoot walk between my tent and my friend's tent. I became frozen in fear, sweating profusely, and my heart was pounding fast. I heard pinecones tossed at my tent.

Janice told Perez that she checked the next morning and was able to see the pinecones at the backside of her tent. On another night the front zipper of her tent was being unzipped. Thinking she was going to die she yelled, "No, no!" and the creature ran off.

The third and last night of their camping trip turned out to be the scariest of all. She told Perez:

> I heard a rather large, massive bigfoot pounding the

ground as he walked. I was very much frightened to say the least.

[The next] morning as we all sat around in our camp chairs drinking coffee, I looked down at my hiking boots and I picked up a pinecone with some needles attached. Bigfoot had gifted me.

It's the God's honest truth I am telling you all. I will never sleep in a tent alone again. There was a clan of bigfoot that visited our campsite. True story, I swear on the Holy Bible.

One wonders what would have happened if Janice had allowed the tent zipper to become completely unzipped? Perhaps because these were women camping in several tents the bigfoot clan that she speaks about were not afraid of them, but more curious in fact.

Baily is 16 miles as the crow flies from the Jefferson, Colorado area. Both of these small towns are in Park County which is directly west of Denver and Littleton on Colorado Highway 285 going west into the mountains of central Colorado. Baily is said to be the bigfoot sighting area of Colorado and is home to The Sasquatch Outpost (149 Main St, Baily, CO 80421) which is a bigfoot museum and gift shop. The operators assure their customers that bigfoot is active in the area.

Violent Bigfoot Attack at Stoneman Lake near Flagstaff

Perhaps Janice, in the story above, was lucky that a bigfoot did not unzip her tent flap and grab her. The Flagstaff area has had a number of bigfoot reports and some of them are quite frightening. Flagstaff is one of the areas known for the Mogollon Monster. In her book *The Mogollon Monster, Arizona's Bigfoot,*[69] Susan Farnsworth tells us of a strange incident that happened near Flagstaff and Stoneman Lake in August of 1963. The area known as Stoneman Lake is eight miles from Interstate 17 today, but that Interstate was just being built at that time. Even today dirt roads leading from Stoneman Lake along the Mogollon Rim go through remote areas known for bigfoot, such as Happy Jack.

Farnsworth tells us that various newspapers in 1963 told of a truck driver, traveling with his wife, who had parked his truck by the side of the road near Stoneman Lake to spend the night. During the night something terrible happened to the couple and they were attacked.

The truck driver was later found pummeled to death and the wife was found nearby, having escaped from the attacker. It was said that the woman was "brutalized" with several large claw marks down her back and legs. She had been apparently sexually assaulted. She described the attacker as an apelike creature with long hair.

The police had no suspects at all and at one point speculated that her husband had been killed with a club that may have had spikes in it because his body was badly torn apart. With no explanation as to who had murdered the truck driver the police struggled for answers. The police speculated that it may have been a bear or a "crazed hermit."[69]

This curious incident, apparently quite famous around Flagstaff in late 1963, seems to indicate sexual assault—by a bigfoot. With her husband beaten and torn apart outside their truck the woman was dragged and beaten and sexually assaulted. She somehow survived and escaped. This shocking account is genuinely scary and it may indicate what has happened to various missing female hikers. More on that in other chapters.

The police were clearly baffled by this horrific murder and then sexual assault of the woman. Had a bear actually done this? It is not what the woman apparently reported. While the coining of the term "bigfoot" had happened five years earlier in California, perhaps the police just did not know about bigfoot at the time. That a crazy, naked, hairy hermit had killed the husband with a club and then sexually assaulted the woman seemed to be their best guess. Needless to say, no one was ever arrested for the crime and it has faded into obscurity at this point.

Tales of Bigfoot in the Chuska Mountains

The Chuska Mountains are an elongated north-south range on the Colorado Plateau within the Navajo Nation. These mountains lie north of Gallup, New Mexico and are partly in Arizona and partly in New Mexico. The ranges highest elevations approach 10,000 feet and it has large tracts of pine forests. It is also known for bigfoot sightings.

The highest point is Roof Butte (9,823 feet), near the northern end of the range in Arizona. Other high points include the satellite Beautiful Mountain (9,386 feet) and Lukachukai Mountains (9,465 feet), both also near the northern end. To the north, the Chuskas are separated from the Carrizo Mountains by Red Rock Valley, which is today commonly referred to as Red Valley. The Carrizo Mountains are a smaller range with pine forests that has also had bigfoot sightings. The highest mountain is Pastora Peak (9,413 feet).

One of the interesting things about the Chuska Mountains is that they are mountainous pine forests with good rainfall and winter snowpack, but they are surrounded by desolate desert. This desolate desert has creeks and valleys with shrubs and a few trees but otherwise it is exceptionally barren.

Most of the Chuska range is the Navajo Nation Forest. The Navajo Nation is the largest Indian Reservation in the United States. Trees there were cut and transported more than 50 miles to the east to construct pueblos in Chaco Culture National Historical Park. Following a period of contentious debate, logging in the Chuskas was suspended in 1994.

A paved road, New Mexico Highway 134, crosses the sparsely populated range through Narbona Pass. Narbona Pass was originally called Beesh Lichii'l Bigiizh, or Copper Pass. This pass was the location where Navajo warriors led by the Navajo chief named Narbona decisively defeated a Mexican slaving expedition under Captain Blas de Hinojos. Hinojos left Santa Fe with his men on February 8, 1835 and headed for the Chuska Mountains which he intended to cross into Navajo country.

On 28 February 1835 the group straggled into Copper Pass. Narbona held back his forces, who were hiding on both sides of the pass. Once the Mexican army was single file in the canyon that was the pass, the Navajos poured arrows into the column; those who had guns fired, and some threw stones or rolled rocks into the gorge. Taken by surprise, Hinojos's army was decimated, with most of them killed, including Hinojos himself. A few men made it back to Santa Fe in March of 1835.

The pass was later renamed Washington Pass, after Colonel

John M. Washington. His U.S. Army troops killed Narbona and five other Navajos in a brief clash in 1849. Colonel Washington went on to become the first American governor of New Mexico. In 1992 the Navajo people renamed the pass as Narbona Pass.

So, the Chuska Mountains have a colorful history but are still a remote area in today's world. Very few people live in and around the Chuskas, except for the Canyon de Chelly area.

Newspaper reports in nearby Farmington, New Mexico, often

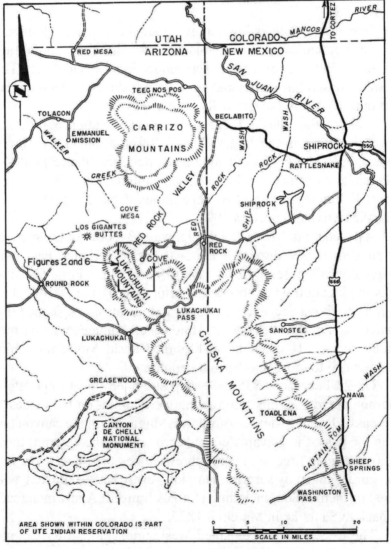

The Chuska Mountains on the Navajo Nation Reservation.

mention bigfoot sightings in the Chuska Mountains or elsewhere nearby. *The Farmington Daily-Times* had a brief story about bigfoot on February 5, 2012. Under the title "Increase in sightings of 'Bigfoot' in Navajo Nation Mountains," the article said:

> There's been an increase in sightings of a "Bigfoot" creature in the Chuska Mountains of the Navajo Nation. There have been sightings of the creature, or its footprints, in January 2011, November 2011 and January 2012.
>
> One man came across Bigfoot when he took his livestock into the mountains. "My animals froze and I saw the thing walk over the hill," Jerry Lewis told *The Farmington Daily-Times* through a Navajo interpreter. "It was taller than 8 or 9 feet, taller than the bushes, upright and hairy."

One of the early reports of bigfoot come from a letter written in 1968 from a Mrs. Cheeseman of the Navajo Nation that two Navajo shepherds in the wooded Chuska Mountains had shot at an 8-foot bigfoot that they had suddenly encountered. The creature ran wounded into a canyon while two other bigfoot helped it.[3, 29]

The Gallup *Independent* newspaper had a story on January 21, 1970 that four youths from Gallup were driving in an area of the Zuni Reservation, south of Gallup, when suddenly a bigfoot was running alongside their car, which was going 45 miles an hour. Armed with guns, they shot at the bigfoot and knocked it down. It then got up and ran away. They estimated the height of the hairy creature to be about 5 feet, 7 inches tall.[29]

A BFRO (Bigfoot Field Researchers Organization) report says that on June 17, 2001 a bigfoot sighting was made in the western Chuska Mountains, near the Canyon de Chelly National Monument. Said the witness:

> I was driving along the washboard dirt road (7) that heads east along the south side of Canyon de Chelly looking for a place to duck into to camp for the night. I was about 7-10 miles east of Chinle driving at about 20 mph. It stepped out from the left side and walked across the road

right in front of me, about 40 feet away or so, right at the edge of the bright part of my headlights, walking briskly but in no hurry crossing the road and slightly away from me at the same time so that it was probably 5 feet ahead when it reached the other side of the road. As soon as it crossed the road and the little swale of a ditch, it bent over just as it was behind a bush as if to take cover as soon as possible. At first, all I kept thinking was, "I just saw an ape of some kind," but I quickly realized what it had to be. It wasn't particularly large, about six feet tall or so, but very solid for its size and uniformly covered in dark brown hair. It never looked at me. I only saw it for about three or four seconds but I saw it clearly. I ended up going back a little, turning north on a paved road that leads to the edge of the canyon, just a mile or so, and turning off into the woods a little to sleep in the back of my truck for the night just two or three miles at most from where the sighting occurred.

Another BFRO report was about an incident that occurred on September 17, 2002 near Rock Springs, New Mexico, just north of Gallup going toward the Chuska Mountains. The witness, an electrical worker, was on Highway 264:

About 20 yards from the truck I saw something walk out from behind a juniper tree that is located on the west side of the dirt road. Right when it stepped out into the lights of the truck, it hesitated and it looked towards me. I stopped the truck at that moment. It then started to walk faster, picked up its stride a little more. It took about 4 steps walking across that road; it did not cross the road in a straight manner, it crossed at an angle on the road and walked behind another juniper tree that is located on the east side of the dirt road. I had stopped the truck as soon as it had stepped out onto the road, my visual contact time with what I now refer to as "the Creature" was about 15 seconds. I waited there to see if it would come back out or if I could see any type of movement, [but] I did not see any. I sat there for a while thinking: what did I just see?

My mind went through an elimination process, I thought, that was not a horse, a cow, a deer or an elk, 4 of the large animals that are prevalent in this area. The creature had a shiny brown hairy coat, it was approximately 7 feet tall— its face was like a monkey's and the eyes were big and black, like a big teardrop shape. Its head was small and it came to a long point towards the back. The torso was skinny, narrow shoulders, the arms and legs were about 3 to 4 inches in diameter, it had elbows and knees but I did not see any hands, fingers or a type of foot or toe structure.

BFRO members Reid and Curt Nelson searched the Chuska Mountains for bigfoot for five days in October 2002. The Nelson brothers put out pheromone traps of apple and other scents to attract bigfoot. These pheromone traps were attracting deer, rather than bigfoot, they said on the BFRO website.

They give a good description of the Chuska area:

The mountains are heavily forested, with ponderosa pine, aspen, gamble oak, spruce and fir at the highest elevations. Pinion pine and juniper grow on the surrounding foothills between 5,500 and 7,000 feet. A desert sagebrush community covers the desert below, which has an average elevation of 5,000 feet. There are numerous small seasonal lakes in the Chuskas. These become quite low in summer,

The Chuska Mountains on the Navajo Nation Reservation.

117

and in the drought of 2002 most dried completely. Mule deer, elk, black bears, mountain lions, bobcats, and coyotes thrive there. Navajo ranchers keep summer camps high in the mountains to tend to their sheep and cattle, which are allowed to free-range graze. They do this until early October or so, when they and their stock head down to winter quarters.

Published reports of sasquatch sightings from this area are rare since few locals are inclined to talk to outsiders about so controversial a subject. There are, however, numerous unpublished reports available to those who would collect them, and Reid, who works as an archeologist for the Navajo Nation, is in an especially good position to hear of them.

This is a good reflection on the Navajo people in that they are very private and generally reluctant to share information, especially to outsiders. Older folks may not even speak English and they have strong beliefs in the paranormal and this means ghosts, witches, skinwalkers and bigfoot.

A report to BFRO stated that on March 5, 2011 a man said he was driving north of Thoreau, New Mexico, east of Gallup, when he saw a figure by the road:

> ...The time was about 8 p.m. As I was traveling on hi-way 612, right when I was exiting the sharp curves, I noticed a figure moving by the road on the right side. I thought it was a very tall person at first but when I looked I noticed that it wasn't human. As I got closer it started to cross the road and almost hit my truck. It stopped and I did not want to stop because the road was ice packed and I didn't want to get stuck or run off the road. I saw the creature a few feet thru my truck's passenger front window. The creature's face looked ape and humanistic. He was probably 7 feet tall because when he got real close to the vehicle I couldn't see his face. He stood way over the truck. I was overwhelmed with fear at this point and just kept going home.

Another report said that on July 16, 2011 an unnamed man and his family were driving through the Chuska Mountains of New Mexico when a bigfoot was encountered on the road. Said the man in the report:

> We were going to the Chuska Mountains on the Navajo reservation for a family reunion. We just left the main paved highway through Narbona Pass, between Sheep Springs, NM and Crystal, NM. We went south on a dirt road, Indian Service Route 32, into the Chuska Mountains. We were about 5-8 miles into the mountains, when we came upon a small hill that curved towards the east, then to the south. As we approached the hill to go up, the road quickly turned right/south. As we reached the top, we saw the full moon and it lit up a flat green pasture that was on top of the hill.
>
> As we made the turn to the right/south I noticed a big black figure standing. As I looked at it, it stood with the full moon behind it, so that all I could see was a black-outlined form. I kept my eyes on the figure while making the turn right. I said to my wife, "Did you see that?!" She said, "What?" I said, "Something is standing over there by the road."
>
> As I looked, I noticed that the figure was standing by a small pond, which was about 10-15 feet from the road. I could see the figure's reflection in the pond, along with the full moon. I would say when I first saw it, it was about 75 feet away. As we got closer, our headlights turned to the right, away from the black figure, but I still could see it, because the moonlight was so bright. It just stood there, still, as if it was waiting for us to leave. I told her [my wife] I was going to pull the truck onto the edge of the road. The road being dirt, and because of the rain, it had been plowed, so there was a ridge of dirt on both sides of the road. So, I pulled the vehicle left towards the "Bigfoot" to flash my headlights on it.
>
> As my headlights flashed the "Bigfoot" turned. We could see the legs (two) turn, the arms (two) turn, and it

started running away from us up a small hill into the trees. It was a quick, smooth run. I mentioned to her that it ran Ninja-like, smooth and stealthy. In less than 5-6 seconds it was in the trees. As it was turning and running, we didn't see any clothing—buttons shining from the headlights/moonlight—we saw a huge mass, a body running on two legs; we never saw any eyes. We noticed the legs and arms, and for sure it ran on two legs up the hill.

We were about 30 feet away from it when it ran up the hill. We could see that it was not a bear or human. It stood at least 7-8 feet tall. It was wider and taller than a person. After it ran away, we were in shock; we sat quietly in the truck, still for about 15 seconds. Then, all of a sudden my oldest daughter screamed and said, "Daddy, what was that." I was shocked that she was awake the whole time. I thought only my wife and I saw it. But, she was terrified, asking me, over and over, "Daddy, what was that?" I couldn't say anything but tell her it was a bigfoot.

My wife and I aren't crazy nor were we believers of bigfoot until now. In fact, we were the biggest skeptics. But we can't deny what we saw. I have to believe it, because it was real."

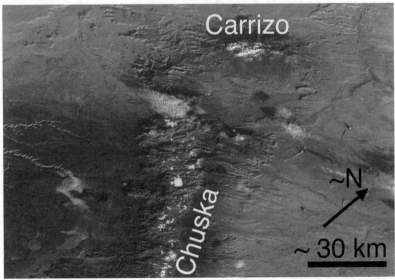

A NASA satellite photo of the Chuska Mountains on the Navajo Nation.

A report to BFRO detailed an encounter on November 3, 2005 at Borrego Pass near Crown Point in western New Mexico. The man wrote:

> I was traveling southeast from Crown Point, NM, on the eastern part of the Navajo Reservation. I was headed home. As I was going through a small canyon (pass) when in the headlights of the vehicle I observed an animal traveling east to west across the highway. It appears to about 6-ft. tall and big; it was walking on two legs and went into a small gully. I pulled the vehicle around and shone the light up the gully and I could not relocate the animal. Due to the darkness and only seeing it through the headlights I could not make out the hair color; it appeared dark.

Bigfoot seems to have found a good hiding place in the Chuska Mountains. They are a high, forested and isolated mountain range in the Navajo Nation, near the Arizona border.

In an article out of Durango, Colorado on May 5, 2020 in the magazine called DGO (dgomag.com) incidents concerning bigfoot in the Four Corners area were highlighted. The article was titled "Does Bigfoot stalk the Four Corners?" and subtitled "Depending on who you ask, Sasquatches live near not just Farmington, but Durango as well." The article, by staff writer Nick Gonzales, tells the incredible story of Brenda Harris and her bigfoot encounters:

> It was the early 1990s when Brenda Harris had her first face-to-face encounter with the unknown. On a hot summer night, Harris had the windows open in her mobile home in Upper Fruitland, on the west side of Farmington, where the metropolitan area spills onto the Navajo Nation. Her husband had left home about 30 minutes earlier, around 10:30 p.m., to start a graveyard shift at the mine. But Brenda was not alone—in addition to her children, ages 4 and 5, the kids' cousins and Harris' brother had come over to stay the night.
>
> The kids were laughing and having a good time when Harris heard something walking on the gravel outside. As

121

the footsteps approached, they were followed by heavy breathing. Harris quieted her kids so she could listen. That's when she heard her family's dogs. They weren't barking; they were crying and whimpering, terrified underneath the front porch. The heavy footsteps then stepped from the gravel onto the porch.

"What is that?" Harris' children asked her. She could only reply honestly with the words "I don't know," repeating herself when her brother asked the same thing. The entire family listened as something came closer, opened the screen door, and turned the doorknob to the front door.

Possibilities flew through Harris' head: perhaps it was a parent of one of the cousins, trying to scare the kids. Harris told her brother that he should open the door and see what it was, but he was too scared to move.

Harris walked up to the door herself and unlocked the deadbolt. As she did, whatever was on the other side of the door let go of the doorknob and went silent. She swung the door open and couldn't believe what she saw.

"All I see is this tall, black creature standing in front of me. You know when you open the door and you say hello to someone? That's how close it was to me," she said. "I didn't get to see the features of the face because it was covered in hair. The color of the hair was black from head to toe, all the way down to the foot. It wasn't very muscular. It was kind of scraggly looking a little bit, maybe a little bit skinny."

Harris and the creature stood there for a moment, looking at each other, before it took off and ran behind the house. The woman turned to her brother, who just looked at her with an expression of "What the heck was that?" She put the children to bed, refusing to tell them she had seen Bigfoot. She closed all the windows and turned the lights off, preparing to go to sleep. But then, the creature came back again, trying to get into the house through the front door. Harris turned the porch light on and it left, but returned about every 15 minutes or so until she would turn the porch light on again.

At about 3 a.m. or so, Harris began to doubt what she saw, thinking perhaps it was a skinwalker, a type of harmful witch in Navajo culture that can take the shape of an animal. Questions continued to mount in her head, prompting her to leave the house to investigate by driving around the property. At one point, one of the dogs came out from underneath the porch to follow her, but got scared and ran back to the house. Harris, who hadn't seen anything while driving around the entire plot at the end of her family's field, did the same and locked up again. As soon as she did, the creature returned.

Harris' master bedroom overlooked the porch, so she opened the curtains and got another good look at the menace. It was 6½ to 7½ feet tall, with long arms, and was covered in black hair. It took off when the woman hit the window, but continued to return until it finally disappeared near daybreak. To this day, she isn't sure what the creature wanted.

Harris told her husband what had happened when he arrived home from work at about 7 a.m. He didn't believe her, so she asked him to come with her for a walk around the house to look for evidence. She wasn't disappointed by what they found in the daylight. Behind the house, she found a long, three-toed footprint matching one popularized by "The Legend of Boggy Creek," a 1972 horror docudrama about the Fouke Monster, a Bigfoot-type creature seen in southwestern Arkansas.

Though this was the first time Harris had seen a Bigfoot, it wasn't the first encounter she'd had with one—and it certainly wouldn't be her last.

As a child growing up in Farmington, Brenda Harris shared a room with her sisters in a mobile home park just south of the Animas River. The girls heard scratching beneath their bedroom window and smelled a bad odor several nights during the summer. They ran to their parent's room and told them what they heard and smelled, but their father's investigations never turned up anything during the

123

night. Tragically, though, the family found a kitten that they had forgotten to bring into the house with its claws sunk into a nearby tree, apparently scared to death. At the base of the tree, they found three-toed footprints, but had no idea what had left them and assumed it was a skinwalker, Harris said.

Harris also remembers listening to a radio show called the "Navajo Hour" as a child during trips to visit her grandmother in Piñon, Arizona. During the show, a woman advised listeners not to go down to the San Juan or Animas rivers because of the presence of a monster. She referred to it using a number of Navajo words, but also called it a sasquatch—a term Harris was unfamiliar with until she saw "The Legend of Boggy Creek" as a teen ...and all of the puzzle pieces started fitting together.

Brenda Harris is a credible witness and has had an unusual encounter with a bigfoot. That the bigfoot kept coming back to the house and trying to get inside is remarkable. This could be for a number of reasons. First, she is a woman who was "friendly" toward the bigfoot, which was probably young and she said, "thin." This bigfoot did not appear to fear her at all and it perceived that she did not fear him.

Harris says that she does not know what the bigfoot wanted. I would say that what he wanted was food. He (or she) knew that there was food in the house and they would like to have some of it.

There is sometimes a sexual motive with bigfoot but that does not seem to be the case in the story told by Brenda Harris. At one point she says she drove around her property with her truck with the headlights blaring across the property and saw nothing. Shortly after going back to the house the bigfoot shows up again. What does it want? Some food. Maybe a few apples, some ears of corn—whatever you've got!

Harris went on to become a founding member of a group called the New Mexico Shadow Seekers. Says the article in the DGO news:

Even after finally seeing the creature in the '90s, Harris

kept quiet about what she'd encountered because she didn't want to upset her family. She remained curious about Bigfoot, though, and talked to her friends and neighbors about their own sightings, which began to grow in number. Finally, around 2009, she had so many people asking her questions about it that it was finally time to come out as a Bigfoot investigator. In 2012, she put together a team of investigators: New Mexico Shadow Seekers, which now posts some of its findings on a YouTube channel. Harris' team gets calls about all sorts of weird creatures in the region: dogmen and lizardmen, chupacabras, gnomes, little green men ... even a centaur. The only reports she is reluctant to investigate are UFOs, because she isn't interested in them, and skinwalkers, because she doesn't want to get mixed up in witchcraft. It seems, though, that most calls she receives are in reference to Bigfoot. In fact, she has hosted an annual Northern New Mexico Bigfoot and Paranormal Conference since 2013, which has drawn Bigfoot enthusiasts from far and wide. (In 2019, she switched it up and had a Bigfoot camp-out.)

Residents of San Juan County tend to report Bigfoot encounters to the Shadow Seekers for practical reasons— the creatures are impacting people's livelihoods, stealing fruits and vegetables from farmland in the summer and fall, and killing animals in the winter and spring. People also report hearing the creature's loud, sometimes lonely or mournful cries and hear or see it tapping on their windows. According to reports, it has red or amber eyes.

The majority of Bigfoot incidents occur near the water, Harris said. Along the San Juan River, people have seen it from Shiprock in the west to Bloomfield in the east. They've also been seen it up the Animas River, toward Aztec, and along the La Plata River, near La Plata, New Mexico, south of Hesperus.

Over time, Harris has learned ways to ward Bigfoot away. For instance, it doesn't like the light. "Back in '86, when I moved out here, hardly anybody ... had street lights on their property. Back in 2009, when this thing kind of exploded and we had all these Bigfoot sightings ... I started telling them, 'Hey, get some lights up. The more light you can have, the better it'll be for you and your animals,'" she said. "Today, when you drive around out here in our area, some of these people now have three or four street lights on their property."

She recommends bringing cat and dog food and livestock feed inside before dark. She also recommends women and children not walk alone outside, as she believes the creatures are drawn to them, especially their laughter. (Harris also says she doesn't think a man could defend himself from Bigfoot alone and recommends they travel in pairs as well.) Finally, as another practical solution for scaring it off your property, she recommends hitting the alarm button on your vehicle key fob—sasquatches dislike claxons as much as anyone.

We see how Harris advises bringing the dog food and livestock feed inside before nightfall—because a bigfoot will steal it! She also feels that it is dangerous for children and women to walk alone at night in the area where she lives. This is because bigfoot—the virtual boogeyman—will snag them, and they might never be seen again.

From what we are learning about bigfoot-sasquatch activity this is correct—bigfoot is most likely to target children or women. An adult male, alone, may be enough to keep bigfoot at bay because bigfoot is afraid of guns and other loud sounds. However, in any physical confrontation between a bigfoot and an adult male human, even with a gun, the bigfoot would probably win.

If a gunshot, honking horn, or other loud sound can deter a bigfoot, all the better. Bigfoot are tough and thought by some to be bulletproof. It has been said that the best way to kill a bigfoot is to shoot it through the eye socket. Bigfoot is dangerous, and this is what makes Brenda Harris's story so fascinating. She seems to have a friendly relationship with this bigfoot.

The DGO news article concludes with an interview with a local cryptozoologist named David Ortiz about his relationship with outdoorsman JC Johnson. Together they formed a group called Crypto Four Corners. Continued the article:

David "Oz" Ortiz, another Farmington resident, got into cryptozoology through his friend JC Johnson, who formed the group Crypto Four Corners in 2004. Ortiz had heard secondhand reports of weird things in the region throughout his life, including a sighting of bigfoot along the Animas River near Flora Vista by a girl he was dating in the early '80s. But he didn't see anything himself until he joined the group, he said.

Among other stuff, the group heard stories of a bigfoot-type creature along the San Juan River between Farmington and Shiprock. In 2009, they investigated Brenda Harris' property for evidence of the cryptid, which was the first time she and Ortiz met. After Johnson passed away in 2018, Crypto Four Corners fell into disarray, and Ortiz has since been investigating as a member of Harris' team.

Since Ortiz started investigating bigfoot, he has had many unusual experiences—a lot of them outside of the region of Harris' sightings. In 2008, Ortiz was riding his mountain bike near the La Plata Mountains on the east side of Montezuma County when he saw an unusual structure. It looked like something had mounted one aspen tree onto another one, so he got off his bike to get a closer look. As he did, he heard what sounded like a pig snorting and looked to see the source: a shadowy figure standing 150 feet away in the aspens. Ortiz shot a photo and the thing responded with a tremendous scream that Ortiz describes as that of a high-pitched voice and a peacock put together. Ortiz got back on his bike and took off, but was chased by the shape, crashing through the forest near the trail. Upon subsequent returns to the area, he has heard more sounds—vocalizations and tree knocking (bigfoot investigators say the creature knocks trees with other objects to produce sounds)—and seen stick-built, teepee-like structures and X marks that are also supposedly signs of bigfoot habitation.

Occasionally, Ortiz's encounters enter the realm of the supernatural. On a drive though the Lukachukai Mountains, southwest of Shiprock, he stopped to take a photo of the moon. As he was setting up his tripod, he heard rustling in the oak brush nearby and got spooked. He shot his photos quickly and got back in his car. As soon as he put it in drive, he felt a surge from behind the vehicle. He couldn't see anything behind him, but days later, he found a large inhuman handprint in the dust on the back window.

He and other former members of Crypto Four Corners were also pelted with rocks this February on Navajo Dam Road near Aztec. During that incident, something left handprints on his car but left no footprints around it, and the rocks seemed to drop from the sky. Stone and log throwing are also, apparently, bigfoot behaviors—Ortiz saw logs thrown about during bigfoot expeditions in east Texas and heard from a friend-of-a-friend who said a bigfoot threw rocks at her in 2003 at Horse Gulch in Durango. Sightings of the unusual seem increasingly common in La Plata County. While selling Ortiz a pair of backcountry skis, a Durango-based judge told him to be careful in the woods because of "strangeness going on out there."

He's also seen Bigfoot-style structures on Missionary Ridge and heard Bigfoot-type growls near Purgatory. For what it's worth, a former city of Durango employee, who prefers to remain anonymous, told DGO she saw a structure like the kind Ortiz describes at the Dalla Mountain Park. She described it as big enough to stand up inside and looked like it would have taken a while to construct. "We were like, how the heck did someone make this?" she said.

Is bigfoot living along the rivers of the Four Corners? And if so, is it throwing rocks at people and trying to get into their houses? It's impossible to say ... but you won't see us near the Animas or the San Juan at night without a flashlight and a camera.

I was a friend of JC Johnson as well, and we went on a camping trip with about seven other friends in the fall of 2016. During that trip Johnson told a number of tales around the campfire that seemed pretty fantastic to me at the time.

Johnson was quite the outdoorsman and had been a rafting guide all over New Mexico, Colorado and Arizona. He told the story of camping at a lake in the Mogollon Rim area of Arizona which had a cliff at one end of the lake. There was a narrow strip of land between the cliff and the lake and he and some friends had pitched their tent there.

Johnson said that during the night big rocks began coming down the cliff near the tent. Johnson said that he and his companions had to stand next to the cliff to avoid the rocks that were coming down at them.

"I stood with my back to the cliff," Johnson told us around the campfire, "and with my pistol I was firing in the air at the cliff's edge directly above me. That's where this bigfoot was throwing rocks at us."

I was a amazed. "So you were standing with your back to the cliff and firing up into the air—did you hit the bigfoot?"

Johnson replied, "It scared him off, I don't think that I hit him."

That night we listened to many of his tales of bigfoot in Arizona and the Four Corners. He also said that there were many encounters with bigfoot near the San Juan River and its various tributaries such as the Animas River. He also told us that he thought that bigfoot would take the scent glands from a skunk—killed by the bigfoot—and use them to make the repulsive skunk smell. He said he thought they used it on infant bigfoot to keep predators

A photo of a bigfoot print taken by a hunter in Colorado, circa 2019.

such as coyotes away from them.

I thought this was an interesting observation. Bigfoot is often described as smelling terrible, like a skunk, or garbage, or wet and dirty. Some witnesses have simply said that it seems that bigfoot does not bathe or ever take a shower. What Johnson was saying was that bigfoot was, in some cases, choosing to smell bad.

Bigfoot have often been seen in the water and they are good swimmers. While swimming or moving through some swamp in Alabama or Florida may not clean a bigfoot very much, when they swim in a river like the San Juan they are likely to get pretty clean. A number of bigfoot accounts, including some from around the Four Corners, claim that the bigfoot did not have a strong smell at all.

So, we know that the degree of bad smell around bigfoot varies greatly. I thought that Johnson's suggestion about the skunk glands had some merit. As most of my readers know, bigfoot in the Southeastern United States is often called a skunk ape.

Bigfoot researcher and author David Weatherly, a personal friend who lives in Arizona, described a bigfoot expedition into the Chuska Mountains in his book *Wood Knocks, Vol. 1.*[20] Weatherly describes a trip he made to the area in 2015 and how he met JC Johnson. He quotes Johnson in the book:

> When you think of New Mexico and the Four Corners, most people won't think of sasquatch, they think all those types of creatures are up in the rainforest of the Pacific Northwest. But we have constant reports here, and this region has a long, long history of sightings. There's plenty of habitat to support these creatures, and if you can get the locals to talk, they'll tell you that the furry ones are here.

One of the most fascinating stories that Weatherly tells is the conversation he had with Johnson's pal Leonard Dan, a Navaho elder and a member of the Crypto Four Corners organization. Dan tells Weatherly that the bigfoot have been around a long, long time in the area. He then tells the amazing story of a baby that was kidnapped on a remote part of the Navajo Nation called Sanostee just east of the northern part of the Chuska Mountains. This apparently happened in the 1940s to a very poor Navajo family picking pinion nuts in a scrubby area. The elder Dan told him:

They say one time that, this family, they were starving. This was way back. I guess they had no food and there was hardly no game that year and what happened was, they were gathering nuts, pinion nuts in this area well southeast of here. They call it Sanostee, that's kind of a hot area too.

This woman left her little baby and they took it and they looked everywhere for it. They even got trackers to come in here and look for it. What they say was a bear took it with the cradle board and everything. My grandfather told me this story, he said a big being took that baby. What they did was raise this little girl.

One day, this guy was riding his horse in the mountains, looking for his horses I guess and he came across this little girl sitting under a juniper tree. She was all naked and had long hair, stringy hair. She was about ten years old by then. From being an infant all the way to ten years old, that's how long she was missing.

This Navajo guy, he tried to talk to her saying "Hi how are you? Are you lost? What's your name?" That little girl, she didn't talk Navajo or anything, she just whooped and grunted noises.

He took her and brought her back down, they had a big meeting and they said, okay whose little girl is this, and the mother, she recognized her right away because her little girl had a birthmark on her shoulder. That's how she knew it was her missing baby.

And everybody was happy that she had returned but they couldn't communicate with her.

Leonard Dan says that the girl continually made whooping sounds and animal grunts when people tried to communicate with her. She was eventually sent to a local school where it was hoped she would get some education and learn to speak the Navaho language. The mother said that the girl continued to have a wild nature and would make whooping sounds deep into the night.

While he was in high school Dan said he encountered the girl in her early teenage years:

> My friend pointed her out and told me that little girl, she was taken by something, a creature, and those creatures, they raised her and she couldn't talk.
>
> And I said, Oh really? I looked at her and I was staring at her and she turned around and looked at me and I just kind of smiled.
>
> She was a nice looking young lady by then, she was sort of pretty, but you could tell, there was a wildness about her and that something didn't look right.
>
> My friend said she was abducted by those wild animals and those animals raised her.[20]

Dan recognized that this was the same girl that his grandfather had told him about. He did not know what happened to this "wild child" in the end. She apparently never communicated what had happened to her as a very young child. Perhaps she really could not recall her early years, having blocked them out when she returned to civilization.

One may wonder how such a thing could happen in this modern era. However, the Navajo Nation is a very large area and many of the Navajos living in small communities in remote parts of the reservation are very poor. They maintain their traditional lifestyle and continue to speak Navajo and have Navajo police and officials. That a little child could go missing and be unreported could easily have occurred 80 years ago.

Weatherly writes about his own experiences with JC Johnson in the Four Corners area and tells the story of fellow Crypto Four Corners member George Harvey and his sister Alex:

> George's sister Alex, recalls an encounter she had on January 4, 2015 with a group of "furry ones" …part of a larger habitation group that migrates throughout the area. Alex was driving a four-wheeler on the homestead, along with her dogs, when she encountered several huge figures hiding behind a cropping of trees. It was at that point that

three bigfoot stepped out, stunning Alex since she had never encountered any of these beings previously. Her brother had mentioned that they did exist, but she never believed the accounts. In fact, this group had been researched by JC Johnson and others in his group for approximately an 8-year period. When Alex told her mother about the encounter, she referred to the bigfoot as her "hairy boys," so their presence was well known.

Like many other reservation reports, Alex's account notes the creatures were massive in size. She describes the largest one being as tall as twelve feet and having dark brown hair. The two that accompanied it were pegged as being ten feet tall, and eight feet tall, respectively. Again eyebrows may be raised at the extreme height claimed, yet the fact remains there are constant reports from the region describing beings of this size.

Alex's description of the creatures mentions they had faces that were mostly hairless with flat, narrow noses and wide foreheads. She further notes that as she sat on the four-wheeler, frozen in shock, the creatures seemed to interact with her dogs, one of them even reaching down to rub the ears of one of the animals.

This is a curious aspect of Alex's encounter since many people report their dogs being attacked or taken away by the hairy creatures, yet in the case of Alex and her family, there seems to be no concern for the safety of the dogs. The nonchalant response of Alex's mother is an example of the calm acceptance Navajos display regarding the creatures in general. While not all residents are happy about the presence of these beings, they do for the most part seem to accept it as part of the reality of life on the reservation.[20]

Yes, this is a curious story in many respects. The witness seems credible as to the 12-foot height of the tallest bigfoot which gives credibility to other reports of a 12-foot sasquatch standing on the side of the road. Even greater heights have been reported.

The story of the friendly dogs and a bigfoot scratching the ear of one of the dogs is very unusual. Usually dogs are terrified by bigfoot. In some cases dogs have attacked a bigfoot and usually they are killed by the bigfoot who punches them and tears them to pieces.

There have been a few fascinating tales of a bigfoot having a pet dog or wolf who stays by the side of the bigfoot. There is even one instance, that of the Minerva, Ohio, incident, where a bigfoot was seen with a wolf and a fully grown mountain lion.

I would venture to guess that in case of the George and Alex Harvey family's bigfoot encounters that they had been so frequent that the dogs and the grandmother tolerated the bigfoot and were friendly to them. It is possible that the bigfoot had given the dogs some food in the years before this encounter, or had at least let the dogs know that the bigfoot did not intend to harm them. The dogs were probably present when the grandmother encountered her "furry friends" and she would tell them to be calm. Therefore, when Alex met them on her quad-runner, she was shocked, but the dogs had met this bigfoot family before.

Weatherly also tells the curious tale of the "Crown Point Howler." Crown Point is a town of 3,000 on the Navajo Reservation in New Mexico. The area is riddled with ravines and dirt roads. There are very few paved roads in the area. Starting around 2011 an eerie howling began, usually between midnight and two a.m. This creepy howling was coming from different places outside of town and was not the sound of coyotes, elk, or wild dogs. The howling made the hairs on the back of peoples necks stand up.

The disturbing howling made people uneasy. Said one man, "You hear it, sends chills down the spine of a lot of people, and the way I hear it from my neighbors and my wife, they don't want to hear it again."[20]

A woman said, "It starts out as a very low, raspy growl and ends up like a big man yelling. It sounds like something in pain. There's something human about it, but not quite."

Weatherly says that the Navajo police have an official policy to investigate any paranormal incident that they hear of from the locals and this includes investigating the Crown Point Howler. Navajos have a wide variety of supernatural beliefs, including the belief in witches, skinwalkers, little people and hairy boogeymen. The Navajo police at Crown Point did one investigation in late

A petroglyph near the Zuni Reservation of a creature with big hands and feet.

2011 where they set up a listening point to catch the creature but this turned up nothing. Then they did a second operation six weeks later after residents continued to tell the police that they were hearing the howling.

This time the Navajo police focused on a canyon near Crown Point that contained many caves and was believed to be the place where the Howler lived. There were reports of dogs being killed by some unknown attacker. A cave was identified by following a foul odor and at one point two glowing eyes were captured by a flashlight. It was thought to be the bigfoot they were searching for but they assumed that it went deeper into the cavern system.[20]

The Crown Point Howler apparently still howls during the night from time to time. Perhaps he moved on to some other area where he could do his howling. Was he howling because he was in pain? Had he been hurt somehow? Perhaps from a bullet fired from the rifle of one of Crown Point's residents? Maybe he had hurt his foot somewhere, stepping in the wrong rocky place as he bounded over some sharp rocks. A number of bigfoot reports have had to do with a "crippled" bigfoot where one of the footprints shows that one foot is not normal.

We can also think of the little girl raised for some years by a bigfoot family. She would howl into the night and we must think that that is just a natural thing for a bigfoot to do—howl!

Tales of the Mogollon Monster

In my book *Bigfoot Nation* I tell many stories of the Mogollon Monster, which is a general term for the many bigfoot in the forests of northeastern Arizona along Mogollon Mountain and the Mogollon Rim, which runs from Alpine and Heber past Payson to Flagstaff, Williams and Prescott.

In the mid-1940s there was a well-known story circulated around northern Arizona about kids at a Boy Scout camp near Payson that had a frightening encounter with a bigfoot one night. A scout named Don Davis, 13 years old at the time, was camping with other scouts near Tonto Creek close to the small town of Pine, when something in the night woke him up as it rummaged though the boys' belongings. Not knowing who would be doing this in the middle of the night, Davis called out to the noisemaker who then came and stood near him. Later, Davis, who died in 2002, described what he saw:

> There, standing still less than four feet in front of me was a monster-like man... The creature was huge. Its eyes were deep set and hard to see, but they seemed expressionless. His face seemed pretty much devoid of hair, but there seemed to be hair along the sides of his face. His chest, shoulders and arms were massive, especially the upper arms; easily upwards of 6 inches in diameter, perhaps much, much more. I could see he was pretty hairy, but didn't observe really how thick the body hair was. The face/head was very square; square sides and squared-up chin, like a box.[59]

Another similar story is about a scout in a mummy sleeping bag with the drawstring drawn tightly over his face. During the night he woke up and found something scratching at his bag as if trying to find out how to get into it. Looking out through the hood the scout saw the large creature picking up several other scouts who had been asleep in their bags, as if to carry them away. The scouts screamed and struggled and bigfoot dropped them and ran away. This story, whose exact date is unknown, was told at many a campfire around Payson in the 1950s.[69]

In her book *The Mogollon Monster, Arizona's Bigfoot,*[69] Susan Farnsworth tells the story of Kent and Sarah Johnson, who along with their daughter Lacy, were hunting near Greens Peak on the White Mountain Apache Reservation, 30 miles east of Springerville in the fall of 1962. Kent, an avid hunter, had Sarah let him off at a certain spot on a remote logging road and told her to drive up the road for a mile or so and wait for him.

Sarah drove the car to a spot where the road split and stopped the car. Suddenly the family dog, a cocker spaniel that loved to chase squirrels and rabbits, went crazy barking and trying to get out of the car. With a leash on the dog, Sarah and Lacy opened the doors and let the animal out of the car. The mother and daughter noted an odd odor in the air and the dog continued to pull on her leash, gagging and coughing as the collar choked her neck.

Suddenly the leash broke and the dog ran barking into the woods toward the foul smell.

They called for the dog and walked a bit into the forest. The dog came running back and they saw something that they thought at first was a log, somehow being dragged by the dog. It turned out that the log was actually a bigfoot, chasing the dog from a distance.

The dog collapsed in their arms when it returned to Sarah and Lacy and suddenly a large rock came flying from a distance and landed on the hood of the car. Just then Kent arrived to ask what was going on. They showed him the dent in the hood and told him to get in the car. Just as Kent got in the car a large rock—big enough to kill him—landed where he had just been standing. The family drove away and vowed never to return to Greens Peak.[69]

A report on January 23, 1971 in the northern Arizona newspaper the *Daily Sun* concerned two students at Northern Arizona University in Flagstaff claiming that a bigfoot had looked in their parked car at 1:00 a.m., probably while they were involved in some sexual activity. In a state of shock they went to the police station and reported it.[3]

A letter from Yarnell, Arizona to Dennis Gates discussed in John Green's *Sasquatch: The Apes among Us*[29] said that in summer of 1975 a man driving in the area saw a bigfoot running down the road behind his car. He stopped his car and got out to look at the creature, which then ran away. The next day he saw it again on the mountainside, "lumbering along, its arms swinging and extending below its knees."

Susan Farnsworth, in her second book with Mogollon Monster expert Mitchell Waite, says that on October 27, 1975 two hunters, Lance and Steve, were in the Greens Peak Wilderness near the White Mountain Apache Reservation when they encountered bigfoot activity. Steve saw a bear and another creature fighting, and heard the ferocious roar of the bear and the shrill scream of the adversary—which he at first mistook to be the scream of a woman.

The bear suddenly took off and ran defeated down the mountain, and everything was quiet. Steve cautiously moved toward the area and then discovered a small hollow that had six dead deer lying inside, each without a head. He stared at the sight for some moments and then realized that this was a stash of dead deer hidden by a bigfoot, and the bear had been coming to steal some of it. Realizing the danger he was in, he quickly went in search of his friend and the two of them immediately left.[70]

The September 2006 White Mountain Apache Nation reports are particularly interesting because a number of Apache Nation police officers were involved, and reports were made to the police department that tended to show the seriousness of the encounters. Local television news crews were dispatched to interview witnesses on September 2, 2006, and a story appeared on Tucson's Channel 3 website, azstarnet.com, under the headline "Apaches Go Public with Bigfoot Sightings."

Another report came from the same area on November 6, 2006, published by *The Arizona Republic* with the headline "Ft. Apache reports spur Bigfoot hunt." In the article it was mentioned that a police report had been made by White Mountain tribal Officer Katherine Montoya (who was mentioned in the Channel 3 story), who responded to a call at 2:30 a.m. on August 14 when Barry and Tammy Lupe of Whiteriver called 911 to report an unhumanly large prowler peering through their window. Officer Montoya reported what she witnessed when she arrived at the Lupe residence:

> It stood approximately 6'7" tall. It appeared to be about 220 pounds or more. It had exceptionally long arms; it did not appear to be wearing any clothes, and just appeared black. When it turned towards me, the most obvious feature was its eyes. The skin around his eyes was a lighter color than the rest of the face. It appeared almost white while the rest of the suspect was black. I could smell a distinct odor, like a stinkbug. You know, when you squish a stinkbug it smells. It never made any sounds until it crashed through the fence [while running away].

Officer Montoya's suspect was, by her own admission, a large, hairy, stinky apeman. Officer Montoya had just met the Mogollon Monster.[11]

It was reported in early 2009 that a forest service employee was driving north on a remote forest service road outside of Reserve,

New Mexico designated FR41, that dead ends at Cienega Canyon. He spotted a tall bigfoot along the road near the canyon and the end of the road. Cienega Canyon is in the rugged and remote San Francisco Mountains, a largely uninhabited wilderness in a little-populated section of New Mexico.

A report on the BFRO website came from a high-level healthcare professional who said he was driving from Denver to Albuquerque, New Mexico on October 18, 2013 and stopped at a gas station in Las Vegas, New Mexico at one in the morning to get gas. He was travelling with his wife who went into the gas station, located just off of Interstate 25, and he decided to urinate in the desert in back of the station. As he walked back to the car he saw a bigfoot that was 8- to 10-feet tall, covered in dark brown matted hair. Said his report:

> As I turned and looked over my left shoulder, I saw an enormous, lurking animal. The animal was crouched over, almost as if taking cover in the sparse and cold vegetation. In fact, I think the creature watched me the whole time, and did not make so much as a noise. However, the creature noticed when I saw it. The creature stood up, and quickly lumbered into the dark, away from the direction of the parking lot. The one attribute of the creature that resounded with me was how heavy the footfall was. It sounded like somebody dropping a sack of potatoes over and over again. And it was fast. I observed the creature for about 8-11 seconds, from the moment it realized I saw it, to watching the animal dart into the wood line. Due to radiant light from the parking lot, I could make steady detail of the fleeing creature.

He said that the creature had a strong, foul odor and "massive, human-like hands." Although he had a concealed handgun in his possession, he was "scared stiff" and couldn't sleep for several nights after the sighting. It took him weeks to tell his wife about the incident.

The Baffling Disappearance of Dale Stehling

Yes, there are quite a few stories of people encountering bigfoot in the Southwest over the years. There have been a few disappearances that may have been caused by bigfoot as well. One baffling disappearance in the Four Corners area was that of Mitchell Dale Stehling, whose body suddenly appeared seven years after he mysteriously vanished from Mesa Verde National Park in southwest Colorado.

In September of 2020 it was announced by Mesa Verde National Park Superintendent Cliff Spencer that the remains of a lost hiker, Stehling, had been found in a remote section in the park, west of Durango, Colorado. Stehling had gone missing in the Mesa Verde National Park in 2013 and had now been discovered seven

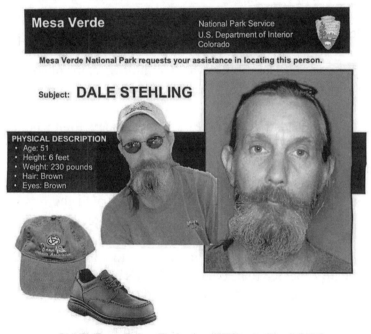

A poster for the missing hiker Dale Stehling.

years later—in an area that had already been searched. There are a number of mysteries surrounding the Stehling case including how he vanished and why he was ultimately found in an area that is completely off limits to all hikers and even Park personnel. It is an area that stretches eastward from Mesa Verde towards Durango.

I happened to go to grade school and junior high in Durango and I know that area fairly well. As a young family we visited Mesa Verde several times over the years, often with relatives who were visiting us from New York, Ohio, California or elsewhere. So I was particularly interested in the case of Stehling and wondered what had happened to this day hiker who suddenly vanished.

Let us look at the story that the *Durango Herald* ran on September 17, 2020 under the title: "End of a mystery? Human remains found at Mesa Verde National Park could solve 2013 disappearance." The subtitle was "Credible tip came in Wednesday, park superintendent says." The story by Jonathan Romeo reads:

> Search and rescue crews on Thursday found human remains at Mesa Verde National Park, which authorities believe belong to a Texas man who went missing in 2013. Mesa Verde National Park Superintendent Cliff Spencer said an anonymous tip Wednesday indicated the remains of Mitchell Dale Stehling were in a remote section in the park, west of Durango.
>
> Based on information included in the tip, Spencer said the tip appeared to be credible. "That's why we're checking it out," Spencer said earlier Thursday. "He ID'd aspects of the case that lead us to believe it's credible." Spencer said Thursday that search crews found human remains in the afternoon. The tip did not provide an exact location, but descriptions in the tip gave search crews a good idea where it was.
>
> As of 5 p.m., authorities had not determined whether the remains were Stehling's. Spencer did not know whether personal belongings were found on the scene. "We're still processing the scene," he said.
>
> A final determination likely will be made by Montezuma County Coroner George Deavers. He did not return calls

Thursday for comment.

Spencer said the body was found "quite a distance away" from where Stehling was last seen. The area, which took search crews about two hours to reach, was searched in 2013 when Stehling went missing. Spencer was unsure late Thursday whether crews would return Friday to continue processing the scene.

Stehling went missing on June 9, 2013, while visiting the park. According to past reports, Stehling and his family, from Goliad, Texas, were on an extended road trip visiting national parks throughout the West.

About 4:30 p.m., Stehling decided to hike alone to the Spruce Tree House, one of Mesa Verde's most popular ancient cliff dwellings, about a quarter-mile hike. When Stehling did not return after about two hours, his wife alerted the park, kicking off what would be a massive search mission.

It was determined Stehling had taken the Petroglyph Point Trail, a longer path that connects to the Spruce Tree House trail and has some more difficult hiking terrain. Stehling was reportedly seen by a group at the petroglyph panel. He then left and was never seen again. A search began that night and grew in the following days to include up to 70 personnel, search dogs and helicopters. Searches continued over the years—most recently in November— but no trace of Stehling has turned up.

Confounding searchers and compounding the mystery of Stehling's disappearance, the 52,500-acre Mesa Verde National Park is not large compared with other national parks. For example, Yellowstone National Park is more than 2.2 million acres, and Rocky Mountain National Park is 265,769 acres. Stehling was presumed to have died in the wilderness, though the case remained open. Spencer said Stehling's family has been notified. Attempts to reach Stehling's family on Thursday were not successful.

An update to the article after a few days confirmed that the body found was Stehling's and gave this background from earlier articles about his baffling disappearance:

51-year-old Mitchell Dale Stehling, known by the name Dale, went to the Mesa Verde National Park in Colorado on June 9, 2013, with his wife, Denean, and his parents. He said he was going for a hike to the Spruce Tree House ruin and left at 4.30 pm. The trail is less than a quarter of a mile long and connects to the Petroglyph Point Trail, a 2½-mile loop with cliff exposure that takes off from the Spruce Tree Trail. Witnesses saw him on that trail and spoke to him. However, he failed to return to his family.

Seven years later, on September 17, 2020, his remains were finally discovered by a hiker.

The Stehlings left their hometown of Goliad in Texas in a camper trailer and drove west, as Dale had always wanted to see Colorado. He was an outdoorsman and a keen camper, a man who could spend hours tending to his garden. He knew exactly how to spend that downtime, a day trip to Mesa Verde National Park.

Originally, the Stehlings only planned to drive out to the lookout point and take in the scene from a distance since the trail was rugged, and since Denean was overweight and Dale's parents were elderly, it would have not been possible for them to easily hike it. But being the rugged outdoorsman, Dale Stehling had to get a little closer.

At 4.08 pm, it was hot, temperatures in the park were in the 90-100 degrees range, and the terrain consisted of steep canyons and mesa tops at an elevation between 6,500 and 8,000 feet. The hike to the top of the trail should have taken around an hour.

Mesa Verde (Spanish for "green table") National Park is an American national park and UNESCO World Heritage Site located in Montezuma County, Colorado. The park protects some of the best-preserved Ancestral Puebloan archaeological sites in the United States. Mesa Verde was the first national park of its kind and it was established in 1906 by President Theodore Roosevelt to protect the legacy of the Puebloans who lived in the area for over 700 years. The park occupies 52,485 acres (21,240 ha) near the Four Corners region of the American Southwest. With more than 5,000 sites, including 600 cliff dwellings, it is the largest archaeological preserve in the United States. The park is best known for structures such as Cliff Palace, thought to be the largest cliff dwelling in North America. Starting c. 7500 BC Mesa Verde was seasonally inhabited by a group of nomadic Paleo-Indians known as the Foothills Mountain Complex. Later, Archaic people established semi-permanent rock shelters in and around the mesa. By 1000 BC, the Basketmaker culture emerged from the local Archaic population, and by 750 AD the Ancestral Puebloans had developed from the Basketmaker culture. By the end of the 12th century, they began to construct the massive cliff dwellings for which the park is best known. By 1285, following a period of social and environmental instability driven by a series of severe and prolonged droughts, they abandoned the area and moved south to locations in Arizona and New Mexico, including Rio Chama, Pajarito Plateau, and Santa Fe.

On the day he disappeared, his family quickly reported him missing. At first, rangers thought he had gotten off track, and they told his wife to give him a couple more hours. "The park never had a person go missing for more than a couple of hours," said Betty Lieurance, park public information officer.

When he had not returned two hours after he started on the Spruce Tree House hike, an intensive two-week search began that at its peak included 60 searchers, two dog teams, helicopter surveillance, and rope teams that rappelled off cliffs in the Chapin Mesa area. The K-9 team initially showed interest in the area in the first days of the search. The Petroglyph Point Trail follows a cliff base before ascending to the mesa via a series of steep, switchbacking sections with steps cut into the rock.

The day he disappeared was very hot and he didn't have any water with him, but he did have a cellular phone. No one was able to get any response or pings from it after his disappearance. Crucially, phone records showed that he tried to access his voicemail about 7 p.m. that night.

He was wearing a khaki Mesa Verde Museum Association baseball cap, brown tee-shirt, tan/khaki shorts, calf height white socks and Red Wing Oxford walking boots. He also carried his wallet and some cigarettes.

According to Patrick O'Driscoll of National Park Services Media Services (intermountain region), other than the main trails, the majority of Mesa Verde is uncharted territory that is off-limits to hikers.

Jesse Farias, chief ranger for Mesa Verde National Park, said the area has been heavily searched, but with no results, "In November we had a dog team come in and search that area again for human remains, but they did not pick up any hits. When we have search-and-rescue exercises, we go there and continue to look but have not found him."

The authorities said no foul play was suspected. "My gut feeling is that he is out there somewhere and never left the park. There is no reason to think otherwise—there have been no sightings. The case is still open." Not one physical clue has been found and he is presumed to have died in the wilderness.

The park never closed the case on Stehling and still continues to look for him in a limited continued mode, meaning, if a ranger is in the park, he or she will keep in mind that there is an unfound body in the park and be aware of any evidence that may lead to his recovery.

Chief Ranger Farias said a photo of Dale Stehling and notes about his disappearance remain on his wall. On average, about five to 10 people go missing in the park yearly, according to Farias, but Dale Stehling sticks with him.

Farias said the park extended efforts for months to find Stehling, which included calling in close to 100 people at a time to search, scaling cliffs and searching in areas of the park closed to visitors. There are a lot of cliff areas in the park that extend down to the Ute Mountain reservation that is filled with rocks, and Farias said if Stehling fell down a cliff, it would be almost impossible to see him from above or below it. "If he fell off a cliff, if he fell in between a rock area—unless you are looking straight down, even helicopters would not see him," he said.

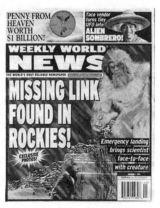

Authorities have shared case files with the family and keep them informed of search activity. But Denean, doesn't think the Rangers did enough to search for her husband. In total, rangers spent two days searching for Stehling before scaling back, she said. A news release cited a lack of evidence as to the reason. One year after he went missing she said, "Now that it's been a year, and the more I reflect on it, honestly, I'm just pissed off. Their attitude was: He was there, he was lost and what are they supposed to do about it?"

But Farias counters this view from Denean saying that rangers at the park searched for Stehling about three months, mostly in a scaled back mode, and continued to keep his disappearance on their radar. Their searches, he said, have and continue to cover a 3- to 5-mile radius around the trail he was last seen on. Mrs. Stehling, however, wanted the search to extend out of the small area as despite her husband's age he could put more miles in a day than they thought, but nothing came of it.

Over the course of 2014, Denean returned to the park three times, expecting answers, expecting to find her husband, expecting some sort of closure, but each time she returned, nothing changed. She believes her husband went off the trail because of confusing signs in the park.

…Perhaps, altitude sickness and dehydration took their toll and he missed the trail and fell over one of the many cliffs.

In the end there was one final update on Dale Stehling in the

Durango Herald that confirmed the remains were of Stehling and that he had been found in an area of the park which is off-limits to hikers:

> After seven years without a trace being found, Park Law Enforcement Rangers, with assistance from ISB and Montezuma County Coroner's Office finally found human remains at the National Park on September 17, 2020.
>
> Mesa Verde National Park Superintendent Cliff Spencer said an anonymous tip the day before indicated the remains of Dale Stehling were in a remote section in the park, west of Durango. The tip did not provide an exact location, but descriptions in the tip gave search crews a good idea where it was. Spencer said the body was found "quite a distance away" from where Stehling was last seen—around 4.2 miles. The area, which took search crews about two hours to reach, was searched in 2013 when Stehling went missing.
>
> Montezuma County Coroner George Deavers said he is "99%" sure the remains are that of Mitchell Dale Stehling because of items found at the scene: a driver's license, credit cards and a Social Security card that had Stehling's information on it. Deavers said he is going to meet with a forensic anthropologist to examine the remains, looking for any signs of trauma or any clues that can explain the circumstances surrounding Stehling's mysterious death. He also said that as of late September, foul play was not suspected and it did not appear he was attacked by an animal.
>
> Because the remains were just bones, Deavers said it was likely impossible to determine a cause of death, unless Stehling had obvious signs of trauma, which he did not. "Just from what I saw, (I'd say) natural causes. But we'll look everything over."
>
> At the time of the discovery, it was unclear whether a DNA test was possible. To take DNA from a bone sample, the bone must have retained some moisture. Many of the bones found at the scene were bleached, but it's possible

there is still some moisture in them. If a DNA test is possible, Deavers said it would take about a year to get results back.

He also said Dale's remains were found by a hiker in an area that is closed to the public, at the bottom of a canyon, and it is believed that is where he died.

The family of Dale Stehling appear to have got closure after a seven year wait. But many questions remain about the circumstances of his disappearance and death.

The remains were found in an area previously searched. The search was extensive over two weeks which included 60 searchers, two dog teams, helicopter surveillance, and rope teams that rappelled off cliffs. The Mesa Verde Park is relatively small, though rugged and hot. Was Dale just missed or did he enter the area where his remains were found after they were searched?

How did Dale get so badly lost on the on the Spruce Tree House hike?

How did he end up 4.2 miles from where he was last seen without water and supplies?

What caused Dale's death?

The forensic anthropologist will have little to work on apart from some bleached bones after seven years.

So, here we have the strange tale of Dale Stehling. Without any water did Stehling become dehydrated and then confused, wandering off the trail farther and farther into the park? But what happened then? Was he kidnapped and killed by a curious bigfoot? Did this bigfoot then dump Stehling's body at a remote part of the park many months—or years—after it had been searched?

It is as if Stehling stepped into a time warp and vanished for a period of time. Even the mainstream media—struggling for an explanation—mentioned that he might have been abducted by aliens who then dumped his body years later.

Maybe he had just wandered off the trail and walked many miles and collapsed between some rocks—but why was he never discovered before in the earlier searches? Was it because he wasn't there? Indeed, it seems that Stehling's body was carried away to some hidden spot—I surmise a bigfoot's cave—where it was kept for an extended period of time. It was then dumped in the spot where Stehling was found.

It would seem that Stehling had not walked to the spot where he was ultimately found, as it is a considerable distance—many miles—and in the opposite direction from the trails and visitor's center. He seems to have gotten off the trail in some spot and was then abducted by the bigfoot, who probably killed him within seconds of their encounter. He was taken away to the cave and then discarded months later in a different section of the park.

What did Dale Stehling do wrong that got him killed? It would seem that he was not prepared for a long hike, but apparently made a long hike anyway. He had no water with him or even snacks. Was this his mistake, not sticking to his original plan and going further than he should have down the trail? His wife blamed the confusing signs in the park for her husband's wanderings.

But we get the nagging feeling here that the Stehling case isn't just about someone who wandered off the trail. It is about someone who took a hike and vanished for seven years. Had he been grabbed by bigfoot?

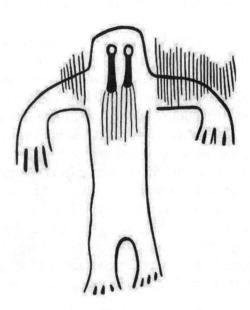

Chapter 5

BIGFOOT BACK EAST

I cooked a bat in a gumbo pan
I drank the blood from a rusty can
Turned me into the Hunger Man
I'm the lover of the bayou
—The Byrds, *Lover of the Bayou*

As JC Johnson (who passed away in 2018) would say, "People are surprised about bigfoot in the Southwest. They don't expect them to be there." It is a similar story with bigfoot in the forests, swamps and mountains of the eastern part of the United States. Accounts have been coming in for two hundred years now, and they keep coming in.

Bigfoot is known from Ontario down through New England and down south to the swamps of Florida and Mississippi. In December of 2021, a video from the backwoods of Georgia was shared on the @CryptidUniversity Instagram account. The video shows shaky footage of what appears to be a large apelike animal with black fur bending over behind some trees in the distance. When the creature fully stands, it looks taller and bigger than a human. It then walks off as the person filming hides behind a tree.

It was reported by the Dailyvoice.com, out of New York City, on August 4, 2020, that a bigfoot was seen swinging through the trees in the Hudson Valley north of the city. The report said that the Hudson Valley's lead researcher of bigfoot told reporters about the incident.

The researcher, Gayle J. Beatty, says she was informed of the sighting on July 2, 2020, when she received a phone call from a woman in Dutchess County, New York, who was working as a landscaper on a property in the Hyde Park area near the Hudson

River. The woman's name is "strictly confidential," as is the precise location of the incident, Beatty said.

The woman described the creature to Beatty as being approximately 6-7 feet in height with reddish-brown hair and said it moved through the trees "like a monkey." The incident happened after the woman, who had been weeding the garden, was told to dump the weeds down a trail a couple of hundred feet behind the barn. After dumping the weeds, the wheelbarrow dropped, making a loud noise, the woman said.

According to Beatty, "Suddenly, from approximately 50-feet away, she sees and hears something crashing through the thick vegetation, parting the brush towards her." Beatty said the creature then jumped in the tree above her, leaving the woman in "shock and disbelief," as it began "using its arms to swing from tree to tree moving away from her." Beatty said she has had several reports from the Hyde Park area over the last few years leading her to believe "there is a clan living there."

Earlier in March of 2020 a black, shaggy bigfoot was seen around a small North Carolina town according to Fox television station WFXB. There report on March 31, 2020 said the small town of Littleton, North Carolina had had a number of sightings during the spring. The station said that Littleton, on the North Carolina-Virginia border, was freaked out over four recent Bigfoot sightings. One of the sightings was by a man taking out his trash; he claimed that he saw a "real tall figure with big hands and black shaggy fur." Other sightings of bigfoot have been made in the same area. Littleton is no stranger to bigfoot sightings and is the home of the Cryptozoology & Paranormal Museum, aka Bigfoot Museum.

Bigfoot Howlers in Upstate New York

The *Adirondack Daily Enterprise* (www.adirondackdaily-enterprise.com) reported on June 29, 2021 that their had been a bigfoot sighting near Massena, a town in the very north of New York, on the Canadian border and near Vermont. The article pointed out that, "In 2020, New Yorkers reported 113 bigfoot sightings, according to Microsoft News. For some north country residents, bigfoots are believed to be residing in their backyards." The article went on to say:

> On June 20 at about 11:30 pm, Massena resident Michael Guimond was driving home on County Route 37 when he spotted what he said was "Something bipedal ran across the road within 50 feet of my car, and was extremely fast." Guimond went on to say that "the thing was brown or gray, shaggy and had arms and legs that moved in a circular motion. I was going 60, as it crossed the road from right to left in less than a second.
>
> It was also the same night that a slew of sightings from other people within the area were reported.

The article went on to describe the story of Aric Lauzon from Louisville, a small town in northern New York, west of Massena. Said the article:

> Aric Lauzon lived at his Louisville home from 2011 to 2015, and he noted before he lived at the home, he was not a bigfoot believer. That all changed in 2011 when Lauzon reported "strange screaming coming from the woods at the back of my house, which went on for miles and miles. I was out there a couple of nights walking my dog when I kept hearing the loud screaming noise. It sounded like nothing I have ever heard before in my life. It sounds like a mix between an elephant and a bear, it goes right through you, it's deafening."
>
> Lauzon also noted that the summer of 2013 was when it started getting bad, Lauzon said. "Every night I would hear this thing screaming. One day I came home from work at 8 a.m. and my neighbors were all outside. While I was at work, a large hairy creature ran through my yard … and destroyed my birdhouse." Big footprints were found on Lauzon's yard and hair stuck in the fence.
>
> Dean Gleason, director of Seaway Valley Bigfoot Research was contacted and conducted a week-long investigation. Gleason began Seaway Valley Bigfoot Research for people to report sightings and experiences

153

they have had. "I used to have a sasquatch sticker on my Jeep, and I had 40 to 50 people come up to me throughout the community and tell me their stories."

With ten years of research under his belt, Gleason believes the animals are harmless unless provoked. He related that, "I've only ever had one get aggressive with me." I've been in the woods with a lot of them and they've always left me alone."

With the assistance of the DEC, Gleason ventured back into the woods around 3 am, Lauzon said. "They were doing tree knocks and the thing was doing tree knocks back. One of them threw a rock into the brush and a minute later something threw the rock back at them and let out a huge roar."

North Carolina Bigfoot Antics

In North Carolina all sorts of bigfoot antics were happening. A woman in Shelby, North Carolina said she was feeding a bigfoot. Meanwhile a man in Hickory was having his own encounter with bigfoot.

According to *The Charlotte Observer* on August 14, 2019, a woman named Vicky Cook says she has been feeding a bigfoot. Said *The Charlotte Observer:*

A Shelby, North Carolina, woman named Vicky Cook says she's seeing something very strange in the woods behind her home. "Sometimes I think this can't be real," Vicky Cook said. "It went in front of my camera." Vicky Cook's video is grainy, but her conscious is clear. "I screamed I didn't know what it was, but that thing was tall!" Cook shouted.

She says the sasquatch sightings started back in March. Footprints are her proof. "I think I've counted about eight different sized prints," said Cook. "This is a juvenile, but look at how long it is. That's a big... big print."

John Bruner who documents sightings across the country and runs the Bigfoot 911 Facebook group said, "It was huge. It was on two legs. It was bipedal. The hair on the head and on the body was real stringy and matted-looking."

Cook says she doesn't want her neighbors going hungry. "Mostly like candy, cookies, they love peanut brittle, chocolate, peanut butter sandwiches," said Cook. "They don't like apples and bananas."

Yes, it might seem like a good idea to be feeding bigfoot, but things can turn sour. There have been a number of reports of widowed, elderly women with orchards on their rural farm having a relationship with a bigfoot, namely feeding the critter, usually by allowing it to eat from the orchard. In one instance the bigfoot would leave dead rabbits as payment for the fruits it was enjoying. In the fields of the Midwest and Eastern US, in the late summer and fall, there is tons of corn (maize) for any bigfoot to gorge himself on.

A few weeks after the *Observer* story the *Hickory Record*, out of Hickory, North Carolina, reported on August 28, 2019 that a local resident, Doug Teague, claimed he had an encounter with a bigfoot. Teague said that the encounter happened in the McDowell County area on August 16, 2019. Teague is part of a bigfoot investigation crew called Catawba Valley Bigfoot Research. Said the article:

> Walking through the woods with his dog, steadfast companion Crazy Daisy, Teague was attempting to recover some trail cameras he'd put up when he heard some wood knocking sounds.
>
> "I just passed it off as a woodpecker," Teague said. Then things changed. Something in the woods was throwing rocks. Teague said he took out his phone and started videoing the experience. He was also able to snap some photos of what he claims is Bigfoot sitting down. When asked how he knows that he didn't take a photo of a bear Teague said: "Bears don't throw rocks."
>
> Crazy Daisy will approach a bear, said Teague, but she won't approach a bigfoot. "She was going nuts but staying close to me," Teague said.

Teague went into the woods not planning on looking for bigfoot at that time of the day. It was about 3 to 4 p.m. in the afternoon and roughly 90 degrees.

Ideal bigfoot investigating conditions occur at early morning or dusk at 40 to 70 degrees with no leaves on the trees, Teague said. Teague has been looking for Bigfoot for nearly a decade. "It's always been an interest," Teague said. "I'm a gorilla freak. I love gorillas." Bigfoot is often described as looking like an oversized gorilla.

Teague said he tries to make it to the Marion area often, which is known in the bigfoot investigating community for being a bigfoot hotspot. Bigfoot investigating has become so popular, that the city hosted their second annual Bigfoot Festival on Sept. 14.

Bigfoot Kidnaps and Releases Toddler

Then we have the case of a missing three-year-old toddler in Craven County, North Carolina, mentioned in Chapter 3. Craven County is on the northern coast of the state, near Nags Head. The Croatan National Forest is in the vicinity.

According to a January 25, 2019 story in *The Charlotte Observer*, the Craven County Sheriff's Office said that Casey Lynn Hathaway, 3, had disappeared on January 22, 2019 from his grandmother's backyard while playing with other children. He was discovered three days later unharmed. Said the article:

> The FBI, state investigators, and the U.S. Marine Corps from nearby bases at Camp Lejeune and Cherry Point joined the effort to find the boy. On January 25, Hathaway was found. He was located by professional search and rescue teams, the FBI said. "Casey is healthy, smiling and talking," Breanna Hathaway wrote. "He said he hung out with a bear for two days. God sent him a friend to keep him safe. God is a good God. Miracles do happen."
>
> Craven County Sheriff Chip Hughes told reporters on Thursday that authorities were able to find the boy after hearing someone call out for their mother. They then found the boy stuck in "a tangle of vines and thorns" about a half-

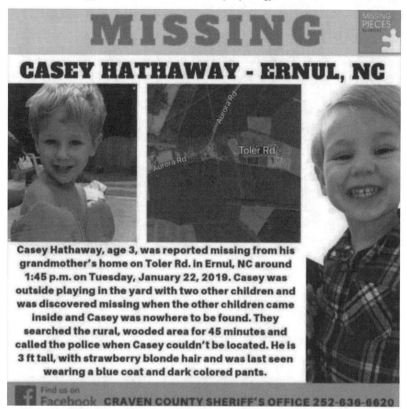

A poster for Casey Hathaway while he was missing.

mile from the place where he disappeared. The boy was discovered "wet, cold and scratched up" but he could talk.

Hundreds of volunteers joined law enforcement agencies to search "treacherous" terrain that is flooded and dotted with sinkholes, the sheriff's office said on Facebook. "Even the trained searchers are having trouble navigating safely," said the post. Helicopters and drones were used in the search but could not find the boy.

It was not immediately clear where Casey was during those two days and what enabled him to stay safe. Posters were made of the missing boy during that time. Later he appeared in a photograph smiling and appearing happy. He must have been in a secluded place for the many searchers to have missed finding him. Was he in some bigfoot den for those two days? Did he eat

157

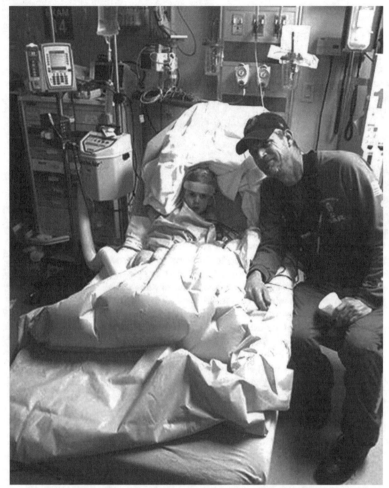

Casey Hathaway with his father in the hospital after being found.

anything during that time?

The young boy told his mother that he had been with a bear for two days. Most park rangers and sheriff's offices will tell you that it would be impossible for a bear to have sheltered little Casey during those two days.

Therefore, who or what had Casey been with for that time? Bigfoot researchers know the answer—it was bigfoot! Sheriff's departments, however, are unlikely to make this diagnosis of the curious case of the boy and the bear.

We might be inclined to think that they boy had wandered into the forest on his own and gotten lost, only to have a bigfoot rescue him and keep him warm for two nights in January. Unfortunately, this is probably not what happened to young Casey. Most probably Casey was being watched by the bigfoot while he played with the other children. As Casey strayed closer to the hidden bigfoot and away from the other children the bigfoot suddenly grabbed Casey in a manner that did not make him scream.

He was brought to the bigfoot's lair where he spent two days and two nights with the bigfoot. One must think that the bigfoot gave him some food, perhaps some dried berries or nuts. With the heavy search that was occurring outside the cave the bigfoot decided to drop the boy back to an area near to where he had been abducted.

Casey was lucky to have been brought back alive. Other young children have not been so lucky. Sometimes they vanish and are never seen again. Sometimes they are found dead, often in an area that has been already been searched. Occasionally they are brought back alive but they have fractured memories of what has happened to them. They simply do not understand it and most of them are too young to understand the bizarre circumstances that they were in. In many cases the children are autistic to some degree.

Miracles do happen, as his mother said, and that is all that really matters in Casey's case. Perhaps as the boy gets older he will remember more of his strange experiences and realize that he is one of the lucky ones.

Man Fires at Bigfoot in Kentucky, Plus Weirdness in Vermont
CNN reported on August 1, 2019 that a couple camping at a national park in Kentucky said they were rousted from their tent by a man who told them he had seen a bigfoot. The man said he fired into the darkness at the bigfoot when it lunged at him. The incident happened in the famous Mammoth Cave National Park.

CNN said:

Law enforcement rangers with the Mammoth Cave National Park responded to the incident involving the camper with the firearm at one of the park's backcountry campsites early Sunday, park spokeswoman Molly Schroer said in a statement. The statement did not confirm a Bigfoot

159

sighting but Schroer said no threat remains in the park.

Federal regulations prohibit the discharge of a firearm in the national park, she said. Park officials know the identity of the person who allegedly fired a weapon; no charges have been filed.

Madelyn Durand and her boyfriend Brad Ginn, who reported the incident to park rangers, said the encounter frightened them. And the attention over the alleged sighting of the cryptozoological mystery known as bigfoot has surprised the Bowling Green, Kentucky, couple. "I was mostly just concerned about him shooting the gun in the middle of the night without him really seeing anything," said Durand, 22.

Durand said she was awakened around 11 p.m. when she heard noises outside their tent. She assumed other campers were being rowdy and drinking. She woke Ginn after a flashlight shined into the tent. "We got out of the tent and saw a man who told us their campsite had been destroyed by someone or something," said Durand, a student at Western Kentucky University.

The man, who was with his young son, showed them his gun on his hip and told them the area was popular for bigfoot sightings, Durand recalled. The couple climbed back into their tent as the man walked away to investigate with his son in tow.

"We heard them coming back about 10 minutes later. We heard them yelling 'I see it!' Durand said. She added: "We saw the flash from his gun, and he shot maybe 20 yards from the side of our tent into the pitch-black darkness."

Durand said she was scared that the gunfire could have struck them. The man with the firearm seemed frightened, too. He told the couple his hands were shaking, they recalled.

"The guy said he saw a bigfoot emerge from the brush and it was coming towards him, so he shot at it," said Ginn, 24, who also attends Western Kentucky University. "We shined a flashlight to see if there was an animal or something. And there was absolutely nothing there,"

Durand said.

So, it would appear that shootouts with bigfoot are still common as of 2019. People shooting at a bigfoot have had mixed results. It does seem to deter the aggressive bigfoot who is stalking someone. Many bigfoot researchers and hunters will carry a pistol with them, but many don't.

The story out of Kentucky is a curious one. It is illegal to discharge a firearm in a National Park, which is to bigfoot's advantage. While this story might be a hoax perpetrated by a gun toting yahoo and his son, it seems like a genuine tale of fear and someone discharging their weapon at something that was frightening them. Was it a bear? This is very likely a bigfoot encounter. The man firing the pistol has never been identified.

Meanwhile in Vermont, the *Barre Montpelier Times Argus* reported on September 11, 2019 that East Montpelier resident Christopher Noel had captured the attention of locals on social media in early September with his bigfoot videos. Recent posts by Noel presented videos of locations in the woods near his home where footprints and stick shelters have been found, as well as audio recordings he made that include strange calls that are not those of "normal" woodland animals. He also showed some casts of bigfoot footprints he had made in central Vermont.

Said the article:

> Noel is convinced they are all made by bigfoot. Noel is a Yale University philosophy graduate who previously taught at the Vermont College of Fine Arts. He is the author of numerous books and writings on the bigfoot, including one that helps identify sasquatch so-called "stick structures" in the forest attributed to dwellings constructed by the creatures. He also leads "Wild Vermont Expeditions" with targeted trips in Vermont for people interested in immersing themselves in the folklore and legend.
>
> Noel said recent evidence uncovered in the area had led him to go public with his discoveries. "I have been researching this species quietly and privately for a number of years," Noel said in an interview Wednesday. "Now

I've decided to come out... and reach out to others who may have information to share with me and learn what I have found out, so we can begin to fill in the picture of the habits, the roots and the behavior of our local population."

Noel said he was returning to visit a man in Worcester on Wednesday who said he had heard strange calls in the woods and had recorded the sounds. "He has heard screams in the middle of the night coming from the mountain that rattled the walls in his house and he's been a hunter and guide for 40 years and knows all the ordinary sounds of the forest, and had never heard anything remotely like that when he first heard it and has now heard it a bunch of times," Noel said. "The volume is just on a completely different level, in the sense that it rattles windows and walls, and you can feel it in your chest, even though you know it's no closer than 100 yards away."

So, we have the yelling and the screaming in Vermont. The howling continues. Decades before, in September of 1985 *The Daily Herald* of Rutland, Vermont ran a story about Bob Davis and his family. The Davis family heard a loud thrashing noise in the woods near their property and called the police. It was about 8:30 in the evening and Ed Davis saw a creature "grunting and screeching" that was "taller than me." His brother went into the woods to investigate and could smell a distinct "swampy smell."[3]

Tales of bigfoot back East are many, including some of the earliest reports of bigfoot. Sadly, we also have stories of vanished children who may have been taken from bigfoot such as the story of an 8-year-old who vanished in Upstate New York in 1971.

The Vanishing of Douglas Legg in the Adirondacks
As part of *The Bigfoot Files* we have the strange case of Douglas Legg, an 8-year-old boy from Syracuse, New York, who vanished from his family's summer home in the Santanoni Nature Preserve in the Adirondacks on July 10, 1971.

The Legg family lived on the edge of the Santanoni Nature Preserve and would go on hikes from their house directly in to the forest. Young Douglas was going on one of these family hikes when his uncle told him to go back to the house and put on pants to protect his legs from the poison ivy that was known to be on the trail.

Douglas obediently headed back to the house. But something happened on the short walk back to the family's cabin. Douglas disappeared and was never seen again.

His disappearance launched the Adirondacks' largest manhunt ever. More than 600 rescuers searched the dense woods of the Santanoni Nature Preserve. US Air Force planes used infrared equipment to try to detect body heat from the boy. An article published in Syracuse's *The Journal* in July 1971 reported that a C131 aircraft also surveyed the area with "a thermo-scanner device used to penetrate the Vietnam foliage." The family even paid for the elite Sierra Madre Search and Rescue Unit to fly in from California.

"It's such a wilderness out there," Patrick Kelleher, the State Police senior investigator, told the Syracuse *Post Star* in 2011.

No trace of Douglas has ever been found, and the search had to be abandoned after 33 days. The family sold their property a few months afterward and moved out of the area.

What happened to Douglas Legg on his way back to his home? Did he wander off the trail and vanish into the forest? Did he get back to his house where he was instantly abducted by someone and driven away? Did he meet a bigfoot on the trail that had been stalking him for months and get abducted?

Unfortunately, this fits the pattern of children who are lone hikers and who vanish from a well-hiked trail near other hikers— and even from their campsite or home. It would appear that Douglas was being watched for quite some time. He played in the backyard that was next to a large forested wilderness area.

It seems that Douglas was being watched by a bigfoot, perhaps a young one. This would have gone on over a period of time— many months. Then, when the family was off on one of their frequent hikes, this bigfoot, watching the group the whole time, saw Douglas leave the group and begin to walk back alone on the trail through the forest. Suddenly the bigfoot struck and Douglas was grabbed by the powerful animal. The young boy may never have had time to scream, but even if he did, probably no one was near enough to hear him.

He was likely taken alive to a bigfoot cave away from the area where the curious bigfoot wanted to examine him. Young children are usually not purposely harmed by a bigfoot when they are kidnapped. They are captives who are vulnerable to the outdoors, night temperatures, and will not be able to eat most of the food that a bigfoot might try to feed them. Wild berries, often plentiful in July, August and September, are thought to be given by bigfoot to abducted children, and it is one of the few things that small children can eat—but not for long.

After a day or two the child will begin to starve to death and either be crying or sleeping all the time. The bigfoot then either returns the child to a spot near where the abduction took place or the child dies "of exhaustion" and remains for some time in the cave. Later it will be discarded but the shoes and clothing will be carefully examined. They may be kept or they may be discarded with the dead child, usually scattered near the body but still some distance away.

This is a sad story of a boy who returned alone through the woods to his house to get some long pants on to protect him from poison ivy. Hey, what about protection from bigfoot?

With the extensive search that occurred after he was reported missing finding no trace of the boy, everyone involved must have been completely baffled. Had a wild animal taken the boy? A cougar or bear? This was a time when law enforcement and searchers might suggest bigfoot as the culprit, but this is not something that the officials are likely to do. Bigfoot abducting a boy cannot be their conclusion. They have to say that they just do not know what happened to Douglas Legg.

Often attention falls on the immediate family as they are always early suspects. In the case of Douglas we have the possibility that he was kidnapped by someone with a car when he returned to his house although the police discounted this.

It seems that Douglas was abducted by a bigfoot who had been watching him for a relatively long period of time. He lived with a wilderness area right next to his home. His parents would naturally be tortured by this disappearance and it is something they would now live with for their entire lives, including the uncle who sent him back to the house. They soon decided to sell their home and move out of the area. Clearly, something was not right about this house, this yard, this trail that led into the forest. This was a family that never wanted to walk that trail again.

Disappearances in the Great Smoky Mountains

The mystery of Douglas Legg is not the only mysterious disappearance of a young child back East. There have been a number of strange disappearances in the Great Smoky Mountains of Tennessee and along the Appalachian Trail.

The Syracuse *Post Star* in 2011 mentions several disappearances in the Great Smoky Mountains of Tennessee. On June 4, 1969, 6-year-old Dennis Martin was scheming with his brother and two other boys in the park's Spence Field while on an annual family camping trip. The group of boys went off into the woods during the evening and then planned on sneaking up on their family to startle them. But when the boys ran and jumped on the adults, Dennis was nowhere to be found. There were several days of searches for Dennis but he had completely disappeared.

After not seeing him for about five minutes and when all of the other children had returned to the campsite, his father became concerned and began searching for him. His father ran down the trail for nearly two miles, until he was sure he could not have gotten any farther. After several hours, they sought help from National Park Service rangers.

The area where Martin disappeared is marked by steep slopes and ravines. Wild animals such as copperhead snakes, bears, feral hogs, and bobcats inhabit the area. A downpour broke out shortly after Martin's disappearance, dumping about three inches of rain. Heavy rains during the first day's search hampered efforts, and heavy mist the next day. Up to 1,400 people were

A shocking news story from the past.

involved in the search effort, potentially obscuring possible clues.

Small footprints were found in the area. The child-sized footprints led to a stream, where they disappeared. The tracks indicated that one foot was barefoot, while the other was in an Oxford (the type of shoe Martin was wearing) or a tennis shoe. Retired park ranger and author Dwight McCarter believes that the prints likely belonged to Martin. A shoe and sock were also found.

By June 22, 56 square miles of ground had been covered. More than a thousand searchers continued to look until June 26, when the search was cut back. The search was abandoned on June 29, and was officially closed down on September 14, 1969. According to Wikipedia, as of 2022, it is still the largest search in the history of Great Smoky Mountains National Park.

The official theories were that he had died of exposure; that a bear had killed him; or that he had been abducted and taken out of the park. Dennis Martin's father was a believer in the last theory. The father offered a US$5,000 (equivalent to $35,286 in 2020) reward for information. Psychics, including the famous psychic Jeanne Dixon, offered clues to the disappearance, but nothing was ever found. According to Wikipedia, a few years after Dennis Martin's disappearance, a ginseng hunter discovered the scattered skeletal remains of a small child in Big Hollow, Tremont, Tennessee. He kept the find to himself until 1985 because of fear that he would be prosecuted for the illegal ginseng. A subsequent search during that year turned up nothing.

What happened to young Dennis Martin? Was he suddenly snatched by a bigfoot and taken away from the area? Why could searchers not find him? He disappeared in the near vicinity of his friends and family but he never yelled or called for help. He simply disappeared. The cost for the Dennis Martin search was $65,000 and nothing was ever found.

The Syracuse *Post Star* mentions two other cases in the Great Smoky Mountains. One case is that of Trenny Lynn Gibson, a 16-year-old girl who disappeared on a school trip in the area in 1976. On October 8 of that year, while on a horticulture field trip with 40 of her classmates, Gibson was hiking along Andrews Bald in the national park. She had left the group and was hiking alone and no one could recall seeing her after 3 p.m. She was reported missing that day and searches continued for months, but no trace of Gibson was ever found.

Another case is of 58-year-old Thelma Pauline Melton who was hiking near Deep Creek Campground in the Great Smoky Mountain National Park. Deep Creek is in North Carolina just near the Tennessee border and is also near the Nantahala National Forest which is essentially a wilderness area. Melton was hiking on a trail she'd been on many times before. On September 25, 1981 she was with friends when she walked ahead of them and disappeared over a hill. They called and searched for her but they couldn't find her. She had suddenly vanished.

Looking for her, they returned to the campground where they all were staying and she did not show up. An extensive search over several days was made for her but no clues to her disappearance were ever found.

What happened to Trenny Lynn Gibson and Thelma Melton? One minute they were walking on a trail in the middle of the day and the next minute they are gone. Did aliens suddenly abduct them? Did they somehow fall off the trail? If so, where? Why are they not found with dogs and other searchers looking for them?

Is it that they have been abducted by a bigfoot? This is a frightening idea, but one that must be considered. We can only hope that they were struck dead by a blow to the head before being abducted. Otherwise they would have spent agonizing days in a bigfoot's cave as they slowly died.

A frightening incident happened in Flintsville, Tennessee on April 26, 1976. Flintsville is a rural town in south central Tennessee, west of Chattanooga. There had been a number of bigfoot reports around the town in the preceding days, including a report of a bigfoot grabbing the aerial of a woman's car and jumping onto its roof. On April 26, Mrs. Jennie Robertson was in her house while her 4-year-old son Gary was playing outside in the evening when she heard her son cry out. She rushed out and said she saw:

...this huge figure coming around the corner of the

house. It was 7 or 8 feet tall and seemed to be all covered with hair. It reached out its long, hairy arm toward Gary and came within a few inches of him before I could grab him and pull him back inside.

Mr. Robertson ran to the door when he realized something was happening and glimpsed a big black shape disappearing into the woods. Six men then tracked the bigfoot and got near enough to fire guns at it. It threw big rocks at them and ran into the bush. The next day they returned to the scene and found 16-inch-long footprints as well as hair and blood.[3]

Bigfoot and UFOs in Pennsylvania

During the1970s there were a number of bigfoot incidents, especially in western Pennsylvania. On the evening of September 27, 1973 two girls were waiting for a lift in rural Westmoreland County, Pennsylvania, southeast of Pittsburgh, when they saw a white, hairy bigfoot with red eyes standing in the nearby woods, apparently watching them. The girls were also surprised to see that it was carrying a luminous sphere in its hand. The girls rushed to their nearby home and told their father who went into the woods for an hour and later told the girls to stay out of the woods. Later it was reported that some sort of UFO was seen in the area, hovering over the forest with a powerful searchlight coming to the ground from the object.

Strange things continued to happen around Greensburg, the county seat of Westmoreland County. In October of 1973, approximately 15 people saw a dome-shaped luminous object near the ground and then later two bigfoot were seen in the area, one about 7 feet tall and the other about 8 feet tall. Then in Uniontown, Pennsylvania in November of 1973 a man was walking his dog one night when he saw a trespasser on his land and called out to him. The figure came toward him and he saw that it was a tall bigfoot with red glowing eyes. Because of wild dogs in woods, the man always carried a revolver and he promptly emptied all six rounds from the pistol into the bigfoot. The creature suddenly vanished but screaming could be heard. The wife also heard the bigfoot making a sound like "a human that was in deep pain."[3]

168

The sightings around Uniontown, Pennsylvania continued in February of 1974. On the night of February 6, a woman, identified as "Mrs. A," was sitting in her house watching television. Around 10 p.m. she heard a noise on her front porch where she kept two large tins of food. Her house was in a wooded area and there were wild dogs that she suspected of rummaging around the porch. She picked up a shotgun and stepped onto the porch expecting to scare off some dogs. Instead she was facing a 7-foot-tall bigfoot that was standing about six feet from her. The bigfoot raised both of its arms above his head and the woman took it to be a sign that he was about to jump at her. She pulled the trigger on her shotgun and with a huge flash the bigfoot was completely gone.

Her phone suddenly rang and it was her daughter's husband who lived in the next house, about 100 feet away, who had heard the shotgun blast. Mrs. A told the man her story and he grabbed his revolver and began walking to her house. Along the way he supposedly encountered four or even five hairy creatures, all seven feet high with glowing red eyes, who emerged from the woods and headed towards him. He fired at them and ran to the house of Mrs. A. Together they decided to phone the police, and while waiting for the sheriff to arrive, noticed what seemed to be a glowing red UFO hovering over the woods near the house. The state police quickly arrived and could find no footprints on the frozen ground but noted that the animals on the property, including a horse, seemed to be acting in a frightened and atypical manner.[3]

Things got even weirder just west of Pittsburgh in Minerva, Ohio, where there was some bigfoot activity. Reports of bigfoot with pet dogs—or perhaps a pet wolf—are extremely rare but they have been filed occasionally, as well as a bigfoot with two large cats, like cougars.

The cats feature in the Cayton family sightings in Paris Township, near Minerva, Ohio on August 21, 1978. The family of nine witnesses were sitting on their porch at 10:30 in the evening when they heard noises near a demolished chicken coop. Several in the family shone flashlights in the direction, some distance

169

away, and saw two pairs of large yellow eyes reflecting the light of their beams. There seemed to be two large animals at their old chicken coop.

At this point, 18-year-old friend Scott Patterson drove to the area in his car to see the animals more clearly. He was astonished to see that the two pairs of eyes belonged to two cougar-like animals. As he watched the cougars, suddenly a large bigfoot strode out of the darkness between the two cougars, as if protecting them.

The large bigfoot then lurched at Patterson in his car and the teenager drove back to the house where they phoned the police. The family all sat in the kitchen in a frightened commotion waiting for the police when the bigfoot looked in the kitchen window and then was clearly seen by outdoor lighting for ten minutes while it stood there in the backyard.

The bigfoot—and accompanying pumas—suddenly left. The local sheriff arrived, deputy James Shannon, who could find nothing, except for the putrid smell which was lingering around the rural home.

The next day Mrs. Cayton and a Mrs. Ackerman saw bigfoot around the house, and this time there were two of them. They called the police again. The authorities told them that they thought they had seen a mother bear with two bear cubs. Mrs. Cayton rejected that analysis.[3] In the summer of 2015 a film was released of the incident called *Minerva Monster*.

With this amazing story, what naturally sticks out is the two cougars that are pets of a bigfoot family. How would this happen? Perhaps a bigfoot killed a mother cougar while her cubs were very young. The bigfoot then raises these cubs as pets until they are fully grown. They then continue to hunt and live together.

The two cougars may have smelled the destroyed chicken coop, which would have had a strong scent of its own. When they got there, however, there were no chickens, to their surprise. The cougars lingered trying to figure out where the birds were when they were seen by the Cayton family. A bigfoot then had to step up when Scott Patterson drove up with his headlights and was flabbergasted to see two cougars and a bigfoot!

So, perhaps we need to give bigfoot more credit than he has typically gotten. He does not like camp fires or cooked food.

However, he can carry a club and have a skin across his shoulder. He can even build crude stick huts and tame such wild animal babies as cougars and wolves or dogs. Not much use in trying to tame bear cubs.

It is said that bigfoot is often imitating humans and is fascinated by children and shoes. Does bigfoot therefore try to imitate humans by having pets as well? In a scenario out of some caveman movie we have a bigfoot grabbing two cougar cubs and raising them as pets. This is amazing. Has bigfoot done this over the millennia or is this a new trend that comes with the realization of humans having pets?

Bigfoot continued to show up in Ohio and surrounding areas during the 1980s with great regularity. A typical account from the time is the one that ran in Dayton's *Ohio Daily News* on June 24, 1980 with the headline, "'Bigfoot' Sightings Scare Socks Off Pair":

> Bellefontaine, Ohio—Does Logan County have a "Big Foot" stalking its wooded hills between West Mansfield and the Union County line? Sheriff's deputies are investigating a sighting by an off-duty Russell's Point police officer who said he saw a "seven-feet-tall, hairy animal" in his barn yard Sunday night and a similar report from Union County last Tuesday. Ray Quay, a Russell's Point police officer who owns a small farm on Twp. Road 132 near West Mansfield, said he was "surprised and dumbfounded" about what he saw Sunday night.
>
> "I was unloading eight pigs I had bought about 11 p.m. I shut off the light in the barn and went around the corner to see what my two dogs were raising Cain about. They never bark when I'm around. I stepped around the corner of the barn and saw this hairy animal. I thought it was a man so I hollered at him. It took off and I've got some weeds out back I haven't mowed and they are waist high or higher and the creature went through them with no problem," Quay said.
>
> Four deputies searched the area but found nothing. Deputies said that last Tuesday Patrick Poling, who lives on County Rd. 142 in Union County east of West Mansfield, was cultivating a field when he said he spotted a creature

walking out of some woods and stride along a road near where the farmer was working.

Poling said he walked over to try to get a better look at the creature, but it ran back into the woods. Poling's description was similar to that of the creature Quay said he saw. Poling said the creature walked up-right all the time. The Lima [bigfoot] research team, a non-profit organization, took measurements and a cast of three claw marks found on the Union County farm. The claw prints are about 40 inches apart. The claw mark has four toes and measures 16 inches by 4 inches, deputies said.

Bigfoot even showed up on the Jack Nicklaus-designed golf course near Dublin, Ohio several times in 1973. Nicklaus designed the Muirfield Village Golf Club in 1966, and it was apparently named after him for some years. In October of 1973 two security guards, plus other witnesses, said they saw an eight-foot "hairy monster" near the course. Later they saw the creature actually on the golf course. The spokesman for the Franklin County Sheriff's Department said that the monster was spotted three times by the guards around the facility. A footprint about 12 inches long and seven inches wide was discovered alongside a creek, and the supervisor of the security firm for the course doubled the number of guards on duty.[38]

We can see that the giant sasquatch of Canada can be all over the place and they can even have pets. While it seems that the bigfoot in the East are a bit smaller than those in the Pacific Northwest they are still huge. It would seem that an adult bigfoot can easily reach 10 or 12 feet tall, no matter where they live.

Chapter 6

THE BIGFOOT PHOTOS

Scientists believe he's a missing link,
Some people think that he's extinct,
Others say something from the battle green,
But, listen to bigfoot's mournful scream.
—Don Jones, *Bigfoot* (1971)

There have been a number of photos taken of bigfoot and sasquatch over the years. While some photos may have been faked, others appear to be authentic. Let us look at some of the famous bigfoot photos that have surfaced. Our first case is an astonishing one that was kept under wraps for a hundred years.

The 1894 Sasquatch Photo from Canada

There is an astonishing photo from Canada taken in 1894 which would seem to be the oldest known photograph of bigfoot. Craig Woolheater posted the photo on his blog at Cryptomundo.com on November 16, 2006. The photo had originally been sent to Tom Biscardi by Lyle Billett of Victoria, Canada.

Fellow Cryptomundo blogger Loren Coleman found the photo on Woolheater's website and posted it again, where I saw it. The photo also appears in the updated version of the 1982 book *Bigfoot Casebook* by Colin and Janet Bord.[4]

It is said that a picture tells a thousand words, and this photo says a lot. It does not seem to be a fake. The photo is cracked from a fold in the upper quarter. A sasquatch is lying on snow with its arms in front so the hairy hands can be seen. The face is hairy but not very detailed. Snowshoes can be seen at the left edge of the photo. There seems to be a fence and a building on the right side, just beneath the crack. The feet of the dead sasquatch are not seen, cropped out of the right side of the photo.

The story that this photo tells us is that in 1894 in the wilds of western Canada some trappers and mountain men encountered a bigfoot and shot him. It may have happened near their cabin. They took a photograph of it. But there is more: the photo had some writing on the back of it, maybe in the hand of Lyle Billett.

The back of the photo bore this text:

The 1894 photo of a dead bigfoot taken in Canada.

Year 1894
Yalikom River Around Lilliott B.C.
Forestry-Hudsonbay Co.
They took the picture and the Guy that was in the picture went
& stole them back from the forestry records (hudsonbay co.) I
believe his last name was Holiday (Don't know the first name)
Never took all pictures (only one) and took pictures of the rest.
(Glass Plate Photography)

This is very interesting information and confirms what some
have suspected for many years: there is something of a cover-
up going on concerning evidence of bigfoot. We now get a more
complete story: There was more than one photo and someone
named Holiday apparently took the photos, or was pictured in one
or more of them. He went to the forestry records of Hudson's Bay
Company where he "stole back" one of the photos—the number of
photos taken of the bigfoot is not known. We might guess that there
were four or five original, glass plate photos.

So, some trappers shot and killed a bigfoot in 1894, and they
worked for Hudson's Bay Company, Canada's earliest trading
company, founded in 1670. Hudson's Bay Company is no ordinary
company; it was the de facto government in large parts of North
America before European states or the United States were able to

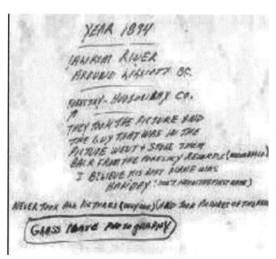

Writing on the back of the photo of the 1894 dead bigfoot in Canada.

175

lay claim to areas in this vast domain. Today it is one of the oldest operating companies in the world. Begun as a fur trading company on the Hudson Bay, it now has its headquarters in the Simpson Tower in Toronto. At one point Hudson's Bay Company had its own country of a sort, called Rupert's Land.

HUDSON'S BAY CO.

At that time, Hudson's Bay Company was one of the largest landowners of the world, with approximately 15% of the landmass of North America. Rupert's Land consisted of lands that were in the Hudson Bay drainage system—basically the land surrounding any rivers that drained into Hudson Bay. It was named after the first governor of the company, Prince Rupert of the Rhine, who was a nephew of Britain's King Charles I. The governor and the Company of Adventurers of England Trading comprised the original group that chartered Hudson's Bay Company.

Rupert's Land and Hudson's Bay Company had their headquarters at the York Factory, a town and fort along the Hayes River leading into Hudson Bay. Once the capital of Rupert's Land, it was closed down by the company in 1957.

The Hudson's Bay Company nominally owned Rupert's Land for 200 years, until about 1870, some 24 years before this photo was allegedly taken—and suppressed. Still, Hudson's Bay Company was very powerful in 1894 and remains a major fixture in the Canadian economy today as the owner of many of Canada's retail chains such as The Bay, Zellers, Fields and Home Outfitters. The company has archives, located in Winnipeg, Manitoba, said to be a collection of the company's records and maps—does it include some bigfoot photos? That is what the writing scribbled on this bigfoot photo suggests.

One has to wonder, if this photo is genuine, why it was not published many years ago, and featured in every bigfoot book written since 1894? Here we have what seems to be some pretty solid evidence of bigfoot-sasquatch that is just what the scientific

Above: The petroglyph panel of the Yakut Tribe in Tule, California that shows the Mayat Datat Wild Man. *Below*: A close-up of the 1894 photo taken at Lillooet, British Columbia. *Below Left*: A curious photo of a bigfoot hunter from the Internet, probably a hoax. *Bottom Right*: A stamp featuring a sasquatch issued by the Canadian government.

Above and Below: Frames from the film
shot by Roger Patterson with Bob Gimlin on
October 20, 1967 in northern California.

Left and Below: Frames from the film shot by Roger Patterson with Bob Gimlin on October 20, 1967.

Top: One of the photos allegedly taken of
bigfoot in November of 1995 by a forest
patrol officer from Tacoma, WA. The
officer preferred to remain anonymous
and presented the photos to Cliff Crook of
Bigfoot Central in Bothell, WA. *Below*: An
automatic camera took the so-called Brents-
Cam photo, circa 2001.

Top: The curious photo allegedly taken of sasquatch in April 2005 by a hidden camera at Moyie Springs in Idaho, near the Canadian border. The circled spot is a piece of bark spit in the air as the creature was apparently eating bark off a tree. *Right and Below*: The interesting photos taken by Randee Chase, a backpacker from Vancouver, WA, on Silver Star Mountain in Gifford Pinchot National Forest, WA, near Mt. St. Helens, on Nov. 17, 2005. At first Chase thought it was a rock, but then it stood up and walked away. © Randee Chase.

The "Tent Flap" photo of bigfoot from 2013.

Top and Left: Two photos of a bigfoot taken near the Hoffstadt Bluffs close to Mount St. Helens on May 9, 2002 and sent to the Bigfoot Research Organization (BFRO).

Right: One of the photos taken in 2000 of a skunk ape lurking in a woman's back yard along the Myakka River in Sarasota County, Florida.

One of the Bigfoot Crossing signs around Bailey, Colorado.

Above: Two photos of a bigfoot by a river in Virginia taken in July of 2014.

Above: The photo of bigfoot crossing a river in Michigan 2021.

Above: The drone photo of bigfoot in Idaho in 2016.

Above: A photo of bigfoot from a Canadian trail cam in 2012.

Above: The astonishing photo of a bigfoot in Idaho taken on September 3, 2021.

Above: A screengrab of the video of bigfoot taken in Washington May 17, 2021.

community says they are looking for. In fact, these folks from Hudson's Bay Company not only have some photos of a dead bigfoot, at one time (say the photos) they actually had a dead bigfoot! We are talking here about bigfoot steaks, bigfoot fur, a bigfoot head, bigfoot paws and all that.

Since Hudson's Bay Company specialized in dead animals and their fur, one would think that this animal—whatever it was— was carefully skinned and preserved. Was its head mounted and displayed in the den of some chairman of the company? That seems far-fetched today, but perhaps back in 1894 it might have been seen, perhaps surrounded by some secrecy, in some Canadian or British aristocrat's personal collection.

Because of my interest in bigfoot and other hidden animals, I've often been asked the question, "Why isn't there more evidence for bigfoot than just stories? Where are the photos and where are the dead bodies that must have been found over the years?"

I have typically said in answer to these questions, that one does not see a dead bear or mountain lion on the trail when walking through the Rocky Mountains or the Pacific Northwest. Though these animals are known to exist, one rarely sees them at all and never a dead one just lying there in the forest. The carcass would only be there for a few hours, days or weeks, and many animals that are about to die (of old age or disease) go off somewhere very far out of the way.

But now we have another explanation. One that is startling to the researcher and the skeptic alike—that evidence of bigfoot, including good photos and preserved bodies, has been gathered but kept a secret. "But why?" you ask. Why wouldn't Hudson's Bay Company just publish its photos and display a mummified bigfoot to gawking tourists in Toronto? Why would the Canadian government (or American or British) suppress evidence of bigfoot? Don't we live in a transparent society where everything that exists—and there are clear photos and bodies of—would be shown to interested viewers around the world? Or do we live in world where some things are suppressed, including evidence of bigfoot?

Add to the suppression of real bigfoot evidence some hoax bigfoot cases that everyone can laugh at, and you have a subject that appears to be just fantasy and tall tales. Some things are just too shocking to the status quo—strange mutations or missing links that make us question traditional religious beliefs or the tenets of mankind's sacred pillars of science and reason. If all the experts and scholars have been so wrong for decades, what are we supposed to believe from them?

In the case of this photo, part of a series apparently, a professional photographer must have been involved. Photography, until recently, was expensive and rare; it required professional photographers with expensive, heavy equipment. Having a photograph taken in 1894 was a big deal, glass plate photography being very time consuming for each individual photo. Taking such photos in the wilderness would have been quite an endeavor. Photography for the common man took many decades to reach even the Kodak Brownie and Instamatic periods of the 1940s and 1960s. Then, finally, common folk could have a simple camera with them to take photos when they were on long camping trips and hikes in remote mountain areas.

This is one of the great hopes of the current digital photo revolution, especially because cameras (even video cameras), are now part of most mobile phones that are in the possession of more and more people every day. In theory, the sheer number of cell phone cameras in use today should result in more bigfoot, ghost and anomalous photos being snapped than ever before.

Also, what of this location in British Columbia? I found that if I searched the Internet for the Yalikom River, as written on the back of the photo, what I found was the Yalakom River which is a tributary to the Bridge River which is a principal tributary to the Fraser River, a major part of Rupert's Land territory. Plus, I was able to find out that the Yalakom River enters the Bridge River near the town of Lilooet, which is apparently the town mentioned as Lilliott.

Lilooet is apparently one of the oldest towns in North America. It is so old that its age is not known. It is considered to be one of the oldest continuously inhabited locations in North America, reckoned by archaeologists to have been inhabited for several thousand years. The town attracted large seasonal and permanent populations of native peoples because of the confluence of several main streams with the Fraser, and also because of a rock shelf just above the confluence of the Bridge River that is an obstacle to the annual migration of salmon—an abundant food source.

Did this salmon-shelf cause the downfall of our unfortunate sasquatch, shot by a trapper in the employ of Hudson's Bay Company? According to the information on Lilooet this natural shelf along the riverbed is an important salmon station on the Fraser-Bridge-Yalakom River:

> This rock shelf, known in gold rush times as the Lower Fountain, was reputedly made by the trickster Coyote, leaping back and forth across the river to create platforms for people to catch and dry fish on. This location, named Sat' or Setl in the native language and known as the Bridge River Rapids or Six Mile in English, is the busiest fishing site on the Fraser above its mouth and there are numerous drying racks scattered around the banks of the river canyon around it.

We now have the final scene of the tragic bigfoot in our photograph: he had come to Lilooet (Lilliott as spelled on the backside of the photo) to get some salmon which was known to be plentiful at this spot. While Native Americans who had lived in the area for thousands of years knew not to bother the sasquatch that came to this area of plenty, this poor beast was shot and killed by the Europeans now penetrating the area for Hudson's Bay Company. What they found shocked them. They shot and killed it. Then they

Close-up of the 1894 dead bigfoot in Canada.

took a photograph of it. Then someone in the company ordered the photo suppressed.

At some point Mr. Holiday decided to get a copy of the photo that he was part of and knew existed. He probably didn't need to physically break into the building to steal the bigfoot photo(s). He was apparently an employee who walked into the building as he typically did, and then went to the files and stole one of the photos and took photographs of the rest. Having a camera to carry and take photos of documents, like photographs in a file, would be unusual at this time, but certainly could have been done.

For anyone involved in such a photo, this incident would have been something that they thought about a lot; the inability to be able to show a friend the "actual" photograph would have been a tremendous rub. Hence the desire to steal a copy of a photograph that one knows exists, but is kept secret by certain powers for their own purposes.

Yes, it seems that a cryptozoology conspiracy exists. Evidence, including photos and bodies, is kept from the press and public at large. It would seem that government and corporate identities are actively covering up evidence of bigfoot. While the governments of Canada and the United States could be trying to protect bigfoot by suppressing evidence of their existence, some countries use the apeman to promote tourism. Countries like Nepal and Bhutan promote "yeti tourism," but still protect the species with national laws.

It seems incredible, but the reality of the sasquatch—the apemen that live on the fringes of civilization—seems hard to deny when faced with what seems to be an overwhelming amount of evidence. Could all of the stories that have come down to us for nearly 200 years in North America be cases of misidentification of bears, or the occasional escaped circus gorilla? Or hoaxes? That, to me, would be very difficult to swallow.

Circa 1945 Photo of a Bigfoot in the Northwest

Collector of anomalous old photos and news clippings Joe Fex/ Joe Roberts obtained an old photo taken be an unknown person in the Pacific Northwest sometime in the 1940s. Little is known of the photo although it appears to be authentic. The black and

180

white photo shows a hairy bigfoot from the waist up and includes the head and shoulders and the arms. The hands cannot be seen. The creature appears not to have much of a neck but no real facial features can be seen. There are apparently some pine trees behind the bigfoot.

The circa 1945 photo of a bigfoot.

This photo was thought to be the oldest photo of a bigfoot until the 1894 Canada photo surfaced.

When looking at the photo it is surprising how close the subject is. This is a close-up photo of what appears to be a bigfoot standing up. Only the head and upper body can be seen and the matted hair obscures many of the features. Why has the photographer gotten so close to the subject? Were they friends? Is it possible the bigfoot is dead?

This bigfoot being photographed by someone in the Pacific Northwest or Colorado seems to be alive and posing for a portrait. I suspect that this photo was made by someone who had become friendly with a bigfoot, probably by giving them food, and was then able to take this puzzling photograph.

So, with this photo we see how some people, adults, can have some sort of interactive relationship with a bigfoot in which they are largely kept from harm. This is not the case with small children it seems, who are definitely fodder for the Boogeyman.

The 1965 Zach Hamilton Photo in the *San Francisco Chronicle*

The first modern photo of a bigfoot was published in 1965 in the *San Francisco Chronicle.* It was published in an article called "The Mountain Giants."

According to Elwood Baumann[5] the photo was part of a roll of film that a grizzled old mountain man named Zach Hamilton brought to Dick Russell, the assistant manager of Brooks Cameras in San Francisco. The year was about 1962 and Zach Hamilton told

Russell that he had just come in from the Three Sisters wilderness area in Oregon where he had been stalked by a hairy monster. He wasn't sure, but he thought that he might have gotten some photographs of the creature with his cheap little camera.

Zach Hamilton never returned for the developed roll of film and it sat for three years at the Brooks Cameras shop. One day Dick Russell looked at the photos and noticed that several had images of bigfoot on them. He put them back in their file, waiting for Mr. Hamilton to come and get his photos when he saw one of a series of articles in the *San Francisco Chronicle* about bigfoot and "the Mountain Giants."

He then gave the photos to staff at the *San Francisco Chronicle* who were very excited about them. Several of the photos showed a huge, hulking, apelike or manlike creature. It had long arms and rather short legs and was entirely covered with dark hair. The head

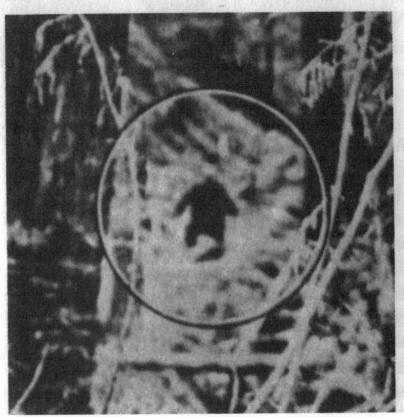

The Zach Hamilton photo from the Three Sisters Wilderness, Oregon.

San Francisco Chronicle

THE VOICE OF THE WEST

FINAL HOME EDITION ★   MONDAY, DECEMBER 6, 1965   10 C

The Mountain Giants

A comparison of a man and the "man-animal," compiled from reports based
on the numerous eyewitness sightings of the strange mountain creatures.

The *San Francisco Chronicle* featured an article on bigfoot in 1965.

seemed to be set squarely upon a pair of massive shoulders. In spite of the poor quality of the photo it can easily be seen that the creature was enormous. One of the photos was eventually published in an issue of the paper, essentially the last in a series of articles about "the Mountain Giants."

We don't know what happened to the grizzled old Zach Hamilton. He may have never intended to return for the developed roll of film. Perhaps he knew his days were numbered and he would just head back to the Oregon mountains on one last trip. The Three Sisters Wilderness was designated an official wilderness area in 1965 along with a number of other wilderness areas in the central Cascades of Oregon. This area is as remote today as it was in 1962 and the closest town to this area is Santiam Junction, a remote unincorporated community.

183

The photo appears to be genuine and it seems to show a bigfoot running away from the camera. The Zach Hamilton photo will be remembered as the earliest published bigfoot photo, published approximately eight years after the term "bigfoot" was coined.

1967: Roger Patterson and the Bluff Creek Film

One of the most famous, if not the most famous, bigfoot incidents is the October 1967 filming of a female bigfoot at Bluff Creek, California by Roger Patterson and Bob Gimlin. As I said earlier, as a youngster I had met Roger Patterson in 1967. It was later that year that Patterson was to film the most controversial of all sasquatch photos and movie footage.

Patterson was a former rodeo rider who took an interest in bigfoot after reading Ivan T. Sanderson's book *Abominable Snowmen: Legend Come to Life*.[9] Patterson was born in Wall, South Dakota (famous for Wall Drug and its billboards across the country) on February 14, 1926 and died on January 15, 1972. Starting around 1958, Patterson and his friend, Bob Gimlin, began going into Washington State to gather follow-up reports on sasquatch sightings and explore remote areas of wilderness where the apemen were reported to live.

During late August and early September of 1967, Patterson and Gimlin were exploring the Mt. St. Helens area. While they were away, friends in Willow Creek, California, phoned Patterson's home to report footprints found in the Bluff Creek area. The tracks, which were said to be of three different sizes, had been found on new logging roads being built in the Bluff Creek region. This same area was the scene of considerable bigfoot activity nine years earlier. It was here in 1958 that Jerry Crew found large human-like footprints. As mentioned above, newspaper stories of this event coined the term "bigfoot."

When he returned home to Yakima, Washington and got the news, Patterson contacted Gimlin and the two men made plans to investigate Bluff Creek, a wilderness area just north of the Hoopa Indian Reservation in the northwest corner of California. Patterson and Gimlin wished to find and film fresh footprints as evidence of the creature's existence in and around Willow Creek, a frontier town that sits near the Oregon border, right in the center of the

A blow-up of one of the frames of the 1967 Patterson film.

Klamath and Six Rivers National Forests. Patterson wanted to make a documentary, and rented a Kodak 16mm handheld movie camera and purchased two 100-foot rolls of color movie film for the expedition. Patterson and Gimlin traveled to the Bluff Creek area in a truck, taking with them three horses.

Patterson and Gimlin set up camp near Bluff Creek and set out on horseback to explore the area. Patterson used 76 feet of the first film roll gathering footage of the scenery to be used as a backdrop, plus took shots of both himself and Gimlin.

Not much happened for the first seven days, Patterson claimed, but in the early afternoon of October 20, 1967 Patterson and Gimlin spotted a female sasquatch down on the creek's gravel sandbar. Patterson's horse reared in alarm at the sight of the creature, bringing both horse and rider to the ground, with Patterson pinned beneath the animal.

Since Patterson was an experienced horseman, he quickly disengaged himself and grabbed his camera. While running toward the creature, he took 24 feet of color film footage. During this time, the female bigfoot quickly but calmly walked away across the sandbar into the woods.

During all this, Gimlin watched the bigfoot, his rifle in hand, in case his friend was attacked by the creature. He did not point it at the creature, however. The two had previously agreed that under no circumstances would they shoot a bigfoot unless in self-protection. The female bigfoot was estimated to be seven feet three inches in height and weigh 700 pounds; she left footprints 14½ inches long by six inches wide.

Patterson and Gimlin

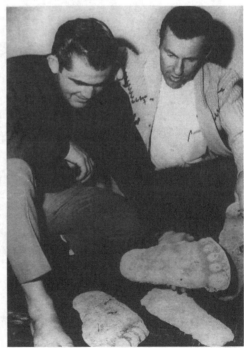

Bob Gimlin, left, with Roger Patterson c.1967.

decided not to pursue the bigfoot into the woods for fear of a possible confrontation with the creature and perhaps others of its kind.

The film gained instant fame. The very clear, daylight footage has been subjected to many attempts both to debunk and authenticate it. Some qualified scientists have judged the film a hoax featuring a man in a gorilla suit, while other scientists contend the film depicts an animal unknown to science, claiming it would be virtually impossible for a human to replicate the subject's gait and muscle movement. Indeed, if it is a hoax, it is a very good one.

In his book *The Making of Bigfoot*,[25] Greg Long claims that it is a man in a gorilla suit named Bob Hieronymus who lived near Patterson in Yakima, Washington. However, Long has difficulty in explaining why Patterson would want to fake a female bigfoot and suggests that black bags were sewn onto the gorilla suit to make the breasts.

Both men continually dismissed allegations that they had hoaxed the footage by filming a man wearing a fake sasquatch suit. Patterson swore on his deathbed that the footage was authentic and he had encountered and filmed a large bipedal animal unknown to science. Gimlin avoided appearing in public and discussing the subject until about the year 2000, when he began to make appearances at bigfoot conferences and give some interviews. I met Gimlin in 2014 at a conference in Los Angeles. He was hanging out at a booth that sold posters and had a poster of the famous Bluff Creek bigfoot. He was friendly and sincere and dismissed any notion that it was a hoax.

The documentary featuring the Bluff Creek footage of the female sasquatch was eventually released as a film entitled *Sasquatch, the Legend of Bigfoot*. Though there was little scientific interest in the film or the Bluff Creek footage, Patterson was still able to capitalize on it. Beyond the documentary, the film generated a fair amount of publicity. Patterson appeared on several popular television shows such as the Merv Griffin and Joey Bishop talk shows.

Today, still photos from the film are the most familiar of all sasquatch pictures. Entire books, skeptical and otherwise, have been written around this event. Hopefully, more film footage of bigfoot will emerge. In fact there are now a number of good photos of sasquatch as can be seen in the color section of this book. Everyone has a camera and video now on their smart phone, so we should be getting more photos. Although, unfortunately, some of it will probably be deliberate hoaxing, part of the fun will be sifting through the video footage as it comes to us—fast and furious.

1968: Flying over Bigfoot

On January 6, 1968, two men were piloting a light plane over Yosemite Park. The pilot was Robert James and his passenger was Leroy Larwick. As they flew over a remote area known as Confidence Ridge they both saw a brown fuzzy creature below the aircraft. The creature seemed to be 10 or 12 feet tall as it walked on the ridge on two legs.

James and Larwick wondered if it was bigfoot as it did not look like a bear. They took another pass at the creature and Larwick took a photograph of a huge bigfoot. They landed and returned to the spot where they had made the sighting, where they said they found 20-inch-long footprints.[3] They took photographs of the prints but their photo taken from the airplane has never been released. We might think that it was just a bad, fuzzy photo that didn't show anything, or perhaps it is one of the great, lost bigfoot photos of all time!

The 1976 Wycliff, BC Photo of Sasaquatch

Another unpublished photo was taken on the evening of September 3, 1976. On that date Barbara Pretula claimed that she saw a bigfoot behind her store in Wycliff, British Columbia (a small ski town near Kimberley in southern British Columbia, near the U.S. border). She said it was black with a light-haired stomach and was 6 or 7 feet tall. She managed to take a Polaroid photo of the creature but the flash of the camera frightened it and it ran into the bush. Said Pretula: "I was about 15 feet from it when I took the picture. It didn't see me come up, I snuck around beside the building. It was just looking down on its hind legs." The fuzzy photo purportedly shows the size and shape of the sasquatch. Apparently the photo has never been published.[7]

Earlier that day in Wycliff a fireman named Mickey McLelland reported that he and a friend plus several other witnesses saw a sasquatch in a field north of Kimberley, British Columbia. McLelland described the bigfoot as 7 feet tall with black hair and a tan-colored chest and long arms. McLelland and his friend got out of their car and chased the bigfoot who ran down the road at a quick pace. The two returned to their car and began to chase the bigfoot down the road, clocking it at 50 miles per hour when the bigfoot suddenly veered into the forest. There were two other cars that were parked in the area with 6 to 8 witnesses who all saw the whole event which took nearly four minutes. This may have been the same sasquatch that was apparently lurking behind Barbara Pretula's store in Wycliff about half an hour later.[7]

1975: The Legend of Bigfoot Film Hoax

In 1975 the famous hunter and trapper Ivan Marx produced and starred in an oddball documentary called: *The Legend of Bigfoot. The Legend of Bigfoot* is a unique film by all standards. It is the true story of Ivan Marx, a professional tracker, who becomes obsessed by bigfoot and sets out to film, capture and/or kill a bigfoot.

The film starts with a shot of Marx in his signature red flannel shirt, introducing himself and his topic. Apparently shot in a combination of 16 mm and 35 mm film, the documentary is like an extended episode of the 1960s television show *Wild Kingdom,* or some Lion's Club presentation on big game hunting—except the quarry this time is the elusive bigfoot. But, for Ivan Marx, bigfoot is not so elusive. With his amazing tracking ability, Marx is able to find bigfoot just about everywhere he goes!

In fact, as the movie goes on, it is astonishing how Marx is able to find—and film—bigfoot from the Arctic Circle to the American Southwest. The bizarre mix of seemingly real bigfoot footage with Marx's authentic backwoodsman style (and the gnawing sense that it just isn't quite real) makes the film a genuine curiosity that is quite amusing. If the various shots of bigfoot in this movie were genuine, then Marx would be the most prolific photographer of bigfoot ever

Ivan Marx from his movie.

to live—or conversely, the biggest hoaxer of bigfoot who ever lived. Indeed, the latter is more probable. But is everything hoaxed in the film? Definitely not. Was Marx a believer in bigfoot? Well, it would seem that he did believe in bigfoot, but hoaxed film footage of the beast anyway. Either way, the saga of Ivan Marx is a fascinating story.

Ivan Marx's California bigfoot.

Marx tells us at the beginning of the film that he is a professional tracker who, working occasionally for the government, "removed" rogue animals from areas where they were presumably killing livestock and such. Marx first heard of bigfoot in Kodiak, Alaska where ranchers claimed it was killing their cows. Interested by the stories he heard, Marx began a quest to track down the mysterious beast and bring back proof of its existence.

Marx first travels to the Petrified Forest of Arizona where 700-year-old petroglyphs reveal mysterious man-like creatures with mighty big hands. Marx then finds footprints 18 inches long in 52-inch strides that could only have been made by a critter in excess of 500 pounds. The hair samples he finds nearby were tested and "couldn't be matched with any known animal."

He heads up to the Yukon in his VW bug where lumberjacks show him some rock cairns that could only have been made by bigfoot because they are in an inaccessible area. After this there is a segment about the gold rush and Marx muses how the influx of gold miners must have had quite an impact on the local bigfoot population, and concludes that bigfoot must hide himself to survive.

Farther north, Marx expounds upon a theory that a local has told him: that the reason no one has found any bigfoot remains is because the creatures carry their dead thousands of miles north to bury them in crevasses that open up in glaciers in the summer. He is told by the local Eskimos that bigfoot breeds in the mating grounds of the Alaskan moose. We are treated here to scenes of Glacier Bay and a glacier falling into the ocean, followed by Marx's obligatory moose mating shots and an extended interlude of the Northern Lights.

Ivan Marx's bigfoot showering.

It's time for some more (faked?) bigfoot shots, though. Marx sets up some walkie-talkies on the tundra and waits. Then things get kind of kooky. We're shown footage of something in the early light of dawn that Marx says is the glowing eyes of a bigfoot. It's odd footage, that's for sure, though it seems like a puppet with flashlights for eyes more than anything else. Marx later confesses that it must have been swamp gas. One begins to guess that Ivan Marx is a heavy drinker, among other things.

Winter is coming up in the Arctic, so Marx knows he has to find bigfoot fast. He charters a plane and finds a young Bigfoot standing on a sandbar in a river and gets crystal clear, daylight shots of the dark biped. After footage of some hunters shooting caribou, Marx beds down in Beaver Swamp where he finds more of the giant hairy critters. This time there are two of them splashing around in the water and getting some of that famous stink off of themselves.

With that, the film winds up as best it can, and Marx seems satisfied at last with the evidence for bigfoot that he has presented. Thank God he never shot one of the beasts, though the film has plenty of animal gore and death in it. What is particularly captivating about the movie is that Marx seems so genuine in his demeanor and in his earnestness to capture bigfoot, yet the hoax is so blatantly apparent. It's like Marlin Perkins in the aforementioned *Wild Kingdom* drinking a bottle of Yukon Jack and filming a sasquatch around practically every corner of the woods he stumbles upon.

1995: Bigfoot Central and the Cliff Crook Photograph

191

The Bigfoot Photos

Not much happened during the 1980s as far as bigfoot photos go. However some photographs of a sasquatch were released in December of 1995. According to an article in *Fortean Times* (No. 93, Dec. 1996), a forest patrol officer from Tacoma, Washington, who wishes to remain anonymous for fear of losing his job, had an encounter with a giant apelike creature and was able to take a series of 35 mm photos. The ranger then called Cliff Crook at the sasquatch-monitoring group named Bigfoot Central.

Bigfoot Central is located in Cliff Crook's living room in Bothell, Washington. Crook held a news conference on December 9, 1995 to satisfy the mounting interest over the photos. Crook told the conference that the ranger had taken 14 photographs of the sasquatch but eight of them were dark because fleeting clouds blocked the sun on his 50 mm telephoto lens. The ranger said that he heard a splashing noise to his left while hiking along a ridge in Washington state's Snoqualmie National Forest. He went to

One of the photos allegedly taken in 1995 and given to Cliff Crook.

investigate the noise. Then, from a high bank, he observed the eight-foot creature just 30 yards away in a swampy lagoon. He used up what remained of his roll of film.

The photos are sensational, clearly depicting a hairy bigfoot creature with its head low on a pair of massive shoulders. One photography analyst declared that he had found tiny diamond shapes in the image indicating that it was a digitally created image. Cliff Crook countered that the analyst was examining a laser print and not an original.

Skeptics believe that the photo was digitally created, probably in Photoshop, while some think that it is genuine. Genuine bigfoot photos would be welcomed by all cryptozoologists, but fakes occur from time to time. The Cliff Crook photo continues to fascinate researchers over 20 years later, and as time has passed the opinion is that the Cliff Crook photos may well be genuine.

2005 Photos of Bigfoot on Trail Camera and Mountain Crest

In 2005 an astonishing photograph of a bigfoot was taken by a trail camera in northern Idaho. Little is known about the photo except that it was sold to *The National Enquirer*. The color photograph shows the head and upper body of a bigfoot in the snow. He is near a fallen log with snow on it and his dark, hairy body has blobs of snow on it as well. Most notable about the photo is the grimace

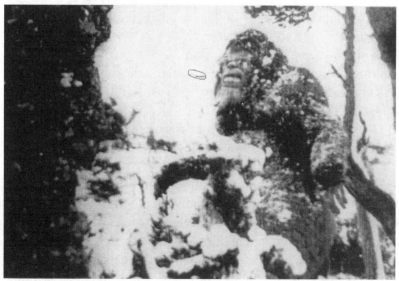

The 2005 trail-cam photo from northern Idaho. See the color section.

One of the 2005 series of photos of a bigfoot on Silver Star Mountain.

that the animal is making, as if in pain, and his teeth can be seen. It is also thought to be spitting out a bit of tree bark it was chewing. The photo seems to be a genuine photo of bigfoot and no one has claimed to have hoaxed it.

A close-up of the bigfoot.

On November 17, 2005, a backpacker from Vancouver, Washington took a series of four photos on Silver Star Mountain in Gifford Pinchot National Forest. He says he doesn't know what the figure was, but he does not believe it was another hiker or backpacker. The photos are inconclusive, but they are potentially relevant. The figure you see could be a bigfoot. See the color section to view these photos.

Video Footage of Bigfoot Chasing a Car Emerges in Russia

The video, which was reportedly recorded in 2016 but shown in 2019 on Russian television, shows a car in Bashkortostan being pursued by an unknown creature that appears to be a bigfoot, yeti, or giant ape. It was reportedly filmed by three girls and a man who can be heard talking and shouting during the footage, seemingly

Two screen-grab photos from the Russian video of a bigfoot chasing a car..

quite terrified by what was pursuing them. The video is somewhat difficult to make out due to the shakiness and poor resolution but shows what appears to be a humanoid creature attempting to catch up to a vehicle that is struggling to escape from the scene. Ultimately it's difficult to know what to make of the footage— certainly the video has been gaining a lot of attention in Russia and people seem to be taking it quite seriously.

Sasquatch Filmed in Utah?

An intriguing piece of footage out of Utah was uploaded to the Coast to Coast website and it appears to show a sizeable creature, probably a bigfoot, lurking on the side of a mountain near Provo. The strange scene was recorded by a man named Austin M. Craig on January 2, 2019. It subsequently popped up on YouTube a few days later and has since caught the attention of bigfoot enthusiasts online.

In the video, Craig can be heard marveling at the massive size of the mystery creature that is "just chilling" on a mountain out in the distance. Although the oddity is rather indistinct and open to interpretation, there is one moment during the footage where it does appear as if the creature is walking in a bipedal fashion. Asked by someone if it could be a human, Craig expressed skepticism about that possibility and notes how it is situated at a fairly distant point on the mountain, yet still stands out considerably, suggesting that the creature is quite large.

195

A screen-shot from the Provo, Utah video taken on January 23, 2019.

Craig says he subsequently drove down a nearby road to get a better look at the potential sasquatch and captured additional footage of what he says is the creature sitting on a rock, although it's quite difficult to discern where it is in that portion of the video. Craig and his companions then went up into the mountains in an attempt to try to solve the mystery of what they had seen, and a friend back on the ground was able to watch the group from the vantage point of the first video; he noted that they looked much smaller than the creature filmed earlier in the day. (coasttocoastam. com, 23 Jan 2019)

Traffic Camera in Oregon Captures Image of Bigfoot?

Drivers near Hood River in December of 2019 called the Oregon State Police and reported a bigfoot sighting along I-84 in the middle of the night. The ODOT camera managed to capture the sighting! According to the Umatilla/Morrow County Watch, the caller described the thing as "dwarfing the guard rail" and "too big to be a bear" not to mention it was walking upright. The dispatcher immediately checked the ODOT camera and saw an image...and it certainly looks like something is there. What do you think? Bigfoot sure looks to be walking there. (Radio Station 98.3 The Key online pages, 23 Dec 2019) https://keyw.com/real-bigfoot-sighting-in-hood-river-freaks-out-driver-photo/

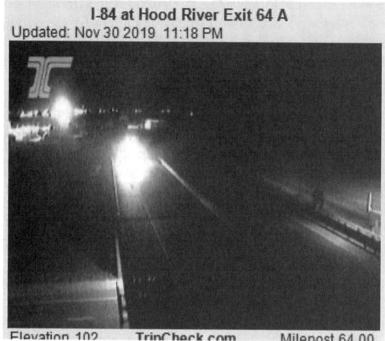

A screen-shot from the Hood River exit taken on November 30, 2019.

Astonishing Bigfoot Film from Washington State

Bigfoot is on the move in the mountains of Washington, if the highway cameras of the Washington Department of Transport

A screen-shot of the Washington ADOT video in January 2020. **197**

are to be believed. On January 23, 2020 the state's transportation agency tweeted a video from Snoqualmie Pass that was the most interesting video clip that had been released in a long time. The 31-second clip, recorded on the Interstate 90 wildlife bridge, shows a bulky humanoid figure striding across the snow.

Before disappearing over the crest, it stops and momentarily looks back toward the camera in a move very similar to the famous 1967 Patterson film. Snoqualmie Pass is a 40-mile drive east from the Seattle area. (*The Mercury News*, 27 Jan 2020)

The 31-second film clip can be seen at the website: bigfootmovies.net

Quad Rider Films What He Claims is a Bigfoot with a Club

A quad rider in Washington State filmed in October 2020 what he says is a bigfoot holding a large stick. The rider was wearing a helmet cam and captured a dark figure running with a large stick-like club across the trail.

The rider said, "While visiting my family in Washington State, my brother and I were taking turns riding my parents' quad. He came back and said he saw a bigfoot. I thought he was making it up until we played back the video. I don't know if someone was in the woods messing with us or something but whatever it is freaks me out."

The brief video may be a hoax, but if so it is a pretty good one!

A screen-shot from the May 2021 video from Washington.

A photo of a bigfoot crossing a river in Michigan in 2021.

The video can be seen at: https://tinyurl.com/yfpt7yhe. (Nexus Newsfeed, 14 May 2021)

Bigfoot Photographed Crossing River in Michigan

A video captured early in July 2021 has some convinced that a bigfoot was spotted crossing a Michigan river with a baby in its arms. The clip has garnered nearly 150,000 views on YouTube as people debate whether the brown figure was really a bigfoot, or just a hunter crossing the water. The footage was submitted to the Rocky Mountain Sasquatch Organization by a person identified as "Eddie V.," who claims his cousin was kayaking in Michigan's Cass River in the beginning of July when he spotted the creature.

"Not sure what it is, but I have sent it to a few people to see what they say," Eddie said. "Some say it's bigfoot carrying baby bigfoot. Others say it's bigfoot carrying a deer."

The Sasquatch Organization zoomed in on the grainy video and slowed it down so viewers could get a better look. Indeed, a large brown figure carrying something can be seen moving through the river at a quick pace. However, viewers in the comments section had differing opinions on what Eddie's cousin actually captured. Some suggested that the figure was "a guy in waders" crossing the water, noting that the area is a popular fishing and hunting spot. Others were convinced. "What else could it be?" one commenter

A screen-grab of a bigfoot filmed in Idaho on September 3, 2021.

wrote. (B100 Quad Cities News, b100quadcities.com, 19 July 2021)

Dramatic New Footage of Bigfoot in Idaho

Dramatic footage from September 2021 claims to show a new sighting of bigfoot. The video, filmed in Idaho and uploaded to the Nv Tv YouTube channel, suggests that the sighting "simply can't be a man in a suit" for a number of reasons. They cite the "amount of detail" on the sasquatch's body and the fact it's "massive in size" as reasons to believe the footage of the infamous creature is real.

However, viewers are not entirely convinced, suggesting in the comments on YouTube that it is another hoax. It is interesting to note the well-developed musculature, however, which doesn't seem like it could be produced by a fur suit. (Independent.co.uk, Independent TV, 4 Sept 2021)

Hiker Films Multiple Sasquatch Hiding in Desert Canyon

A peculiar video posted on YouTube in October of 2021 shows what appears to be a mysterious bipedal creature lurking in a desert canyon which some suspect is bigfoot. The curious footage was posted to the YouTube channel "Sasquatch Confessions." The video shows what initially seems to be a simple observation of a rocky desert canyon when a dark form can be seen creeping around in the distance.

When zoomed in it is revealed to be a distinctly bipedal creature that is trying to hide behind some rocks. There seems to be a second bigfoot in the rocks as well, one that is not moving much.

A screen-shot of the desert photos of 2022.

Unfortunately, there is almost no information concerning where or when the scene was filmed nor who submitted the footage. Be that as it may, the puzzling material is rather intriguing since the creature in the footage appears clearer than most suspected sasquatch caught on film. (www.youtube.com/watch?v=yCdSIiJZ0gM, 6 Oct 2021)

Bigfoot Photographed in Iowa

In mid-July, 2021, a man named Jeremy saw a figure while on a walk and fortunately managed to get a picture. This happened in Bernard, Iowa at White Water Canyon. Jeremy swears he saw the figure moving so it wasn't a shadow, and claims he called out to it as well with no response, meaning it probably wasn't a person because

The July 22, 2021 Iowa photo.

we all know anyone in the Midwest would stop to say hi.

Jeremy went on to say:

"I was doing a morning walk at White Water Canyon with my sister, who lives up in Dubuque. I pointed out the figure and my sister laughed saying it was a person. We called out to it but got no response." Jeremy also admitted that he never believed in bigfoot and didn't release his last name because he knows this sounds crazy. "You don't have to believe me. I wouldn't believe me, but

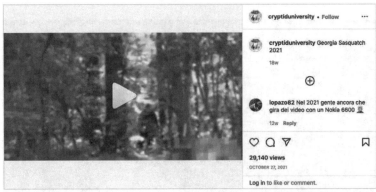

A screen-shot of the Georgia video from January 2022.

now that I've seen whatever that was firsthand... I think I may be a bigfoot believer now." (AM 950 News, koel.com, 22 July 2021)

Bigfoot or Skunk Ape Caught on Camera in Georgia

Someone recently filmed what they claim is a bigfoot in the woods of Georgia. The video, which was shared by the @ CryptidUniversity Instagram account, shows shaky footage of what appears to be a large apelike animal with black fur bending over behind some trees in the distance. When the creature fully stands, it looks taller and bigger than a human. It then walks off as the person filming hides behind a tree.

Commenters on the video are torn as to whether it is real, with some writing things like, "Best footage I've seen in a while—that thing was huge," while others said, "They do all sorts of things for attention down in Georgia." Seth Breedslove, the documentary filmmaker behind *On the Trail of Bigfoot*, told the *Daily Star*:

> The subject seems to be looking down at the ground as it turns indicating it might be a person in a suit who is having some difficulty judging the forest floor beneath them. It makes me think this is more than likely a hoax. The thing does appear to be large though, so maybe it's real? These videos always leave us with more questions than answers.

The Southeast has its own version of bigfoot called a skunk ape. Named because of its odor, the creature has been spotted in Georgia, Florida, Alabama and other southern states for hundreds

A screen-shot from the Amarillo, Texas video on May 21, 2022.

of years. (wbznewsradio.iheart.com, 7 Dec 2021)

Skinwalker Caught on Camera in Texas?

Something strange was seen lurking outside a Texas zoo in May of 2022, and while the city has several theories, its identification is still a mystery. Security cameras at the Amarillo Zoo captured the mysterious creature "in the dark and early morning hours" of Saturday, May 21, according to a June 8 news release from the city. A still photo from the recording shows the life form outside the zoo's perimeter fence at 1:25 a.m.

"Was it a person with a strange hat who likes to walk at night?" the city asked. "A large coyote on its hind legs? A Chupacabra? It is a mystery–for Amarillo to help solve."

As the visitor's identity remains unknown, the Texas Panhandle city has declared it an "Unidentified Amarillo Object"—or UAO, for short. But city officials hope someone may be able to offer a better explanation.

"We just want to let the Amarillo community have some fun with this," Director of Parks and Recreation Michael Kashuba said in the news release. "... It is definitely a strange and interesting image. Maybe Amarillo can help solve the mystery of our UAO."

The Bigfoot Photos

The city said it does not have video footage of the encounter to share, so eager UAO detectives will have to use the still image to crack the case. Is it a curious skinwalker, wolfman, or someone in a costume?

"It is important to note that this entity was outside the Amarillo Zoo," Kashuba said. "There were no signs of attempted entry into the zoo. No animals or individuals were harmed. There were no signs of criminal activity or vandalism." (*Fort Worth Star Telegram*, 8 June 2022)

That concludes our rundown of bigfoot photos. There are others that we are not mentioning and some are simply anonymous photos that are put up on the Internet with no accompanying story. One would think that there would be more photos of bigfoot now that there are so many smart phones out there. Everyone is a cameraman these days. But, can you keep your cool and take a photo when you are confronted by a bigfoot?

The Don Jones single "Bigfoot."

Chapter 7

Taking a Selfie with Bigfoot?

The open road where the hopeless come
To see if hope still runs
Nothing to do now but drop it and roll
Into the lights of the open road
—John Hiatt, *The Open Road*

In May of 1956 near Marshall, Michigan, three friends (ages unknown) were sleeping out in the woods when a "huge, hair-covered creature" with green eyes "as big as light bulbs" and smelling "like something rotten" picked up Otto Collins and Philip Williams in their sleeping bags, holding one under each arm. Their companion Herman Williams grabbed his rifle which scared the bigfoot who then dropped the men and ran into the woods.[3]

We don't know if bigfoot was trying to abduct the teenagers or just trying to scare them, but the encounter certainly terrified the boys. It would seem that one of the occupations of various bigfoot, mainly young males, is to abduct children and examine them. While this may be just a curiosity with some young bigfoot it is usually traumatizing to a young child who is kidnapped by a bigfoot. Many times they will not survive their abduction—even if the bigfoot means them no harm.

Some children are abducted in their sleeping bags—straight out of the tent, as we see in the above account. There are other tales of bigfoot unzipping a tent and such. There is the curious "Tent Flap" photo of bigfoot put on the Internet by an unknown photographer.

And then we have the strange story of the boy who may have taken a selfie with a bigfoot.

On July 19, 1991, a Boy Scout named Jared Negrete went on

his first overnight camping trip with his troop in the San Bernardino National Forest and vanished.

Jared Negrete.

Negrete was 12 years old and described in articles at the time as a shy and pudgy kid. He was with five other Scouts and their troop leader when they left Camp Tahquitz to hike up 11,500-foot Mount San Gorgonio, the highest peak in Southern California. It is south of Big Bear Lake and most of the area is wilderness, although it is near to metropolitan Los Angeles.

As the group of seven hiked up the mountain, Jared fell behind and was struggling. As he fell behind and was apparently told to stay behind, he simply vanished. When the other five scouts and their adult troop leader returned down the trail to the parking lot, they did not see Jared. They had not seen him on the trail and he was not at the parking lot and the van that had brought them.

Differing reports have him either wandering off the trail, falling behind after stopping to tie his shoe, or being told to hang back for the troop to collect him on the way back down from the summit. Whatever the case, he was never seen again. He completely disappeared.

Rescue teams began searching around the clock and eventually turned up Jared's backpack, some candy wrappers, beef jerky and a camera. Twelve photographs were developed from the camera. They were mostly landscapes, but the last one was of Jared's eyes and nose, taken after he went missing. The photo, seen here, is an extreme close-up of his eyes and nose. His eyes are open and it shows that he is alive. But where is he? How did he discard his backpack and camera and then disappear?

The camera was discovered in the same area as the other items, but after a 16-day search that included five helicopters, rangers on horseback and infrared cameras, Jared Negrete could not be found. According to a *Los Angeles Times* story on July 28, 1991:

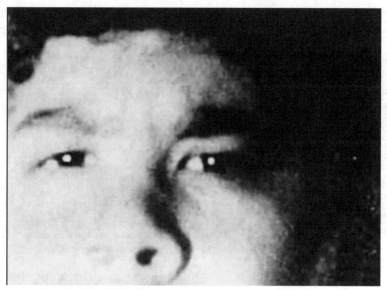

The final "selfie" taken by Jared Negrete—or by a bigfoot?

A 12-year-old Boy Scout, lost in the wilderness of the San Bernardino Mountains for the past nine days, may have taken a picture of himself after he became separated from his troop, family members said Sunday.

Twelve snapshots were developed from a camera found by searchers combing 11,500-foot Mt. San Gorgonio on Saturday for Jared Negrete, who has been missing since July 19.

Most of the photos were landscape scenes apparently taken before the boy became lost. But the final picture on the roll of film was a photograph of the Scout's eyes and nose, taken with the aid of the camera's flash attachment, possibly at night after the youth disappeared. Family members said it appeared Jared pointed his camera at his face and snapped the picture.

"Evidently, the flash went off so we determined it was rather late in the evening," said Harvey Beach, one of Jared's uncles.

Beach and another uncle, Leo Cortez, said they believed the boy lost the camera while sliding down a portion of the mountainside within days of his disappearance.

"He was on his bottom sliding down to a lower area

207

The "selfie" that Jared Negrete took as published in a newspaper.

and water," Beach said. The camera was found in the same general area where searchers discovered beef jerky and candy wrappers believed to have been dropped by the Scout.

"Jared always carried some goodies with him" and also had a two-quart water canteen, said Cortez, who has accompanied the boy on short hikes.

The film, food wrappers and earlier tracks helped rescuers narrow the search area to the south fork of Whitewater River, north of Mt. San Gorgonio, from the entire brush and boulder-covered mountain face.

And because of the discoveries, about 100 volunteers will continue the search today "full force," said San Bernardino County Sheriff's Deputy Bill Lenew.

"There are areas in the south fork where someone could survive an extended period of time," said Lenew, but as time passes "the chances of survival are a big issue."

While nearly a dozen uncles and cousins gathered near the search area, the youth's parents remained at their home in El Monte. The family has been having a "terrible time" since the 5-foot, 2-inch, 150-pound boy disappeared while on a Church of Jesus Christ of Latter-day Saints Scout outing, Beach said.

In addition to searchers on foot and on horseback,

helicopters have been used to scan the brutal terrain. Infrared monitors were installed at a number of high points Saturday night in hopes of spotting the boy in the dark. Only deer and other animals were detected by the monitors, authorities said.

But, despite the hope that the family had that the boy would still be found alive after several days, Jared Negrete was never found. What happened to Jared Negrete? Had he really taken that last photo? Had someone or something taken that photo—shortly before he disappeared? Why would Jared leave the trail? He was tired and simply had to wait for the others to return. Even if he had decided to go back to the trailhead, no great distance away, he would have stayed on the trail. It just doesn't make any sense that Jared would move off the trail by himself. He must have been taken away from the trail.

The strange selfie photo of Jared is one of the more unusual parts of an already strange tale. It does not seem that Jared wanted to take a photo of himself and this certainly wasn't the photo he wanted to take. Is it possible that Jared was standing there near the trail taking some photos when he was suddenly attacked? During this attack he took a photo of his nose and eye. The flash apparently went off but this does not mean that it was taken in the evening. Nothing can really be seen in the photo. Perhaps in the struggle the photo was actually taken by a bigfoot. This would be a first.

While his backpack, camera and other items were found, the clothing that Jared was wearing has never been

A newspaper story about Jared Negrete.

found, nor his body. Why would he discard his camera and backpack anyway? The whole story makes little sense to traditional investigators. They are looking at a story that seems to make no sense. Who could be kidnapping a 12-year-old in the middle of the forest? Could Jared have done this all on his own and disappear?

Perhaps a bigfoot had been watching the group and when Jared was now alone the creature decided to kidnap the boy. Jared may have survived this initial abduction and found himself in that terrible place—bigfoot's cave.

While bigfoot looked through Jared's stuff he was able to take his camera and take his last photo. It would seem that the bigfoot was right next to him or perhaps in front of him when Jared took his last photo. Perhaps at this point, because of the flash of the camera, the bigfoot struck Jared and killed him. This would have been a good thing for Jared because otherwise he would have been alive in the cave for more days until he starved or was killed by the bigfoot.

These animals are so strong that it is impossible to overpower them and escape from the cave you are in. These caves are in craggy, hard to reach areas with often narrow accesses. The bigfoot may try to feed you, but you will eventually die as a captive of bigfoot. The bigfoot will throw your backpack and sometimes other clothes back to where you had been abducted. The dead body of Jared may have been discarded elsewhere or may be still in the cave in which he died. The bigfoot has long moved on and this hidden location may never be found.

Something terrible happened to Jared Negrete while he sat by himself on the trail in the San Bernardino National Forest that day. In many ways he is the perfect story of the Boy Scout who was last in line on the trail and suddenly disappeared! We will probably never know what happened to this young Scout on his first camping trip. We can only be glad of the many scout outings that did not end in this way.

Chapter 8

BIGFOOT IN CALIFORNIA AND THE PACIFIC NORTHWEST

In my rearview mirror
My life is getting clearer
The sunset sighs and slowly disappears
These trinkets once were treasure
Life changes like the weather
—Bon Jovi, *Lost Highway*

As I chronicled in chapter two, the term "bigfoot" was created in California in 1958 when a road construction worker named Jerry Crew walked up to his bulldozer in the wilderness of northern California and found a circle of enormous footprints around the vehicle. This area was 17,000 square miles of mountain forest that had never been explored or settled in the past. Except for this road gang, the area was completely uninhabited and the roads they were creating were the first sign of civilization in the huge area. Crew eventually made plaster casts of some of the footprints he saw. When asked by the local newspaper who made the footprints he replied, "Bigfoot."

It was near this same area that Roger Patterson with his friend Bob Gimlin took the famous film footage of a female bigfoot walking through the forest in October of 1967. This dense forest along the Oregon-California border is kind of ground zero for bigfoot in the United States, although parts of British Columbia may have a denser population of sasquatch than even this part of northern California. At any rate, bigfoot have been frequently sighted in Washington, Idaho, Oregon and California. Sightings go back to the early pioneer days and continue to this day.

Yes, plenty of bigfoot activity is still happening in California. In January of 2021 a Garberville, California man named Rick Bates encountered a bigfoot on the highway while he was driving back from a trip to Oregon. He then went to the local news at kymkemp.com who reported his story on February 6, 2021.

Bates told them and BFRO that he saw the bigfoot between Benbow Inn and Richason Grove. Bates wrote on the BFRO website:

> I was driving home from Brookings Oregon on January 23, 2021. I was south bound on highway 101 south of Garberville, California, and south of the Benbow Inn. The road makes a few turns and the speed limit drops in the area. As I rounded a sweeping right hand turn I saw a figure on the southbound shoulder of the highway. I was the only vehicle in the area about 8:15 PM. My speed was about 45-50 MPH as I passed the figure. The figure was laying on the shoulder of the road on its right side. I estimated the height to be about 7 feet. I was looking at the creature's back and noticed it had broad shoulders and a thick torso shape. While the shape was similar to a human it was not human. It was not a bear either. I could see muscular features in its glutes and a head on the shoulders that was somewhat tapered toward the top and being held off the ground. Its hair was a chocolate brown and very course. The hair was not fur like of a bear at all.
>
> I turned around a distance past the spot and returned to where I had seen it. No other vehicles had gone north or south from the time I saw the creature to the time I returned to its location (2 minutes estimate). When I got to the spot where I had seen it, the creature it was gone. As an avid hunter and fisherman I spend a lot of time in the woods. I spent every summer camping in that area as well as a kid. I have never seen anything like what I saw just this evening.

Then, in July of 2020 a hiker from San Ramon, California

Saeed Emadi and his daughter.

named Saeed Emadi vanished while hiking at the El Dorado County Reservoir. San Ramon is south of Walnut Creek in the eastern San Francisco Bay Area. El Dorado County is a large county that is east of Sacramento, the capital of California. It contains a great deal of wilderness and two reservoirs named Union Valley Reservoir and Ice House Reservoir which are near each other. Emadi was hiking near the Ice House Reservoir with friends. The Tahoe National Forest is to the north.

According to numerous newspaper accounts such as the *Sacramento Bee* (sacbee.com), on July 8, 2020 Saeed Emadi, 66, went hiking with friends. He got separated from the group of longtime friends and became lost after splitting up from his party.

According to the El Dorado County Sheriff's Office, Emadi became separated from his hiking partners while crossing the southern fork of Silver Creek. He called his friends with his cell phone at about 3:30 pm, after becoming separated, according to the sheriff's office. He told them he was on a hill near a road and that the lake was below him. The friends responded by calling the authorities. That's the last anyone heard from him as there were no further cell phone calls and he did not respond to any calls made to him.

On the day Emadi went missing he was wearing a hat, headphones, a button-down shirt, shorts, and a pair of tennis shoes. He was 6 feet, 2 inches tall, and about 190 pounds. He was a diabetic and it was likely he did not have his medication with him. Although in good physical shape with day hike experience and a "never quit" attitude, he was not familiar with the heavily wooded terrain and had no climbing experience.

A group of about seventy law enforcement officers and volunteers searched the area without any luck, according to Sgt. Anthony Prencipe. He said the sheriff's office had reduced the search to a limited, ongoing one after the agency used personnel to search 24 hours a day for the first 10 days that Emadi was missing.

The family of Emadi offered a $10,000 reward for any information on Saeed Emadi that led to his discovery. No trace

MISSING HIKER
$10,000 REWARD

THIS IS THE DAY
SAEED WENT MISSING

SAEED EMADI - AGE 66; HEIGHT 6'3"; WEIGHT 190; MIDDLE EASTERN

WEARING	light stripe shorts, white button up shirt, blue tennis shoes, and gray ball cap. Wearing black and silver headphones
PLS	S. FORK OF SILVER CREEK AT **ICE HOUSE LAKE RESERVOIR** 38°49.182N 120°18.945W 38.91970, -120.31575 10 S 0733042 4300192
TERRAIN	Heavily wooded and brush covered ravine Class 1&2
CIRCS	Saeed was separated from his hiking partners when he crossed the creek and continued around the lake. Saeed has day hike experience, he is unfamiliar with the area. Good physical shape. "Never Quit" attitude. **AMATEUR HIKER/NO CLIMBING EXPERIENCE. DIABETIC**

CONTACT the **El Dorado Sheriff Department** emergency line: **(530) 626-4911/911** and Zhila Emadi via Facebook

Do not interfere w/search & rescue and do not move evidence. Record photos and geo-coordinates

Total reward amount distributed is not to exceed $10,000. Money will be provided on the condition that it leads to the whereabouts of Saeed Emadi.

Proceed at your own risk using your own equipment at your own cost
Inexperienced hikers/climbers please avoid the area

A reward poster for Saeed Emadi.

of him or his belongings has ever been found despite numerous searches.

What happened to Saeed Emadi? Why did he not make any more calls or answer his phone? He apparently had phone service. Did something terrible happen to Emadi shortly after making the phone call to his friends? He told them he could see the lake and the highway. Why could he not be found despite huge searches that went on over ten days?

Did Emadi just wander off into the wilderness to die? Was he suddenly attacked by a bigfoot and then carried out of the area?

Although the terrain around the reservoirs is rugged and forested, there are many trails and viewpoints where one can see the nearby roads. Many campsites are in the area. For Emadi to not find a trail to get to a nearby road is baffling to me. It seems that he was abducted and removed from the area.

Sadly, we may surmise that Emadi was being watched by a bigfoot who followed the hiker's trail as he stumbled on alone. Shortly after he made his phone call he was suddenly attacked by the bigfoot. Being an adult male, Saeed Emadi was probably struck with a powerful blow to the head and neck and then carried dead or unconscious out of the district to an area miles away from where the attack and abduction took place.

Saeed Emadi would have died shortly after the abduction if he was not already dead. His shoes, hat and other things would be examined over and over again by the bigfoot. Eventually the decaying body would be discarded. Perhaps it would be taken back to the area where the abduction occurred or more likely discarded in a remote ravine where the corpse would never be seen. His body may be discovered one day, we just don't know. Meanwhile the $10,000 reward for any information on Saeed Emadi still stands.

Family of Six Bigfoot Seen Near Fresno Lake

Then we have the story of the bigfoot family that showed up shortly after Saeed Emadi's disappearance near Fresno, California in October of 2020. This is an area of California that is directly south of El Dorado County. The Fresno Fox television affiliate KMPH, Fox 26 News reported on the incident, referencing local paranormal expert Jeffrey Gonzalez:

…the most recent California Bigfoot sighting was in early October near Avocado Lake in the eastern part of Fresno County. Gonzalez says a local farmer saw a family of five or six Bigfoot running on his ranch in the middle of the night. "One of them, which was extremely tall, had a pig over its shoulder. And the five scattered and the one with the pig was running so fast it didn't see an irrigation pipe and it tripped, with the pig flying over," says Gonzalez.

This story intrigued Gonzalez but did not surprise him. In the last five years, there have been three bigfoot sightings, all in the same area in East Fresno County. "I would have never guessed in a million years that you would have told me there were bigfoot on Shields or Ashlan Avenue. Right? So, I want to know what's going on. Is this for real?" says Gonzalez.

He says five years ago a woman called him saying her two sons had seen a bigfoot in their orchard one afternoon. A few years later, Gonzalez received a call from a man who said he saw five bigfoot in an orchard across the street from his house. Turns out it was the same orchard where the boys had seen the bigfoot years before. And now, a local farmer says he, too, has seen five bigfoot on his property.

"What are the odds of three people, three different families, who don't know each other, within a radius of 2 to 3 miles, come and tell me what they witness, and it matches up," says Gonzalez. (Fox 26 News, kmph.com/news, 12 Oct 2020)

This fascinating story reminds us that there are whole bigfoot families out there. Perhaps daddy bigfoot wants to show his kids how to steal pigs and chickens. The whole family is there for something out of a cartoon bigfoot movie with the tall bigfoot grabbing a pig and carrying it away with him, only to trip and fall. No word on whether the pig ran off, so perhaps it was dead from a powerful blow from the bigfoot, coming down from the mountains to the orchard and farm for a quick smash and grab. Yes, bigfoot is well known to raid chicken coops and barns during his sordid excursions into the nearby highways and byways of civilization.

That we have this family of six bigfoot shows us that bigfoot is not dying out and there are families out there with kids, male and female, who will have to go out on their own one day and search for a mate. The myth of the lone bigfoot out there with only a dwindling few companions may be completely wrong. Tribes of bigfoot exist all over the United States and Canada and they will travel long distances to find mates and go on their own "long treks" or "walkabouts" that bigfoot and sasquatch seems wont to do.

It should be noted here that bigfoot and sasquatch are deemed to be good swimmers. There are numerous accounts, from the coastal region of British Columbia, even islands, to the swamps of Mississippi, of bigfoot creatures swimming in lakes and rivers.

Two Women Disappear in Washington State

On October 17, 2019 a 28-year-old single woman named Rachel Lakoduk went missing after telling her family she planned to hike in the North Cascades of Washington State. She left her home at Moses Lake, Washington to hike the Hidden Lake Trail. She parked her car at the trailhead and then headed down that trail. Nearly two years later her body was discovered far from the trail in August of 2021.

Said an article in the local KING 5 news on November 4, 2019 under the title "Ground searches for missing North Cascades hiker suspended":

> Rachel Lakoduk, 28, went missing on Oct. 17 after telling her family she planned to hike the Hidden Lake Trail in the North Cascades.
>
> Over the weekend, search and rescue crews were again unable to locate a 28-year-old hiker who went missing in the North Cascades on Oct. 17.
>
> Skagit County Undersheriff Chad Clark told KING 5 "nothing was located" during the latest search. Ground search efforts are being suspended with the possibility of more air searches in the near future, depending on the weather, according to Clark.
>
> Rachel Lakoduk left Moses Lake on Oct. 17 telling

Rachel Lakoduk.

her family she planned to hike the Hidden Lake Trail to a lookout cabin and spend the night. She hasn't been seen since.

Then it was announced on August 14, 2021—two years later—that they had found the body of Rachel Lakoduk. Said an Associated Press report on August 17 under the title "Searchers find body of missing hiker in North Cascades":

> The body of a 28-year-old hiker who went missing in the North Cascades nearly two years ago was found over the weekend by a private search and rescue group. Rachel Lakoduk of Moses Lake went missing Oct. 17, 2019 after telling her family she planned to hike the Hidden Lake Trail to a lookout cabin and spend the night, KING5 reported. During the initial search for Lakoduk, her vehicle was found at the trailhead. However, search crews reported that it didn't appear she had made it to the lookout tower. Over the weekend, her remains were found by a large search group. Lakoduk's mother, Elizabeth Tripp, posted on Facebook Monday morning: "Our beloved Rachel's remains arrived off the mountain yesterday."

Tripp said her heart is both thankful and broken.

"Thankful for all the courageous people who searched for Rachel for the past two years," she said. "Thankful for the outpouring of love from people around the world. Thankful for the prayers sent up for us. Thankful that I was able to kiss my baby's remains goodbye.

"Sometimes there are just no words for a broken heart."

Some additional details were given in a further report from iFIBER ONE News on August 16, 2021:

The close friend of a missing Moses Lake woman who was found dead in the wild this weekend in Skagit County disclosed more about the discovery of Rachel Lakoduk. The remains of the deceased 28-year-old were found Saturday in the Hidden Lake area just west of Marblemount. Lakoduk didn't come home after going on a solo hike in mid-October of 2019.

Emily Sawyer of Moses Lake spoke to iFIBER ONE News on Sunday night. Sawyer says Lakoduk was found in her sleeping bag. Sawyer says Lakoduk's final resting place was far off trail on a 50-degree slope in a depression under a fallen tree.

Sawyer indicated that Rachel likely used the depression to seek refuge from the elements; it is not believed that Rachel was killed by the tree, but used it to shield herself from the snow.

Sawyer says search parties were able to identify Rachel's remains based on her clothing and equipment as well as her red hair. Sawyer says some of Lakoduk's remains were scattered.

Sawyer confirmed that Rachel's remains have been removed from where she supposedly died and are now in the possession of the Skagit County Coroner.

An autopsy will be performed soon to confirm the cause of Rachel's death.

Another article had the headline: "Body of woman who went

missing in 2019 found far from trail she was hiking in North Cascades."

> The body of a Moses Lake woman who went missing in the North Cascades almost two years ago has been recovered.
> Rachel Lakoduk, 28, went on a solo hike toward Hidden Lake lookout cabin in the Mount Baker-Snoqualmie National Forest in October 2019. Bad weather set in, and Rachel didn't return from the hike.
> Rescuers found no trace of her at the time, but friends and family continued to organize volunteer searches, and over the weekend a search party found Rachel's body and gear far off the trail.
> The precise cause of her death wasn't yet known today; the Skagit County coroner's office is investigating.

So we have the strange story of Rachel Lakoduk and her discovery two years after her disappearance. She was in an area far from the trail. Why is that? How did she get to where she was? Was she brought there after her death? What happened to Rachel?

She was planning on spending the night at a lookout cabin. Did she make it there? Investigators are indicating that she did not make it to that cabin. Bad weather had set in and this is always a factor. But why did she stray so far from the trail? Why was she not found in the previous searches —searches that utilized dogs?

She was said to have been found in her sleeping bag but parts of her body were found elsewhere. Why would she have died in this sleeping bag beneath a tree? Would she have frozen to death? It does not seem so. What caused her death?

In fact, we have never gotten a precise cause of death. Were the

Rachel Lakoduk.

bones in her neck broken? Did she have some trauma to the skull? We will probably never know of any results.

Was Rachel Lakoduk ambushed by a bigfoot and taken to his bigfoot cave far from the abduction? Perhaps she had been in her sleeping bag at the time, perhaps under a large pine tree while she waited out the storm that pelted the area with snow for an evening. Was she taken with her sleeping bag by a bigfoot who strangled her and otherwise abused her?

After having her dead body in his cave for amusement for a year or so, the bigfoot might decide to remove the partially mummified body back to the general vicinity of where the person had been snatched. It will be deposited at a randomly chosen spot, often remote but sometimes in obvious areas that had been searched before. In some cases the people have apparently been thrown over a cliff or similar area. We will see some of these cases as we continue.

It should also be noted in the Rachel Lakoduk story is that she may have been stalked by a bigfoot over some time. If Rachel Lakoduk was in the habit of making these solo hikes into the relative wilderness of the area she may have been watched over the months and years by those who silently watch humans from behind a bush or tree.

A year tan the Lakoduk case earlier on August 1, 2018, a 28-year-old woman named Samantha Sayers went for a day hike by herself on Vesper Peak in the Northern Cascade Mountains of Washington State. While seen by fellow hikers earlier that day, Sayers vanished and was never seen again.

Vesper Peak is a peak along the Mountain Loop Highway region of the North Cascades. Vesper Peak is part of the Mount Baker-Snoqualmie National Forest—a massive wilderness area that extends more than 140 miles (230 km) along the western slopes of the Cascade Range.

This huge area is a core area for bigfoot in the Pacific Northwest. Along with the northern woods of California—where the famous Patterson photos were taken—and the Mount Hood area of Oregon, the Mount Baker–Snoqualmie National Forest is a vast area of wilderness that is populated by bears, cougars, elk, moose and bigfoot.

A road called the Cascade River Road comes out from the town of Marblemount and heads toward Vesper Peak, passing the Cascade River Community Club. A side road called NF-1540 then goes north to the Hidden Lake Lookout Trailhead. Samantha Sayers took this road on August 1, 2018.

In late July she had been looking for hiking partners on Facebook from her Belltown, Seattle apartment. "Seattle friends," she wrote, "I'm going hiking this Wednesday and tackling Vesper Peak… Message me if you want to tag along." Nobody took her up on it and Sayers drove to the Hidden Lake Lookout Trailhead about two hours northeast of Seattle. Sayers signed her name in the logbook at the trailhead at 10 a.m.

Sayers probably started up Hidden Lake Trail with a brisk step but it is unknown what happened to her after that.

Back in Seattle her boyfriend Kevin Dares, around six p.m., became worried and he drove to the trailhead. There he found her

Samantha Sayers at 28 years old.

car, the only automobile in the lot. He then searched part of the trail using a flashlight he'd bought on the way. He then called 911 to report her missing.

A search for Sayers began that lasted for 22 days—the longest in the history of Washington State. There seemed to be no trace of Samantha Sayers. Nothing was found of her and she had essentially vanished.

Social media in the Seattle area exploded on this case and the mystery of Samantha Sayers became a popular subject. Various theories on Sayers' disappearance were batted around online. Psychics sent tips to the police with such vague advice as "Sam is near rocks, trees and water." Someone reported seeing Samantha in a Walmart in Spokane, Washington, acting strangely. Someone claimed she was on an episode of "The Bachelorette." Her mother began posting frequent updates and seemed to think that her daughter—who had a shaved, tattooed head—was still alive. She also seemed to have some suspicion of Kevin Dares, Samantha's boyfriend.

The police had four possible theories of Samantha's disappearance and they all revolved around her falling into an icy crevasse or slipping into Vesper Lake. One would think she would have been found had she drowned in Vesper Lake. That she may have been abducted was not part of any police theories. By the way, the name Vesper refers to an evening song. It also refers to evening prayers, and then it's usually used in the plural as vespers.

In an article that appeared in the *Seattle Times* on August 23, 2019 under the title "A year after officials called off search for hiker Sam Sayers, her mother is still looking," said:

> Samantha Sayers was last seen Aug. 1, 2018, while on a solo day-hike up Vesper Peak in the North Cascades.
>
> It was easy for fellow hikers to remember the young woman with the bald, tattooed head and the wide, easy smile. One saw her eating a sandwich. Another saw her descending the south side of the summit.
>
> But Sayers, 28, never made it home to her Belltown apartment.
>
> For 22 days, more than a dozen agencies and countless

volunteers scoured the mountain's steep, jagged terrain. Helicopters clattered overhead. King County Search and Rescue conducted an air search using thermal imaging cameras. Three K-9 teams searched for her scent. Nothing more was found than a possible boot print.

On Aug. 23, 2018, the Snohomish County Sheriff's Office suspended the search after spending thousands of hours on Vesper.

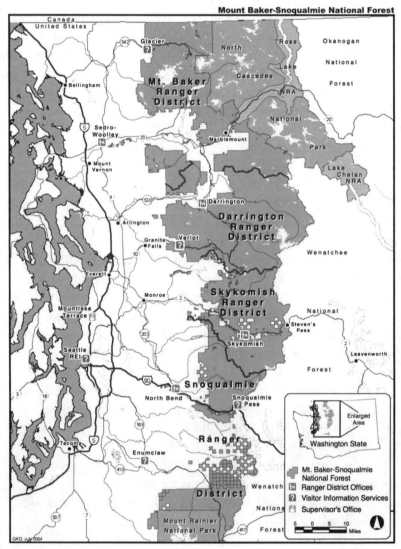

A map around the Mt. Baker and Snoqualmie area of the Cascade Mountains.

But Sayers' mother, Lisa, refuses to give up hope that her daughter is alive. Somewhere. "We're not searching the mountain," Lisa Sayers said Wednesday from her home in Pennsylvania. "We don't think she stayed on the mountain."

The family has hired a team of investigators that has asked Lisa Sayers not share anything about what, if anything, they have gleaned.

"I'm not going to say who we're working with," she said. "But we have not stopped. We still believe she is alive."

Earlier this month, her boyfriend, Kevin Dares, held a service in her memory on the peak where she disappeared—and where officials determined there were "four possibilities for mishap," all involving slips into an icy crevasse or into Vesper Lake.

The service included the installation of an iron cross with a hammered-metal oval inscribed with Sayers' name and birth date and the title "Queen of the Stars."

In a long post on Facebook, Dares thanked the 15 people who attended—some who flew in to remember their friend.

Dares went on to describe how the two met on Tinder in 2015, and about Sayers' excitement about her work as a "properties artisan" at Seattle Rep, and how driven she was in everything she did: Cleaning Airbnbs, flipping houses, hiking and traveling.

And he wrote about how hard people tried to find her, to no avail.

"As we choose life, adjust to new realities and consciously put one foot in front of the other," Dares wrote, "we can also recognize that we never move on. We will forever carry Samantha within us and through every step we take."

Lisa Sayers didn't participate in the Vesper Peak service, and has had no contact with Dares. "I don't want to talk about it," she said. "We don't care what the people there are doing."

In June, Lisa Sayers' cancer returned after 11 years of being in remission. Through six chemotherapy treatments—and facing two more—she hasn't lost the determination to find her daughter.

"Just know that we won't stop until we have our daughter home or we have DNA that will tell us otherwise," she said. "People tell me, 'You just need to have a funeral and move on,' but I say 'No, we don't.'

"Because there is truth out there. And we're going to get it."

So her mother appears to think that Samantha Sayers made it back to the parking lot but did not get into her car. Instead she got into someone else's car and disappeared. Therefore, she may still be alive. It is sad that her boyfriend, Kevin Dares, had to have some suspicion directed at him. He is clearly innocent regarding Samantha's baffling disappearance. As her mother said, "The truth is out there."

It would appear that Sayers never returned from the mountain. She was seen eating a sandwich and descending the south side of the summit. Something happened to her as she descended alone from the rocky peak to the tree line below that and the trail that would ultimately take her back to the trailhead and her car.

Did she meet a bigfoot along the way? Perhaps as she arrived at the tree line where the forest began again from the rocky alpine heights. Was she stunned and kidnapped by the powerful creature? Was she then carried away out of the area to a bigfoot cave miles

A portion of the Snoqualmie National Forest.

away from where she was last seen? This bigfoot was probably watching Samantha for some time before he finally struck—maybe with a soft blow to the head. In this isolated area even a soft blow to the head would not be necessary as no one would be able to hear her scream. This bigfoot would have been observing other hikers in the area as well and know if any were within earshot.

She would have been taken back to the bigfoot's cave where she would have died very shortly if she were not already dead. Her shoes and other artifacts would have been looked over for some time. Eventually these artifacts—or some of them—would have been scattered with her remains in a remote ravine. Perhaps her remains will be found one day, but I rather doubt it.

Bigfoot Goes to Idaho

A year earlier in March of 2017, a northern Idaho woman told police she crashed into a deer because she was distracted by a sasquatch in her rearview mirror. This occurred in the Moscow-Pullman area which is in northern Idaho along the Washington border. It occurred near the small town of Potlatch that has the Saint Joe National Forest to the north and the Nez Pierce Clearwater National Forest to the south. Perhaps this is where the famous rock group Credence Clearwater Revival got part of their name.

First the *Moscow-Pullman Daily News* reported on March 26, 2017, that a 50-year-old Tensed, Idaho, woman was driving south on U.S. Highway 95 when she struck a deer. The woman told Benewah County Sheriff's officials that she saw a sasquatch chasing a deer on the side of the road while she was driving. She said she checked one of her mirrors to get a second look at the beast and when she looked up, the deer ran in front of her and she struck it. She kept driving and reported the incident to the police. The Sheriff's officials marked the incident as a vehicle versus deer collision but did not report any evidence of a bigfoot.

The *Idaho State Journal* out of Pocatello, Idaho had this follow-up story on April 3, 2017 under the title of "Local researcher says recent Idaho Bigfoot sighting seems credible":

A northern Idaho woman recently made national news after she blamed a car crash on a sasquatch. Now a noted local Bigfoot researcher is saying that her story seems credible on the surface. Dr. Jeff Meldrum, professor of anatomy and anthropology at Idaho State University, has been researching Bigfoot sightings for years, and he said the woman's claim is not out of the realm of possibility.

According to an article in the Moscow-Pullman Daily News, the woman, a 50-year-old resident of the town of Tensed, told police she saw a sasquatch chasing a deer on the side of the road last Wednesday night while driving on U.S. Highway 95 near the Idaho/Washington border. Then, she checked her rearview mirror to get a second look at what she described as a 7- to 8-foot tall "shaggy" creature. But when she looked up, the deer ran in front of her and she struck the animal with her Subaru Forester. Even though Meldrum has not interviewed the woman making the claims, he said the story does seem credible due to how she handled the sighting in the aftermath of the crash.

"It's intriguing because she sounds like a very credible witness," he said, noting that there is no suggestion that she was inebriated or delusional. "Her first response was to report it to the sheriff and not post it on Facebook."

Meldrum also said that the whole scenario seems plausible, especially considering the time of year and the location of the crash, which occurred near a heavily wooded national forest.

"The most common places to see a Bigfoot is on a highway at night or adjacent to a body of water," he said. "The whole northern panhandle is prime habitat for a sasquatch. This is also the time of year you would expect a Bigfoot to be chasing deer, when it's malnourished at the end of winter."

Though Meldrum said this is all speculation at this point, he does say there are some other possibilities to explain the sighting. The woman could have merely misinterpreted what she saw chasing the deer. While it could have been a bear emerging from its winter den and looking for a meal, Meldrum said that explanation seems unlikely.

"A bear isn't going to be chasing deer on its hind legs," Meldrum said. "The bear would have taken one or two steps before going back on four legs." There's also the possibility that the woman was being pranked. In 2012, a man dressed in a Bigfoot costume was trying to drum up sightings of the creature along a Montana highway.

Instead, he ended up getting struck by two cars and killed. But what fascinates Meldrum most about the case in northern Idaho is how much interest the story has generated. It has already been picked up by multiple national news organizations such as Fox News and was one of the top trending stories on Facebook this weekend.

"What's interesting is the attention it has gotten," he said. "It isn't obviously involving a crazy person and it doesn't seem like a prank. I think it struck a chord because it was just so mundane, but it smacks of a credible encounter."

In the end, the Associated Press reported that police marked the incident allegedly involving Bigfoot as a vehicle versus deer collision.

On the evenings of April 14 and 15, Meldrum will make two presentations at the National Oregon/California Trail Center in Montpelier regarding the subject of Bigfoot.

The first presentation, entitled "Sasquatch and Other Wildmen: The Search for Relict Hominoids," will be held on Friday at 7:30 p.m. Meldrum will discuss the shifting attitude of science towards cryptic man-like species, such as sasquatch, surviving into the present alongside humans in various remote corners of the globe.

Meldrum will also hold a book signing beginning at 6 p.m. in the lobby of the center.

The second presentation, entitled "50 Years of the Patterson-Gimlin Film," will be held on Saturday at 7:30 p.m. The year 2017 marks the 50th anniversary of the controversial film footage depicting what alleges to be a Bigfoot in northern California. Meldrum will discuss his findings regarding the film. He will be available from 1 to 7 p.m. for questions and book signing.

So here is a good newspaper story about bigfoot in Idaho, but there was more. Meldrum is a respected bigfoot researcher and is the author of *Sasquatch: Legend Meets Science*.[32] It was probably this book that he was autographing at the April, 2017 event. This event also shows that investigation and study of sasquatch is a respected one, not just in Idaho but in many states.

Idaho became something of a hotspot when in June of 2016 it was reported that a video was made of a bigfoot south of the town of Pocatello. The *Idaho State Journal* out of Pocatello, a newspaper that is used to publishing bigfoot stories, reported on June 30, 2016 that a bigfoot had been seen in broad daylight near Hawkins Reservoir, south of Pocatello. It had been video taped as well.

A still shot of the figure in the video is reproduced here and in the color section. The video was available at XtremeIdaho.com. However that page no longer exists and the video has been taken down from YouTube. The article said:

> An online video of an alleged Bigfoot sighting in Southeast Idaho has been creating quite a stir over the past few days.
>
> The 2-minute, 24-second video, entitled "Possible bigfoot in Idaho!! Flying the drone around and ran across this," was posted on YouTube on June 2.
>
> The duration of the video consists of drone footage over a clearing near the Hawkins Reservoir west of Downey in Southeast Idaho. The reservoir is located approximately 35 miles south of Pocatello.
>
> A mysterious hairy figure, seemingly running on two legs, becomes visible at approximately the 25-second mark. It then runs across a field and into a wooded area as the drone flies over the area.
>
> The videographer, who wishes to remain anonymous due to fears of public ridicule, said he initially thought the figure he captured was just an animal. However, he noticed the figure seemed to be running upright, which grabbed his attention.

"I said, 'wait a minute, that's not right,'" he said. A still shot from the footage, which was provided by the videographer, indicates the figure is hairy and light brown in color.

However, since the YouTube footage was shared to Idaho State Journal's Facebook page late Sunday evening, numerous commentators on the page noted how difficult it is to actually see the running figure in the video. Even the YouTube video description recommends viewing the video on a large computer monitor.

The drone is quite high in the sky, and by the time the camera starts to zoom in on the figure, it has disappeared in the wooded area. Because of the difficulty of getting a clear shot of the running figure, Idaho State University professor and noted Bigfoot expert Dr. Jeff Meldrum said the identity of the figure is inconclusive.

"I had to expand the size of the video to clearly see it on my 22-inch computer monitor, and those screens for drone cameras are usually no bigger than a cell phone screen," he said. "How could he have picked up that little speck, and then zoom in and fly directly to the point when it entered the forest?"

Meldrum also said that from his studies of Sasquatch, he said it's unusual for them to be found in the immediate habitat surrounding Hawkins Reservoir. "I can imagine them crossing areas that aren't their prime habitat to get from one place to another or find another member of their species," he said. "But I can't imagine they would do that in broad daylight."

The videographer, who said he has lived in Southeast Idaho for over 30 years, said he isn't sure what the figure in the video is exactly. However, he said his footage has piqued his interest so much that he has invested around $400 in specialized Adobe video software so he can get the clearest, zoomed-in footage of the mysterious figure possible.

The footage was taken approximately a week and a half ago, according to the videographer, who says he commonly uses his drone to take wilderness and wildlife shots from the air.

"I fly my drone everywhere, and I get video of elk, deer, rivers, all kind of things," he said. "Usually pretty views nobody else can see."

Here we have Jeff Meldrum again and he says the video is inconclusive. A furry figure with light brown hair is seen moving into the forest. It looks pretty authentic to me. Being a daylight photo we can really see the color of the hair. Just like humans they have different colored hair, from light brown to dark brown or black. Then there exist the white or silver colored bigfoot which we will discuss in a later chapter.

Also in Idaho was the disappearance and later discovery of two women at the Craters of the Moon National Monument and Preserve. Two women vanished at the Monument while going on a short hike in September of 2013.

Craters of the Moon National Monument and Preserve is a wilderness area in the Snake River Plain in central Idaho. The protected area's features are volcanic and represent one of the best-preserved flood basalt areas in the continental United States. The reserve encompasses three major lava fields and about 400 square miles (1,000 km²) of sagebrush steppe grasslands to cover a total area of 1,117 square miles (2,893 km²). The Devil's Orchard Nature Trail is a sidewalk winding through cinder beds and native vegetation, passing interpretive waysides at one section of the monument and preserve. On this trail you can enjoy a brief and easy stroll as it is a paved half-mile (0.8 km) trail that is wheelchair accessible and meanders through an area of cinder beds scattered with pieces of the North Crater wall.

On September 19, 2013 Amelia Linkert (69 years old) and her friend Jodean "Jo" Elliot-Blakeslee (63 years old) were visiting the Craters of the Moon in a camper that Linkert had purchased. Linkert was a retired teacher and Elliot-Blakeslee was a retired doctor and US Navy Reserve Commander. Both were avid campers and hikers.

The two women parked their camper at a KOA campground in Arco, Idaho and then drove their car to the Preserve where they entered the park at the Visitors Center. They then drove past the Devil's Orchard Nature Trail to the Tree Molds trailhead. Here they parked their car and left their two Labradoodle dogs in the back seat. They were apparently going for a very short walk from the car. They walked out onto the Tree Molds trail and then vanished.

Amelia (Amy) Linkert.

They were not reported missing until September 23 and a formal search did not start until September 24. Their car was found at the Tree Molds trailhead with their dogs still in the back seat and their phones and purses in the front seat. A body was found a day later which was initially thought to be Elliot-Blakeslee but was actually Linkert. In fact, Elliot-Blakeslee would not be found until a month later.

The *Minneapolis Star Tribune* had this story on September 29, 2013 about the disappearance and identification of Amelia Linkert under the headline "Longtime Minneapolis teacher found dead in Idaho after hiking tragedy":

> Amelia Linkert was back home in Rosemount, visiting relatives two months ago with a twinkle in her eye. The longtime Minneapolis special education teacher and missionary had purchased a camper as a retirement gift and was ready to explore. She was to celebrate her 70th birthday last Thursday.
>
> Linkert, who moved to Idaho seven years ago, was planning a second trip to the lava-strewn landscape of Craters of the Moon National Monument in her adopted home state.
>
> "She was very happy and excited about going on this trip," her younger sister, Margaret Poirier of Cottage Grove, said Saturday after authorities notified her that a

body found Wednesday was Linkert's. She had died of exposure.

At first, Butte County deputies and U.S. park rangers in Idaho believed they found the body of Linkert's friend, 63-year-old doctor Jodean Elliot-Blakeslee. But dental records confirmed it was Linkert.

"Obviously, they left the trail for some reason and a tragedy occurred," her sister said. "My heart goes out to Jo's family, who had reached a bit of closure. Our family is concerned and distressed they can't find her."

As searchers continued to comb the rocky terrain with a helicopter, dogs and 70 volunteers, spokeswoman Lori Iverson said Saturday that Linkert had been dead for a few days when her body was found. The women left the trailhead Thursday, Sept. 19, and searchers began looking for them Tuesday.

Jo Elliot-Blakeslee was finally discovered a month later around October 22 by a helicopter about a mile from the discovery site of Amelia Linkert. A *New York Daily News* article for October 24, 2013 had the headline of "Missing Idaho hiker found dead after government shutdown hinders search" and said:

A missing hiker turned up dead in a national park on Tuesday after the government shutdown forced many rescuers to postpone their search for her. The body of Jo Elliot-Blakeslee, 63, was found

Missing

AMY LINKERT AND JO ELLIOTT-BLAKESLEE

LAST SEEN: THURSDAY SEPT. 19TH, 2013
FROM: CRATERS OF THE MOON
NATIONAL MONUMENT
ARCO, IDAHO

IF YOU HAVE ANY INFORMATION
PLEASE CALL: ARCO POLICE DEPT. (208) 527-8553
OR
BUTTE COUNTY SHERIFFS OFFICE (208) 527-1300

A poster for Linkert and Elliot-Blakeslee.

in Craters of the Moon National Monument and Preserve in central Idaho just a mile from where the body of her hiking partner, Amy Linkert, 69, was discovered late last month, park rangers said.

"They were such beautiful people. I can't believe they're no longer in our lives," Elliott-Blakeslee's friend Susie Hart told the Idaho Statesman. "We're so glad that Amy's and Jo's paths crossed ours. We're the lucky ones."

The pair was reported missing Sept. 24, but the federal government shutdown, which went into effect Oct. 1, hindered the search. Unpaid yet undeterred, ten park service rangers continued to look for Elliott-Blakeslee on foot without access to government resources, such as search helicopters, dogs or planes, reported ABC News.

Elliott-Blakeslee's body was finally located in the lava fields northwest of the Tree Molds Trail during a helicopter search. Authorities are awaiting autopsy results to determine the cause of her death. It is believed that Linkert died of exposure, and she showed signs of dehydration.

"We hope that this will bring closure to her family, friends and all those who have been involved in the search," said Park Superintendent Dan Buckley in a news release. "We join the family in thanking the searchers and local communities for the tremendous outpouring of support that we have received throughout this intense effort."

How and why were Jo and Amy separated? Did one get injured before the other by the jagged lava rocks in the area?

Why was Jo found so far from the trailhead car park and why did it take over a month to find her body despite numerous flyovers by helicopters? The rock in the area can obscure bodies easily.

Although the authorities have dismissed foul play, it seems unlikely that the two just left their dogs behind and went wandering in this potentially dangerous terrain without supplies. What made them leave the pickup truck behind and then separate? As the family member said they were both keen hikers and survivalists, not naive and not inexperienced in these wilderness areas. A sad end to these ladies' lives in the amazing scenery of the Craters of the Moon National Monument.

This is a bizarre and sad story. What happened to these women? They were apparently going for a short hike and had left their dogs and phones in the car. It would seem that within minutes of their leaving the car and walking up the trail something happened to them. There do not seem to have been any other visitors in the area at the time and theirs was the only automobile in the fairly remote car park and trailhead.

What could have happened to these two women so quickly into their hike? The authorities seem to think that they ventured off the trail for some unknown reason and then one of them got hurt. The other one then wandered for days in the lava fields trying to get help. They both eventually collapsed and died of exhaustion and dehydration.

Yet, why were searchers unable to find Jo Elliot-Blakeslee for more than a month? Was it that she was not there before the time that she was found? These lava fields and cinder cones have hundreds or even thousands of small caves in them. Some of these caves can include lava tubes and such that can go for long distances

Craters of the Moon National Park in Idaho.

underground, even miles. These tubes and extended caves can still have occasional skylights and open areas where light can reach into these dark places during certain times of the day. If you were a bigfoot living in this area and you wanted a cave, you would have hundreds to choose from.

It would seem that these two older female hikers thought they would explore the beginnings of this trail and leave the dogs in the car. Because of the dangerous lava fields they might have that thought the dogs would run off and either cut up their footpads or fall into one of the caves and crags.

The women must have been instantly grabbed and incapacitated. They may have yelled but there was no one to hear them. For their sake, let's hope they were killed at the time of their abduction and not later. Perhaps they were taken back to one of the bigfoot's caves deep in the lava fields. These lava fields have trees and brush as well.

The body of Linkert was discarded early on and the body of Elliot-Blakeslee was discarded nearly a month later, it would seem. Both had probably been dead since the day of their disappearance. We are not told of any missing clothing and this might be for the privacy of the families and that Elliot-Blakeslee had been exposed to the elements for more than a month.

This is a tragic case of two women going for a short walk and ending up in Bigfoot Hell. Idaho is a hotbed of bigfoot activity as are the neighboring states and Canadian provinces. Even a short hike can become a deadly experience in these wilderness areas and national parks.

The Disappearance of Maureen Kelly

Back in Washington State we have the strange case of Maureen Kelly in 2013. On June 9, 2013 Maureen Leianuhea "Anu" Kelly, 19, disappeared from Canyon Creek Campground in the Gifford Pinchot National Forest near Cougar.

Kelly was from Vancouver, Washington and was with a group of friends at Canyon Creek Campground camping out for the night. She left the group at around 5 pm saying she was going on a "spiritual quest" and would be back by midnight. She took off her shoes and all her clothes and was wearing only a belt pack around her waist that contained some knives, matches, and a compass.

She failed to return that night and her friends reported her missing in the early morning hours of June 10. Kelly was never seen again. Was this just misadventure in the forest, abduction, or had something else happened to her?

Gifford Pinchot National Forest is located in southern Washington just north of the town of Portland. It has an area of 1.32 million acres (5300 km²), extending along the western slopes of Cascade Range from Mount Rainier National Park to the Columbia River. It has old-growth forests, high mountain meadows, several glaciers, and numerous volcanic peaks. The forest's highest point is at 12,276 feet at the top of Mount Adams, the second tallest volcano in the state after Rainier.

The Skamania County Sheriff's Department initiated a one-week-long search for Kelly. Undersheriff Dave Cox said, "She had talked about doing this spiritual quest for evidently quite some time. The folks that she was with, they felt that this was something she needed to do. It's a rough remote area with a lot of timber and brush. It's going to be a tough go for her, especially with no shoes."

While Undersheriff Cox admitted that it was "a little bit unusual" for a 19-year-old to leave a campsite nude, save for a belt pack, he said there was no indication that she was on drugs at the time of her disappearance.

The extensive search of the area turned up no clues. Search teams using dogs determined that she crossed Canyon Creek and headed north, climbing upwards towards Forest Service Road 54, but then lost the trail. Cox said the weather interfered with the search. A thick cloud covering prevented helicopters from scanning the Canyon Creek area for signs of Kelly from the air, limiting rescue crews to search on land only. During the night, temperatures

Maureen Kelly.

dipped into the forties with some light rain. Without any clothes, she would have quickly succumbed to exposure if she did not stay dry.

Investigators believe it's likely that Kelly probably died in a mishap in the wilderness, but her body has never been found and her case remains unsolved. Did she just vanish into the wilderness or was she abducted by a bigfoot? Would a nude woman really venture very far from a campsite on a chilly evening? It was still light outside when she left the camp and she probably would have turned around before it became dark. But something else happened.

Was she walking along the trail from the campsite, being watched the entire time by a bigfoot? She may not have walked very far when she was suddenly attacked and abducted. Throwing her over his shoulder, he trudged through the forest to his cave in a completely different area of the Gifford Pinchot National Forest. Sadly we will never know what happened to Maureen "Anu" Kelly and her body will probably never be found. I guess that one lesson we might learn here is not to go on spiritual quests into the forest without a companion.

Bigfoot In Alaska

Let us not forget that Alaska is also in the Pacific Northwest and there have been plenty of bigfoot reports from up there as well, often on the islands of the lower part of that state.

One such island is Revillagigedo where there have been a number of recent sightings. Ketchikan is the main town on the island and is the sixth largest city in Alaska. Revillagigedo Island is the 12th largest island in the United States and much of it is forested wilderness. The island is traditional Tlingit territory.

The *Anchorage Daily News* reported on May 18, 2011 an article under the title: "Bigfoot sighting in Ketchikan?" Said the article in which we learn that the Tlingit word for bigfoot is "Kushtaka":

> Driving up the Alcan Highway through Canada, there is a whole stretch of Canadian towns along the road touting their bigfoot-rich properties, a tourist draw for those who believe in the unsubstantiated animal.
>
> Alaska is well-known for its hulking wildlife—bears,

239

moose, caribou and sea lions are among the biggest draws—but when it comes to the elusive bigfoot, there seems to be a dearth of sightings for a state so enveloped in the woods that play home to the legendary beast in other parts of the world.

Maybe the Bigfoot's northern cousin, the yeti, is a more appropriate fit for Alaska, where half the state hangs above the Arctic Circle.

But recently, YouTube user putua76 posted a shaky video that purports to capture the unconfirmed creature on tape near Ketchikan, Alaska.

From the original upload:

I was on a logging road in Ketchikan hiking with my friend when I saw it! Boy did my heart start racing!! It was about 40 yards from the road! Not sure if it knew I was there or not, because the noise of flowing water from the stream. It seemed to travel fast! It made my hair stand up!! At one point you can see a whitish yellowish thing in its hand! I believe it was skunk cabbage. Not sure, but it is in bloom.

You see it jump and after that point it just seems to disappear. There was a lot of brush and trees between it and I, I could not tell where it had gone. It was a scary sort of exciting feeling at the same time!! We went to search for tracks but the riverbed where we thought it was walking was full of perfect skipping rocks, we found no prints! If there is a Bigfoot, Sasquatch, or Kushtaka I swear I saw him!!

According to the Bigfoot Field Researchers Organization, this would be the first reported sighting of a bigfoot in Ketchikan, although there have been 21 previous sightings in Alaska, eight of which have occurred in Fairbanks or "Southeast Fairbanks."

As with all bigfoot video the creature is hard to see, hidden behind trees and partially or totally obscured, giving just enough evidence for the skeptics to dispute and just enough for the believers to support. So is there a bigfoot in Alaska? We'll leave that up to you.

This person saw the bigfoot on one of the many logging roads that go inland from the coast into the interior of the island. However, there have been more than 21 previous sightings in Alaska, and those are just the ones that are in the BFRO database.

Researcher J. Robert Alley has numerous bigfoot incidents in his book *Raincoast Sasquatch*.[12] Alley relates several stories about Revilla' Island, which is the local name for Revillagigedo, named after a Spanish lord.

One of the stories takes place on the nearby island of Annette Island, just south of Ketchikan and Revilla' Island. A man was just south of the town of Metlakatla when he encountered a bigfoot. The man had been walking a gravel road into the mountains when he suddenly saw something running across the road. In the brief encounter the man saw a seven-foot-high bigfoot with light brown fur running quickly across the road.

Another encounter described by a Mrs. K.W. who was driving south on the North Tongass Highway on Revilla' when she saw a bigfoot:

> Late one afternoon in the late 70s, summertime, I had been driving southbound, toward Ketchikan with passengers, coming up on the scenic viewpoint that overlooks Tongass Narrows. As I came around a curve, I noticed a seven-foot, dark, hair-covered creature standing on the right-hand side of the road, just at the edge of the forest. It was on two legs and jumped quickly into the trees and was gone. But it stayed upright as it disappeared into the trees![12]

Alley says that this area of Ketchikan has had numerous sightings. One was by five youths in 1955 and another by a Ketchikan cyclist in 1998. That sighting, by a cyclist named Gerald P. happened in broad daylight in August of 1998.

The cyclist had been visiting friends at the end of the North Tongass Highway at Settler's Cove and was on his bike headed southbound down the highway. The highway is mostly downhill with heavy forest on either side and ditches from the construction of the highway. The cyclist told Alley:

> I had just slowed down from seeing how fast I could go, when I suddenly noticed something standing in the ditch on my left as I went by, less than 20 feet away. It was big and looked like it weighed maybe 275 to 300 pounds, with long arms and dark brown fur. I got a lungful of the most awful gagging smell, like a combination of rotten meat, urine and damp earth. It was opposite me in the bottom of the ditch with its head and shoulders bending down. It was shaped about like a man but larger; it would have been about seven feet tall if it had stood up straight. The hair on the body was a couple of inches long. The hair on the top of the head was longer and matted. Its head was bent over as I went by.
>
> It didn't look up, and I don't think it heard me coast up to where it was. I couldn't see its two legs well, just from the tops of the thighs up, but it was reaching down and looked like it was digging at something in the slope of the ditch nearest me. There were flies buzzing all around it.
>
> It smelled so bad it made me want to throw up. It was shaggy and not really heavily built, it kind of looked like it wasn't doing too well, kind of on the thin side. I know it wasn't a bear. I couldn't see its arms from the forearms down. I thought it might have a dead dog it was digging at or something because of the smell. Its head was down and I couldn't see a neck or its face.
>
> I was scared and started pedaling real hard and heard crunching sounds like wood breaking behind me as I went past. I was scared—I felt my hair go up. I thought maybe it was coming after me, but after fifty feet or so I looked back and it was gone. I guess it went back into the woods on that side. The smell really made me want to gag. I didn't stop pedaling once till I got home in town.[12]

Not all the bigfoot on Revilla' Island were quite as stinky as this one passed by the cyclist. Other witnesses said that they did not hear any sound or smell any odor. Alley goes on to describe some sightings south of Ketchikan at Bugge's Beach, a half north of the town of Saxman. In 1986 some campers witnessed a tall, dark haired sasquatch walk down the trail early in the morning, passing near them.

Alley says there was another sighting in the same area in 1999. Saxman resident Mike V. told Alley that he and a friend had seen a sasquatch from their parked car on a logging road north of Saxman. Said Mike V.:

> ...Some time after midnight we were all surprised to see a seven-foot, dark brown or black, upright creature walk real smooth across the road. It walked into the light about a hundred feet in front of us, left to right.
>
> It was swinging its arms and was heay built. It didn't turn to look at the headlights and continued into the trees. That was it, we stayed a while but it didn't come back.

Alley gives a few more examples of people seeing a bigfoot from their car. Then there is another encounter, in 2001 with a rather stinky sasquatch. This sighting was from a 28-year-old cannery worker named Doug Johnson:

> It was the night of June 8, 2001, and I was taking a drive to the end of the road a few miles past Herring Cove to enjoy the clear skies. It was about 9:30 at night, not really dark and I saw this creature crossing the road just before Achilles Creek, from right to left about 55 yards ahead, walking on two legs across the gravel road, swinging its arms. It was about six feet tall, I would say, and it was covered all over with dark hair, shiny—like it was dripping wet. It was crossing from the Oceanside of the highway, going toward the steep inland side of the road. Before it stepped into the forest I got a good look at how heavy it was built. I'd guess about 300 pounds, anyhow. I didn't slow down and it didn't even seem to turn to look at my car or anything, it was gone in a couple of steps. It was, like, a bit spooky, y'know. I didn't see any other wildlife on that trip. One thing I remember was that there was a lot

of stink to that stretch of the road. I never stopped later to see tracks or anything, but there is a little clam beach just through the trees at that spot, I've fished there before, a pretty quiet spot.[12]

Alley says that just a few weeks later another sighting was made in the same area. On the night of July 4, 2001 a man and his wife and son were taking a stroll along South Tongass Highway when they suddenly saw a dark brown, hairy figure running away from them toward Herring Cove.

Alley also discusses bigfoot sightings on Prince of Wales Island, which is just to the west of Revillagigedo. The Prince of Wales Island is the fourth-largest island in the United States, after Hawaii, Kodiak Island, and Puerto Rico. Alley says that Prince of Wales Island has more logging roads than anywhere in Alaska and it is up these remote logging roads that are hardly used today thats one encounter sasquatch.

Alley says that the main Klawock-Hollis Highway that crosses Prince of Wales Island is also a good place to view bigfoot. In fact, he says that if someone was wanting to see a sasquatch, traveling this highway at night for a month might get you a sighting.

Alley also discusses and has a few photos of dead cedar trees that have been torn up by their roots and then shoved back into the ground with the roots sticking upward. One such tree was photographed in 1999 by Al Jackson and shows a huge, dead 12-foot cedar log that has been thrust upside down into a swampy area east of Klawock Lake on Prince of Wales Island.

Only a bigfoot could do this. Is it a sign from bigfoot that this is his territory? Or is it a sign of a bigfoot wanting to show his strength? Alley also offers photos of other cedars in the vicinity that are uprooted and shoved into the wet ground. This is important information as it shows the efforts a bigfoot will go to mark his territory or to scare off humans. In other areas of the forests in North America the ground would be too hard to shove an uprooted tree into, so they would probably use other signs. We will discuss this more later.

Among the sightings on Prince of Wales Island was that of a hunter who was walking up a gravel road on August 1, 1987, near

Al Jackson and an upturned tree on Prince Edward Island, 1999.

Lab Bay, when he saw a dark haired sasquatch, about five feet tall, moving along the tree line near him. In 1984, near Lab Bay, two sets of footprints of different sizes were found walking together.

A sighting on the Klawock-Hollis Highway in 1993 was by a Mr. I.W. He and his wife were driving back to Klawock at 2:30 am when they saw a dark-haired sasquatch crossing the road in front of them. The husband exclaimed, "Look, a bear," to which his wife responded, "Yes, but look at that! Since when does a bear walk on two legs."[12]

Alley was also told by a Mr. S.W. that he had been driving the Klawock-Hollis Highway with his son one night during the summer of 1997. It was raining lightly when the two spotted a dark haired form in their headlights that was 9 to 10 feet tall. It went from the middle of the highway to the right side of the road, and "wasn't a bear."

Alley also relates the story of Stan Edenshaw and his cousin Mickey Calhoun who often travelled the Hydaburg Highway on Prince of Wales Island. One night in early July 1997 the two were driving at 2:00 am when they saw a 7 to 8 foot hairy man step into the middle of the highway in front of their car. Said Stan Edenshaw:

> It never even looked at us. It was chocolate brown colored and covered all over in six-inch-long hair or fur. ...I don't know exactly but it looked like it would have weighed at least three, maybe four, hundred pounds. We noticed that it hadn't any hair on its face, palms or bottoms of its feet. Mickey wanted to stop and look for tracks and stuff, but I wanted to keep driving. I didn't feel like stopping—if you know what I mean—and we kept driving on to Hydaburg.
>
> It was something that kind of shakes you up for a while, so when we got to Hydaburg, we didn't just hit the sack, we stayed up to tell my grandmother about it. She knew about these hairy men. "People used to see them regularly around twelve mile in the years past," she said. We reported it to the police but besides that, only to our family.[12]

This wild and sparsely populated island seems to be a good place to see a bigfoot. It is interesting to note that they reported it to the police. The police on that island must have gotten a number of bigfoot reports over the years. They, like a lot of police departments in the Pacific Northwest, are probably completely aware of sasquatch in their forests, but they are unlikely to talk about it. With bigfoot, as much as the authorities are concerned, it is better to avoid the subject.

Alley tells several more tales in the year 2002 which are all similar: drivers see a tall, dark and furry bigfoot crossing the road as they drive into town. One witness said that they were surprised to see one so close to town. Indeed, Alaska seems to have more than its share of bigfoot!

He's a real Nowhere Man,
Sitting in his Nowhere Land
Making all his Nowhere Plans for Nobody
—Beatles, *Nowhere Man*

Strange Disappearances at Yosemite National Park

Finally, we need to look at the many strange disappearances at Yosemite National Park. Yosemite National Park is in California's Sierra Nevada Mountains and is famed for its giant, ancient sequoia trees, and the iconic vista of towering Bridalveil Fall and the granite cliffs of El Capitan and Half Dome. President Lincoln signed the Yosemite Grant of 1864 which declared Yosemite federally preserved land. In Yosemite Village there are shops, restaurants, lodging, the Yosemite Museum and the Ansel Adams Gallery. A free bus service takes hikers and other visitors on its roads.

Yosemite receives thousands of visitors a year and occasionally the lone hiker goes missing at the park or nearby. Is a bigfoot or two kidnapping and murdering hikers in this area?

The online San Francisco news site SFGATE (sfgate.com) had a story on November 18, 2021 entitled "The 12 people went missing in Yosemite National Park and haven't been seen again." The story, by Katie Dowd, went on to discuss the recent September

2021 case of missing hiker Joel Thomazin:

With more than 750 miles of trails, Yosemite National Park is a vast, unspoiled wilderness, making it a hiker's dream. But it can quickly become a search-and-rescue nightmare when someone goes missing.

Joel Thomazin, 31, of Denair in Stanislaus County went missing on Sept. 6 on a solo hike in the park. The United States Army reservist planned to hike from Hetch Hetchy to Lake Eleanor, returning Sept. 9. A park ranger saw him on the first day of his hike near a steep section of O'Shaughnesy Dam. That's believed to be the last known sighting of Thomazin.

After months of extensive searching, Thomazin is presumed by his family to have died on that hike. On Dec. 4, his family is planning a memorial service in Turlock, and they're currently raising funds on GoFundMe to help his wife and 2-year-old son.

"Though it's unlikely he is alive, without proof of his whereabouts, Joel is considered a missing person," a post on the GoFundMe explains. "In the state of California, it can take five years to get a death certificate for a missing

A valley view of the Merced River in Yosemite National Park.

Joel Thomazin vanished in Yosemite on September 6, 2021.

person which means his wife, Amanda, can't collect on the things normally available to help bridge the gap such as Joel's life insurance, social security, etc."

Sadly, Thomazin is not the only person who has disappeared without a trace in the massive park. The National Park Service keeps track of cold cases on its website, where it lists a number of still-unsolved Yosemite disappearances.

Here are cases the park service is still hoping to close someday:

Richard Judd, 72, went missing on a day hike from Lower Merced Pass Lake to Red Peak Pass on July 25, 2021. He is 5-foot-11 with brown eyes and gray hair and a beard. He reportedly used white trekking poles and a navy blue daypack and was wearing a dark blue shirt and gray hiking pants when he went missing.

Sandra Johnsen Hughes, 54, has been missing since July 4, 2020. She was camping by herself in the Sierra National Forest when she was involved in a solo vehicle crash. Witnesses who saw her at the crash scene said she refused help. Since the last known sightings of Johnsen-

Richard Judd vanished in Yosemite on July 25, 2021.

Hughes, her sleeping bag and campsite were found abandoned.

Hughes is 5-foot-3 and 150 pounds with brown hair and brown eyes.

Peter Jackson, 74, went missing after texting his son on Sept. 17, 2016, that he was hiking to Yosemite. His campsite was found undisturbed at White Wolf Campground, but no sign of Jackson was found. In 2019, his backpack was discovered between Aspen Valley and Smith Peak. He is 5-foot-10 and 155 pounds, with a gray hair and beard and blue eyes.

George Penca, 30, disappeared on a hike with fellow church members on June 17, 2011. According to his hiking companions, he became separated from the group and was last seen at the top of Upper Yosemite Falls. He is 5-foot-10 and 240 pounds with brown hair and blue eyes, and was last seen wearing either a black T-shirt or tank top and gray sweatpants with a white stripe down the leg.

250

GEORGE PENCA

30 years old, 5'10", 240 pounds
Dark brown hair about 4 inches long, blue eyes, stocky build, speaks English.
Last seen wearing gray sweatpants with white stripe, a black t-shirt that says
"D & B" or a black tank top, gray/blue running shoes, had a blue cloth bag.

Photos taken Friday 6/17/11

Last seen at the top of Upper Yosemite Falls on Friday 06/17/11, at 2:40 pm

**If you were near the top of Upper Yosemite Falls, the Upper Falls Trail, or
any trail between the Valley and Tioga Road on Friday or Saturday 06/17
or 6/18 please call the Yosemite National Park Search and Rescue Office
at (209) 372-0311 or (209)372-0252 whether you have seen George or not.
Your information will help us focus the search area. If you have trouble
getting through you can call (209) 379-1992 at any hour.**

A poster for George Penca who vanished in Yosemite June 17, 2011.

The George Penca case is particularly troublesome. On June
17, 2011, George Penca, 30, went hiking at the Upper Yosemite
Falls in Yosemite National Park. George was from Hawthorne
in California and was visiting the National Park with his church
group of 80 people of which around 20 people were walking the
Upper Yosemite Fall trail that day.

The group separated at the top, with the hikers going back down
at their own pace. George most likely fell behind the main group.
His friends assumed he'd hiked back to the Yosemite Valley floor
earlier and didn't report him missing until 9 p.m. that evening. In
the meantime, George had vanished off the trail.

251

Initial search efforts began on June 17, 2011, after George was reported missing and a full-scale search and rescue operation was initiated the next day. The massive search could not find any trace of George Penca. On June 23, 2011, search efforts transitioned to a limited continuous search. After nearly one week of intensive searching, park rangers did not find any clues as to George's whereabouts.

What happened to Penca? His bag, clothes or remains have never been located. He was the last guy on the trail and he vanished. Was he abducted by a bigfoot? Unfortunately this seems to be the likely conclusion.

The SFGATE article then continued its list of the missing with the disappearance of Michael Ficery in 2005:

> Michael Ficery, 51, was believed to be hiking in Tiltill Valley on June 21, 2005, when he went missing. He is 5-foot-10 and 165 pounds with shoulder-length gray hair and was last seen wearing a faded blue T-shirt, olive or khaki shorts and a faded red scarf. He also wears glasses.

> Walther H. Reinhard, 66, went missing on Sept. 19, 2002, in Yosemite National Park. National Park Service/ Handout Walther H. Reinhard, 66, likely went for a hike on the White Wolf Trailhead around Sept. 19, 2002; his car was found at the trailhead a few weeks later. He was 5-foot-8 and 145 pounds with graying hair. It is not known what he was wearing, although he often hiked with a large fanny pack.

> Ruthanne Ruppert, 49, was supposed to be going on a backpacking trip on Aug. 14, 2000, but reportedly had to delay it because of an infection. She was last seen either at the Yosemite Medical Clinic or Curry Village that day, and

Ruthanne Ruppert.

witnesses believe she may have gone on a day hike from Yosemite Falls to Foresta. In 2008, her backpack was found near Fireplace Creek, which is along that route. She is 5-foot-5 and 140 pounds with brown hair and eyes; one of her eyes is a prosthetic.

The case of Ruthanne Ruppert is another strange case where she completely vanishes from a short hike in the afternoon. An exhaustive search for her finds nothing. Eight years later her backpack is discovered in 2008 in a drainage area of Fireplace Creek. There was no other sign of her and her disappearance remains unsolved. Was Ruppert abducted and killed by a bigfoot who then discarded her backpack eight years later? Her body was probably discarded as well, but will never be found.

The SFGATE article continued on, reporting on Kieran Burke, a visitor from Ireland:

Kieran Burke, 45, was visiting from Dublin, Ireland, on a hiking trip in April 2000. He was discovered missing on April 6, 2000, when park staff noticed he hadn't checked out of his lodging. He was last seen the day before at Curry Village, possibly on his way to hike alone. His family said he was an experienced hiker. He is 6 feet tall and 180 pounds with black hair and blue eyes.

David Paul Morrison, 28, set off from Yosemite Valley to hike Half Dome in the early morning hours of May 25, 1998. He did not return. He is 5-foot-9 and 150 pounds with brown hair and eyes, and was last wearing a gray UCSC sweatshirt, black pants, Nike running shoes and a fanny pack.

Timothy John Barnes, 25, disappeared on a day hike to Polly Dome Lakes on July 5, 1988.

David Paul Morrison.

Witnesses last saw him on the Murphy Creek Trailhead around 9 a.m. He is 6-foot-3 and 180 pounds with dark hair and a mustache, and was last seen wearing a white T-shirt with a red letter "F" on it, gray sweatpants, white tennis shoes and a yellow daypack.

Stacey Ann Arras, 14, departed on a four-day camping trip with her father on July 17, 1981. They rode mules with a group of 10 other campers to Sunrise High Sierra Camp. After arriving, Arras wanted to take a short hike to Sunrise Lakes. She departed with a 77-year-old man in their group. The man quickly wearied and took a break while Arras went onward. She was never seen again. She is 5-foot-5 and 120 pounds with blond hair. She left the camp wearing a white windbreaker, maroon-and-white striped shorts and gray hiking boots.

Dikran Knadjian, 20, was on summer break from Cambridge University in England, where he was a medical school student. He was last seen in Curry Village on July 24, 1972, asking an employee for directions to Half Dome. He is 5-foot-11 and 180 pounds with brown hair and eyes, and was last seen with his Pentax 35mm camera.

This is the end of the article of the vanished people in Yosemite National Park, having happened since 1972.

The Stacey Arras case is particularly strange. Fourteen-year-old Stacey Arras, from Saratoga, California, went on a mule riding trip in July 1981 with her father, George, and eight others in the Sunrise Meadows area of Yosemite National Park in California. After riding a few hours, they stopped at some cabins at Sunrise High Sierra Camp, around three miles southeast of Tenaya Lake.

The group decided to freshen up after the ride, having planned to stay the night. Sunrise camp is 9,400 feet above sea level where nine cabins provide beds for 34 guests and it is set against a lovely alpine meadow facing Mt. Florence and Mt. Clark.

Stacey cleaned up, showered and changed clothes. An older member of the group, Gerald Stuart was sitting on a boulder about

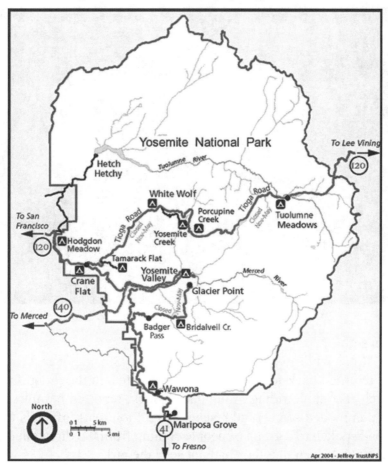

100 feet away from the cabins. Stacey told her Dad she would go for a walk close to where Gerald was sitting to stretch her legs after the mule ride and to take some photos of the views. She asked her Dad if he wanted to go with her, but he told her he'd pass. The last conversation she had with her Dad related to her footwear, where he advised her to change from her flip-flops to hiking boots.

Everybody saw her go walking over to the boulder and take some pictures. Subsequently, she told Gerald Stuart she was going to take a walk to a nearby lake. Stacey planned to take some more pictures of the lake and he offered to accompany her.

After a little while down the hill the elderly man felt tired and sat down; the rest of the group watching from up above saw the man sit down. They all watched as Stacey went on a little further towards the lake, go behind some trees and eventually disappear

255

A view of Bridleveil Falls in Yosemtie.

from sight.

After a while, when Stacey didn't return, Gerald got concerned and returned back to the cabin area and gathered the group for a search. The mule riding group had no luck, reported her missing and summoned search and rescue. Gerald told park officials that he had spoken to a group of people coming from the direction that Stacey had taken, but they had not seen the girl.

A huge search involving 100-150 people, including 67 Mountain Rescue Association volunteers, and sniffer dogs were deployed over 10 days, concentrating on a 3-5 square mile area around Sunrise Lakes. Three helicopters were also used in the search. Despite the efforts of SAR (Search and Rescue) teams, the only thing ever found was the lens cap from Stacey's camera, just inside the tree line from where she walked into the area by the lake.

The police concluded that she had been abducted, but they could not explain it. Was Stacey attacked at the spot where her lens cap was found? Was she suddenly abducted by a bigfoot? Who else would have been capable of abducting her—aliens? No sign of her has ever been found except for the lens cap to her camera.

256

But there are other deaths and vanishings in this wild national park. This list is by no means complete. There are others who have gone missing in Yosemite. One is the shocking death of Evelyn Consuela Rosemann who was found dead at Yosemite in 1968.

The Death of Evelyn Consuela Rosemann

Evelyn Consuela Rosemann, 24, was a masseuse in San Francisco who ventured to Yosemite in October 1968 to do some hiking. She set out on a three-day solo hike and her body was found by three hikers on October 19, 1968, 200 feet from the base of the 594-foot-high Nevada Falls in Yosemite National Park.

According to investigators, Evelyn had somehow "been launched" from the fall or cliff and hadn't jumped. She had also been found partially undressed. During October, the creek leading to the fall is at a very low water level and she would not have been swept away.

She wore a pair of badly torn corduroy pants that were pulled down near her ankles, and her sweater had been pulled up over her head. Another of Evelyn's sweaters was lying on a rock near her feet and her purse was found on the bridge above Nevada Falls.

The autopsy found the cause of death appeared to be a massive head injury sustained in the fall. Parts of her brain were found on a rock fifty feet from her body. The pathologist discovered she had been sexually assaulted either pre- or postmortem with indications of bloodless vaginal lacerations.

Unfortunately, because this dates to 1968 there is little information on Evelyn's case. How did she end up so far from the base of the cliff? The National Park thought it was probably foul play given the vaginal lacerations. The Park Service decided not to publicize the incident with concerns that park visitors might be scared away by publicity about a potential serial killer in the area.

This disturbing case has all the indications of a bigfoot sexual assault and murder. It seems that Evelyn was attacked by a bigfoot on the bridge above Nevada Falls while standing there alone. Afterward

257

she was thrown off the bridge—launched—where she fell to her death, if she were not already dead.

It is said that she had bloodless virginal lacerations so she may have been dead when she was sexually assaulted. Because her body was recovered and autopsied relatively soon after her disappearance and death we have the important evidence that she was sexually assaulted. Did another hiker, some depraved rapist, do this to Evelyn? It would rather seem to be a bigfoot attack.

We must assume that some of the disappearing women around Yosemite and elsewhere may have been abducted and sexually assaulted by a bigfoot. This would not seem to be the case with children or adult males. Children are generally left unharmed by bigfoot when kidnapped, but if not released within a few days, they will die of starvation, trauma and exposure. We do have the curious story told in chapter four of the Navaho baby who survived 10 years with a bigfoot family and later returned to her tribe.

At any rate, it would seem to be very dangerous to hike by oneself in certain areas of Yosemite National Park.

Among the other deaths and disappearances at Yosemite is the 2018 disappearance of Maximillian "Max" L. Schweitzer, 41, in January. Schweitzer's LinkedIn profile claimed he was a Clandestine Analyst at the U.S. Department of Homeland Security.

Schweitzer is believed to have gone to Yosemite around January 1-3, 2018. His rental car was found at the Camp 4 parking on January 5, because the car was reported overdue by the rental company. No family had reported him missing.

He was seen hiking wearing a light-colored, long-sleeve shirt, shorts, and a dark-colored backpack. Max remains missing after his hike in Yosemite. Did Schweitzer succumb to foul play or did he intend to disappear? Was he a victim of a bigfoot?

Another disappearance and death at Yosemite was that of Timothy Nolan who vanished

A Max Schweitzer missing poster.

on September 9, 2015. His body was eventually found on September 15, nearly a week later. Timothy Nolan, 36, had a wilderness permit to backpack from Happy Isles to Tuolumne Meadows and began that hike on September 1. When Nolan failed to show up on September 9 at the trailhead called Happy Isles a search for him began immediately.

The search included park rangers, dog teams and the park's helicopter. No trace of Nolan could be found. Visitors to the park later spotted his body on the afternoon of September 15th. He was found on a well-

Bigfoot sex books do exist.

traveled trail in the High Sierra Camp Loop. The National Park Service would not say how Nolan died, citing privacy concerns. This would make you think that suicide was part of the explanation, but no one has indicated at all that this is the case, and it seems he was a happy hiker until he died.

Online investigations concerning Timothy Nolan's death seem to suggest that he had some sort of accident at the end of his hike. But it would seem that he was abducted and killed by a bigfoot. This is because he disappeared for a week and then was discovered on a well-traveled trail that would have been searched in the week before. There was a helicopter as part of the six-day search as well.

Was Nolan so torn up and disfigured that the authorities did not want to release the condition that the body was in? Or for that matter, the cause of death? Photos would have been taken of the death scene as well. It seems that these photos will never be released.

There were other mysterious deaths in Yosemite National Park in the autumn of 2015. On September 1, the National Park Service announced it had found the body of James Michael Millet, Jr., who had been missing for three weeks. Millet, 39, had gone missing during a planned hike to Upper Yosemite Falls. What caused his death?

Then, on September 6, 2015, Matthew Baldwin, a 24-year-old graduate student studying at the University of Nevada, Reno, was found dead near the El Capitan Gully. He had vanished on August 25 while going on a solo hike. Where had Baldwin been for two weeks? What caused his death? Was it an encounter and abduction by a bigfoot?

It seems that hiking around Yosemite National Park by oneself could be dangerous. In fact, bigfoot himself is dangerous. He is strong and crafty. He can kill or abduct in an instant. He has no compunction about kidnapping little children or abducting adults. He strikes without warning. He will scare you stiff if you encounter him. He is the boogeyman.

Chapter 9

I HEAR YOU KNOCKIN!

Shrunken head and Mardi Gras Beads
Hanging on a rearview mirror on the beach
Keepin' their eyes on the open road
No tellin' where that son-a-bitch goes
—John Hiatt, *The Open Road*

One of the constant themes found in bigfoot research is that of loud sounds in woods of a thick tree branch or club being hit against a tree. If the tree is partly hollow then the sound can be quite deep and carry for long distances.

What is making these strange wood-knocking noises in the woods? While there is the possibility that they are being made by humans either for fun, as a hoax, or they are trying to signal bigfoot themselves—it is generally thought that these noises are being made by bigfoot.

In an article on its webpages, the Kalamazoo radio station WRKR (wrkr.com) published a story on September 27, 2016 entitled "What Does a Wood Knock Warning Deep in the Michigan Woods Mean?"

The author, Eric Meier, said:

Say you're spending some time in the great north woods of Michigan. All of a sudden you hear the distinct sound of wood knocking together. Any idea what that would indicate? Those who believe in the Bigfoot phenomenon say the wood knocking is a warning from the creature not to venture any further into their lands.

261

The possibility of Bigfoot in Michigan came up recently when a viral video claimed to capture an unidentified creature on a trail cam. Odd creatures are no stranger to the Michigan woods. The most commonly spoke of being the Dogman.

This video comes from the Smoky Mountains and contains the sounds purported to be the Bigfoot knocking.

There are several videos then posted on the Radio WRKR website with wood-knocking sounds that can be seen here: https://wrkr.com/wood-knock-warning/

It is all interesting and clearly this Michigan radio station wants to report on the latest bigfoot activity, including wood knocks. The subject of bigfoot screaming and whooping plus knocking on trees with branches is something of a specialty subject but it is a strong theme that runs through bigfoot research, much in the same way as photographing and making casts of bigfoot footprints. Probably the first to display the scream of a bigfoot was Roger Patterson in his early career before Gimlin took the famous film footage.

Arizona cryptozoologist David Weatherly has been investigating paranormal activity including bigfoot for several decades. In 2016 he published the first of his "Journals of Sasquatch Research" which was titled *Wood Knocks: Volume One*.[46]

This book was followed four more volumes also titled *Wood Knocks*. The first volume has articles by David Weatherly, Linda Godfrey, Ken Gerhard, Nick Redfern, Micah Hanks and others. One of the articles is by Lyle Blackburn who wrote the 2012 book *The Beast of Boggy Creek*.[35]

Weatherly collects all kinds of interesting bigfoot/sasquatch tales in his *Wood Knocks* volumes and it is a good title that evokes the nuances of bigfoot research."If you hear some knockin' then better not come rockin," you might say. The warning sign of bigfoot is there for those who want to hear. Let us look at some fairly recent wood knock incidents from the USA.

Strange Knocking in a New York Swamp

A Bigfoot Research Organization (bfro.net) report was filed in 2020 about some strange knocking heard in the Great Croton Swamp south of Pawling, New York. The incident said that the date was May 18, 2020 and that it happened in the small village of Patterson, near the Patterson Rec Center and access to the swamp.

The anonymous witness said:

> I was having a small campfire last night alone with my small dog who at the time was sleeping. First there was something moving through the wooded area to my left. Sounded like it was on two feet and moving towards some neighbors' houses. Wasn't alarmed by this, although it was dark and there was no flashlight; the neighbors do walk through there from time to time. My dog wasn't alerted at all. This part of the incident may be just coincidental but it's what happened next that I'm curious about. About five to ten minutes later to the left of me way off in the distance there was an obvious wood knock then immediately to the right of me in the distance but in that direction is the Great Croton Swamp was a reply wood knock and then immediately after that another from the left. Then nothing. I've never heard anything like that before. It was about 11 pm and the neighborhood was quiet and in my opinion it was an obvious call and response. Are wood knocks usually so instantaneous or do they usually have some time in between? (Bfro.net)

This phenomenon of a knock in one area and then an immediate knock from the opposite direction, or such, would mean that two bigfoot are communicating. This person was not spending the night, appears to have been just having a campfire in his back yard near the rec center of the small town. Had he been in a more remote area and spending the night, he could have been in a dangerous situation.

The Associated Press reported on August 18, 2019 that the Kisatchie National Forest in Central Louisiana was being scoured by bigfoot researchers. The report said that a bigfoot researcher who calls himself "Tex-La" communicates with bigfoot by letting out a series of howls in an area that he and another researcher, named Claude, believe is an area of bigfoot activity. In a demonstration witnessed by the reporter, several seconds went by after the researchers let loose four howls, and then in the distance, four howls answered back. Tex-La and Claude sent out another four howls and after several more seconds, those howls were also answered back. Were they howls from a bigfoot?

"It is what it is. If you choose to believe that's great. If you choose not to believe, that's great, too," said Tex-La. He recorded the howls and will study them later. He says everything has its own distinct sound—even bigfoot.

Claude and Tex-La have left audio devices camouflaged in the trees. Sometimes cameras are left to record nighttime activity. Those recordings, which are hours long, are studied and analyzed. To avoid harassment and ridicule from those who don't believe in bigfoot, Tex-La and Claude from Baton Rouge don't want to disclose their full names or the locations in Kisatchie National Forest where they are researching. "A lot of people don't want to come forward because they don't want to be intimidated," said Tex-La about other bigfoot researchers. Most don't like to discuss their interest in Bigfoot for fear of repercussions in their jobs or social standings in the community. They also want to avoid those who want to prank them. And Tex-La has had his share of pranks played on him over the years.

"It's something you have to approach with an open mind," said Tex-La about researching bigfoot. Kisatchie National Forest spans 600,000 acres across Central Louisiana. Tex-La and Claude are investigating an area between Georgetown and Jena where there have been reports of bigfoot sightings. Claude does most research during the day when he can see tracks, but there are times when he might do a night trek. "Finding a spot is the luck of the draw," said Claude. "This area here is in the middle of highly visible eyewitness activity." Claude said he got fairly good results at the first place he researched. He was able to get photos of bigfoot tracks in that area.

Bigfoot Noises Around Bailey, Colorado

Bailey, Colorado is said to be a hotspot for bigfoot activity. The town has the Sasquatch Outpost, essentially a museum and gift shop, which has put Bigfoot Crossing signs around the town. Bailey is in Park County and just west along Highway 285 is Jefferson, an unincorporated community that is virtually in the center of Colorado.

A recent report of bigfoot comes from a mother and daughter hiking near Jefferson, Colorado on August 28, 2018. According to a BFRO report made shortly after the incident (bfro.net, case 60877) a mother and her daughter were hiking in an area called North Twin Cone when they apparently encountered a bigfoot. Said the woman in her report:

> We were hiking the road at Kenosha Pass on the east side that takes you to the Twin Cones above the tree line. We began our hike at noon and hiked up the road. We reached the Twin Cone tree line area at 3:30 p.m. It was a beautiful and uneventful hike until we were headed back down the road. My daughter had said she thought that she had heard a tree knock and I was being silly and took a rock and knocked [it] on a large rock off of the road and then tossed the rock about 5 feet off of the road. Literally two minutes later we both heard multiple tree knocking and rocks were whizzing past our heads.

Along with her 21-year-old daughter the woman noted an "unbearable" smell and the reality that they were encountering a bigfoot set in. Her daughter began to scream and cry.

The woman said in her report, "I was so startled that I just stood there frozen as this dark figure was staring back at me."

The rock throwing went on for about five minutes and then the woman realized that she had an air horn and blew it three times. This seemed to stop the rock throwing, but the woman thought that the creature was hostile to them. They walked back to their vehicle and left the area about 6:15 p.m. She thought that she and her daughter had been lucky not to have gotten hit by any of the rocks thrown their way.

In another report on the BFRO site filed by Rod Lopez in 2020, he says that he had been camping with his children in the Spring of 2014 near the Lost Creek Wilderness near Bailey when he heard whoops and knocking. He relates how he likes to get away from Denver and camp in this area. Says Lopez of his interesting incident:

> I have a spot near Tarryall Reservoir I have camped at several times before. It's a few miles off the main dirt road up a jeep trail and during the week there are usually not many people there. I like it because it's on a ridgeline overlooking a small valley. It's at the end of the Jeep trail, so on the way up and once I'm there I can easily tell if anyone is in the area or coming up on our camp.
>
> We got there on a Thursday morning and I didn't see anyone on the way nor hear anyone down in the valley below us.
>
> I had heard bigfoot stories like everyone else but never thought about it or gave them much credit. I figured it was like alien abductions or something. Weird stories that happened in people's imaginations but not real. I do know it wasn't on my mind when we arrived. We set up and hung out the entire day around camp. The plan was to stay 3-4 nights. We didn't have a fire because there was a fire ban at the time. That night the kids went to bed as soon as it got dark. I went to bed around 11:30 pm or so.
>
> I was lying in my sleeping bag for about 20 minutes messing with my phone to see if I could get coverage and play some games. I could hear coyotes start to howl and bark down in the valley below us, where I believe they had a few dens. In the middle of this coyote chatter and barking I hear, about a quarter mile in the valley below, this startlingly sound I have never heard before. I have spent years in the mountains. I have heard just about every animal sound there is. With the exception of coyotes,

an occasional owl, ranchers' cattle, and very rarely a screaming mountain lion most animals stay quiet at night. I heard two deep "WHOOOOP" WHOOOP" sounds coming from about a quarter mile in the small valley below. The howling from the coyotes instantly stopped and remained silent.

At first I thought maybe it was some drunk campers messing around. I had driven through the valley the day before and had seen no one there. Again I hear another series of loud whooping calls. I am running through my head what animal it could be. A bear? A mountain lion? Some sort of crane or bird? I hear it again. Did some ape escape the zoo and get loose in the mountains? I start hearing what sounds likes someone beating two large pieces of firewood together. These sounds go on for another good 10-15 minutes.

After it was over I stayed awake for several hours waiting for the noises to return. At the time I am thinking some idiots came in late to camp and were screwing around in the woods. The next day I walk down to the area I heard the noises come from, to check to see if anyone was there. Not a soul. I thought maybe whoever was there had packed up early and left.

We spent the rest of the day at camp and hiking around. Later that afternoon, before dinner I shot some of the rifles I had brought. Amazingly my kids had slept through the previous night's noises and I didn't tell them about it. I didn't want to scare them for no reason. The kids went to bed around 9:30 and I stayed up. I figured I would stay up a bit later to see if the sounds would return.

About midnight I decided to turn in and get some sleep. I lay awake in my sleeping bag for quite awhile. I still couldn't sleep. Eventually I started to nod off thinking nothing was going to happen that night and whoever had been messing around the night before was gone.

I am guessing it was maybe 30 minutes into a very light sleep later that I was startled awake to the sound of two very deep, and loud "WHOOOOP" "WHOOOOP" sounds. This time the sounds were much louder because the sounds were coming from about 70 yards from our camp near the jeep road below us.

I am both half scared and half very pissed. I quickly jump out of the tent. I'm now thinking the jerks from the night before have decided to make this personal and have been stalking our camp and think it's funny to wake us up in the middle of the night. I never go out in the woods without a rifle and a good light. (I have run into idiots out in the woods before.) I heard the whooping noise a couple more times while I started to walk down the slope of the ridge about 25 yards. I was thinking if these people were armed I didn't want to engage in gunfight in the middle of my camp.

I scanned the tree line with my rifle mounted light looking for movement. Each time changing positions after each scan. As I moved a bit further something off to my right and about 30-40 yards away went crashing through the woods. I know what somebody running through the woods sounds like. Whatever this was, it was very big and very heavy. I am thinking, "What the heck, is Shaquille O'Neal with them?" It was running very fast and covering more ground than an average person could. It was also snapping branches and small trees like they were just grass. I could hear the heavy pounding of its large footsteps.

At this point, my heart is pounding in my chest as I hightail it back to the camp. I don't know if this person is running away or trying to flank me.

I was now debating in my head on what to do. Wake the kids (I have no idea to this day how they slept through this) and break camp and leave knowing they will be scared to death when I do?

The downside to that is there will be no one to watch

our backs as we pack up and I get them up, we'll make a lot of noise loading the truck, and the trip outputs us down the jeep trail where I was hearing the noises to begin with. I elect my second option. I find a spot in the trees and shadows where I can observe camp and silhouette anyone approaching against the skyline without silhouetting myself.

If anyone comes up the hill I will hit them with the light and confront and engage them if I have to. I figure anyone sneaking around my camp at night doing these things can't have good intentions.

I didn't sleep the rest of the night. I sat waiting with my back against the tree the entire time. I never told the kids. I made up some excuse why we had to leave early that morning and never explained why I was so exhausted. Though the idea of bigfoot was in the back of my mind that second night, for whatever reason my logical side wanted to explain it off as some assholes playing games in the woods.

Over the next week, after we got back home, I couldn't shake both the question of what those noises were and was there a possibility that it was a bigfoot. I didn't really know what a bigfoot would sound like so I started searching google for "bigfoot sounds." That's when I came across this video.

Lopez then gives us this YouTube video to listen to and then resumes his story:
https://www.youtube.com/watch?v=PuDRpYLsP5c

At point :22 of the video I found the exact noises I heard that night. I have listened to it over a dozen times since. I also did some more research on the area. To my surprise I discovered that not only does the area have many reports of bigfoot sightings and encounters but that it is listed as one of the top 10 places to encounter bigfoot in the United States. I also found out there had been a documentary filmed in the area a few years before and featured in the film was Observatory Peak which I could see from my camp a few miles away. There have been so many sightings in the area that the nearby town of Bailey has since placed bigfoot crossing signs along their small town roads.

Now when I go up to that area my mindset is a bit different. I look over my shoulder a bit more and I search the tree lines for anything that might be watching me. We went backpacking on the other side of the mountain last year. It was hard to sleep because I was waiting to hear those whoops again. I don't know what it was for sure that night but I don't think it was human.

BFRO investigator and co-host of "Finding Bigfoot" on the Animal Planet Channel (2010-2017) Matthew Moneymaker personally looked into this bigfoot report and said:

The location described in this report is in Pike National Forest south of Lost Creek Wilderness. When "Lost Creek Wilderness area" is mentioned as one of the best Bigfoot areas in the country, that does not mean only the designated wilderness area. It means the whole zone around Lost Creek Wilderness, including areas near Bailey.

Bailey is one of many bigfoot hotspots where wood knocking and vocal noises can be heard. The North Woods of Maine has a lot of wood knocking it seems.

That Knock, Knock, Knocking in Maine

In her book *Bigfoot in Maine*,[39] Michelle Souliere tells the curious story of a bigfoot encounter in May of 2007. Souliere says that she got an email from a man named Jeff who told her a curious story about a 16-acre pond on Moro Plantation in Aroostook County named Green Pond.

This pond offered good fishing for trout and Jeff had fished there before a number of times. The road to the pond was a dirt road that dead-ended near the pond. Jeff walked the swampy trail to the pond and then got into waders, a fisherman's float tube, and then put on flippers over his wader boots. This was always quite a tricky process, Jeff told Souliere. However, once he was set in his waders and floatation device, he could move quietly about the pond fishing. It was a still day with no wind and he fished for several hours until about 11 in the morning.

At this time he heard two loud knocks on a ridge on the opposite shoreline of the pond. He thought it an odd sound, like someone swinging a baseball bat twice at a tree.

He continued fishing for about two more hours when he heard a sharp crack that sounded like a large tree limb being snapped from a tree or broken in two. This came from the wooded ridge close to the shore. Jeff continued fishing.

Then there was a single sharp knock coming from the side of the pond where Jeff was fishing. It seemed to have come from the dirt road that leads to the pond. Something had been encircling Jeff and making the knocks. Yet, Jeff ignored this and continued fishing until there was only about an hour of daylight left. Suddenly he heard a great roar come from the direction of his truck.

It lasted for about five seconds and all the hair on Jeff's body stood up. Supremely frightened, he headed for shore as fast as he could. Once he hit the shore he did not bother to take off his fins as he ran and hopped to his truck. Once there he flung off the floatation tube and tore his flippers off, tossing them in the back of the truck. Knowing that the bigfoot must be nearby, Jeff started the truck and drove off while still in his boots and waders. After about half an hour he reached the town of Patten and stopped to check his things and take off the waders. He thought about the whole ordeal and realized that the bigfoot had encircled him while making the knocks.

Jeff said he was back in the same town ten years later and spoke with several people who had also fished in the pond or knew others that had. One person told Jeff they had been at Green Pond and heard a terrible roar that frightened them. Another person told of having pretty large rocks thrown at them while they were in the pond by someone in the distance who could not be seen.

It seems that there are some ponds in the North Woods that one should be careful fishing in! When one hears that knocking, it might be best to leave the area. Such knocking could also bring other bigfoot into the area.

Souliere tells another story of a Jeff Robertson who lived in Livermore Falls in the Androscoggin River area for many years. Robertson told Souliere that in the spring of 2011 he was in the forest behind his house with his son Seth looking for fern fiddles to collect and eat. Suddenly his son called for Jeff to look at something. It was a huge and perfect footprint much larger than his size 12 boot. They took a photo and then noticed other footprints nearby. Each had very clear toes without any claws—a big toe and four smaller toes.

That summer Robertson began to notice strange things around the house and coming from the woods behind his house. He heard loud knocking in the forest that he could not explain. He heard a funny "Whooooo," which was answered by three tree knocks. He heard other vocalizations at night and tree knocking, and his birdfeeder was broken several times. The first time he found it on the ground and simply fixed it and put it back up. This happened again and he fixed it and put it back.

Then, on the third time that the birdfeeder was torn down, Robertson was awake and smoking by the window just before dawn one morning. He saw the broken feeder and just for fun he let out a big "WhooooOOOOooo" as he had heard on the television show *Finding Bigfoot*.

Suddenly a bigfoot about six feet tall with black fur darted out from near the birdfeeder and ran into the woods. Robertson said that the creature turned and look back at him just as it entered the woods. He said that it had dark eyes, a squashed nose, and not much hair on its face. He said that he wanted to yell, "Hey what are you doing?" but he was too afraid at the time. We might assume that the knocking continued for some time after this.[39]

It seems that this may have been a juvenile bigfoot and possibly a female. Taking food from birdfeeders, orchards or chicken coops is a common pastime for bigfoot. That and making wood knocks.

The Mogollon Monster is Knocking

The Mogollon Rim is a large pine forest and wilderness area that stretches from Mogollon Mountain on the New Mexico-Arizona border and Flagstaff, Arizona. There are numerous lakes with wild berry patches and forests full of deer and elk. It is known as the domain of the Mogollon Monster, who is a bigfoot. There must be a substantial community of bigfoot in the area.

There are few towns or even villages in this area, but the ones that are there include towns such as Strawberry and nearby Pine, and villages such as Happy Jack and Clint's Wells.

In the Mogollon Rim area of Arizona, with the nearest town being Strawberry, a man named

Bigfoot gets into politics.

John Johnson reported on July 10, 1999 to Oregonbigfoot.com that he had camped with a friend a few days earlier, and they had a sasquatch visit their camp. Johnson claimed that they heard strange screaming noises like a banshee's one night. On the next night he and his friend heard what sounded like pounding on a hollow log. This occurred off and on through the night and the next morning they discovered an old tree that had been torn to pieces by some powerful being. Said Johnson, "You would have to be Hercules to do this to a tree." (Oregonbigfoot.com file #00503)

A woman reported that on July 12, 2015 she was awoken at a cabin by whooping sounds. She and her two children were staying at a remote cottage 12 miles down a dirt road at an undisclosed spot on the Mogollon Rim. Wrote the woman in her report to BFRO:

> It was a Sunday afternoon and I went to stay at a cabin we rented, with my two children, for the night. We were escaping the heat of Phoenix and it was a beautiful day, clear, sunny and no rain or clouds.
>
> That night we were asleep in the cabin but I kept waking up because I was on a very uncomfortable cot. As I lay there trying to fall asleep again, I heard what sounded like a "whoop." This was followed by a clear wood knock sound. They were about 8-10 seconds apart.

I lay there listening and about 1 minute later, I heard the same "whoop" and again, followed up by another knock about 10 seconds later. They seemed to both come from the same direction (SE of the cabin). I was the only one who heard it as the kids were asleep, and I didn't tell them as I didn't want to spook them. The sounds sounded close, I'm guessing within 50 yards since I was able to hear them while inside the cabin.

...about 10:30, earlier that night, shortly after we climbed in bed, I was trying to fall asleep while the two kids were playing games on their Ipods. All of a sudden a rap noise hit the window on the south side of the cabin. Immediately, the kids look at me and say, "What was that?!" The sound was like a small pebble hitting the window. Again, it was clear and no wind. I played it off to the kids that it was probably just a moth or bug hitting the window, and it may have been just that. But then I heard the whoop and knocks later in the night and wondered if something was watching us. Whenever we camp, we always set up a camera trap, for the fun of it, to see what wanders into the camp. I did so on this night, too, and it was set up in front of the cabin, but it had zero hits on it.

As we drove down the road to the cabin we saw only 2-3 other camping parties along the roughly 12-mile stretch to get to the cabin. It was Sunday afternoon about 2PM when we drove to the cabin. But when we left the next morning about 7AM, they had all left—assumedly the previous afternoon since it was a Sunday. So we were the only ones in the area 12 miles back in the woods. We passed one truck near the main road as we left Monday morning but that was it.

It is interesting that they had set up a camera trap, and that there was no male present at the cabin, just a young mother and two children. With all the other campers having left, perhaps this was the only cabin worth being curious about. Sometimes a camping trip is just a camping trip. Sometimes a camping trip is bigfoot nightmare.

274

On October 6, 2012 it was reported to BFRO that two friends on a motorcycle camping trip heard strange sounds around their campsite south of Jacob Lake near the North Rim of the Grand Canyon. They were sleeping in their tents when, at about 2:30 a.m., they were awakened by screams. The sounds made the hair on their necks stand up and went on for about five minutes. They were convinced that it was bigfoot making the vocalizations.

Sex with bigfoot is taboo.

BFRO reports that on August 15, 2010 a bigfoot disturbed a camper in a high country forest with strange noises. Says the report:

At about 12 AM, I was awoken to the sound of two sticks cracking together near my RV trailer. The knocking sounded as if somebody had two girthy sticks, maybe about 2 inches in diameter, and they were banging them together at a perfect 2 second interval. Sometimes the sticks sounded a little different as if a knot had been struck but the timing was never flawed. ...I have never heard a known animal make this sound, let alone in perfect repetition for the duration that I heard it. But that wasn't the strangest part; the sound was translating through the forest quickly and without making additional sounds. The sound was emanating from an area on the backside of my trailer and receding away. It would then come closer and recede again. This was happening over and over. I would say that it was probably about 20 to 30 yards at the closest and went out an additional 50 to 70 yards away. My campsite was near a primitive road and the sound seemed to parallel the road but I can't be sure.

After lying in bed, listening to this for about 2 minutes, I decided that I needed to do something about this thing that was disturbing my camp. Familiar with the observance that bigfoots knocked wood, a bigfoot did come to mind instantly, but I felt that as the patriarch, I needed to investigate and protect my family. My family members were all three asleep ...I did not turn on any lights and was absolutely silent, feeling around for my clothes, shoes and pistol. Once dressed, I moved silently to the trailer door, being careful not to shake the trailer or create any noises. This was actually quite easy because there is a door adjacent to my bed. I waited until the cracking sound had receded as far away as it sounded like it was going to get. And remember, the sound was emanating from the opposite side of my trailer. I slowly opened the door, again careful not to make a noise. The knocking sound continued. This is the part that freaks me out the most: as soon as I stepped outside, the knocking sound that seemed as far away from me as possible, stopped.

Now the story does not stop there. I had a lousy flashlight (unlit) in one hand and my pistol in the other. I proceeded around the front of my trailer to the other side. Once I was on the other side, I was confronted by the pitch black woods in which I was certain that there were a couple of unknown creatures. Having the distinct feeling that there was something to the rear of my trailer, I shined the lousy flashlight directly towards the rear. This only lit up the two very large pine trees that were about twelve feet in front of me. Shining the flashlight did however elicit a response. As soon as I shone the light, directly in front of me, but on the other side of the trees, perhaps about 20 to 40 yards away, something let out a "whoop, whoop." It was clear, it was distinct and it was amazing. Before this incident, I had never heard on TV that bigfoot made a "whoop, whoop" sound, so I am certain that this was not in my head. At that moment, I knew that there was something different from an elk, a bear, an owl, etc that was disturbing my camp. And I also knew that there was more than one. I felt that this was an alert call signaling any additional creatures to leave the area.

His wife came to the door of the trailer just then and the creature silently disappeared. He said that he thought about the bad odor that was often said to come with bigfoot but he says he did not smell anything at all. The next day he looked for tracks but could not find any. He did find two thick sticks from a ponderosa pine that made a similar sound when he banged them together as the one he had heard in the night.

In July of 2011, a mother camping with her children heard possible late-night vocalizations in the Knoll Lake area of the Mogollon Rim. Said the witness in her report filing with BFRO:

> It was in the middle of the night on a trip when I took my three kids camping. I was awoken by strange noises. The noises sounded like an angry female with a smoker's voice screaming in short bursts. Probably 5- to 10-second bursts every 10 to 20 seconds. The camping area where we were was near Lake Knoll, Arizona. ...I did not sleep the rest of the night. I heard other noises later that night. It sounded like multiple animals fighting but it was more animal sounding... maybe wild boars or something. I asked some of my hunter friends and they could not explain the first sound that I heard. Other than those noises, there was not a sound to be heard. It was dead quiet.

A report to BFRO says that on July 12, 2008, a woman from Phoenix whose family likes to vacation on the Mogollon Rim had a bigfoot encounter on a rainy afternoon near Christopher Creek. They were on a side road off Forest Road 300, the main Rim Road, and it had been raining off and on all afternoon, so the family was reading or napping in their camper van when the woman heard a large animal in the forest outside the trailer and grabbed her camera:

> Not five minutes after I had put my camera down and resumed reading a branch about 4 feet long and 3 to 4 inches round came shooting out of the trees directly at the van like a javelin. It hit the side mirror dead on center, pushing it in towards the van. (It is hard to even move this mirror by hand. The force it took to force it in towards the van had to be tremendous.) The force was such that

it shattered the side mirror into many pieces. There's still a dent on the back metal portion of the mirror from the impact.

They did not see anything more, but that night she could hear a large animal sniffing at the slider window of the van where she was sleeping. The sniffing and huffing noises went on for about five minutes, and suddenly stopped. She did not hear the sound of the animal moving away from the van. In the morning they found that their kitchen had been raided and some food taken, but not by some animal crashing around and tearing bags and knocking things over, but crackers had been removed from their plastic pouches and sausages taken out of tinfoil without tearing it. They returned to the same spot a week later and loud screaming was heard in the afternoon by them and some target shooters.

Yes, it can be said that the Mogollon Monster doesn't like hunters or target shooters! And there might be a lot of screaming and knocking until they are gone from the bigfoot's territory.

Chapter 10

THE OLD WHITE BIGFOOT

Walk into splintered sunlight
Inch your way through dead dreams to another land
Maybe you're tired and broken
Your tongue is twisted with words half spoken and thoughts
unclear
—Grateful Dead, *Box of Rain*

One of the recurring themes in the study of bigfoot and sasquatch is that some of these creatures have white or gray hair. Typically bigfoot have brown or black hair covering their bodies. Are the white-haired bigfoot older bigfoot whose hair has gone silver-white or grey because of old age? Could some of these bigfoot be albinos? The answer to both questions may be yes.

Some sasquatch have been described as albino, but most seem to be white-haired because of old age. Some have been described as having patches of white and brown hair. As we will see there is one case of an "albino" family seen in Washington, but generally the white-haired bigfoot are solitary. They are often seen near towns which makes us wonder if they have been dumpster diving in the middle of the night?

Are these elderly bigfoot who have been cast out of the their clan and are now on the edges of both worlds, that of the bigfoot and that of humans? They become more desperate for food and are loners who have little to lose in their old age. They become dumpster divers and sneak into remote towns to skulk around the garbage cans after midnight.

They often become peeping toms as well, as they may look

into the occasional window or follow a woman through a parking lot late at night.

Perhaps the oldest tale of a light-colored bigfoot is told in Michael Newton's book *Strange Monsters of the Pacific Northwest*[25] where he tells two tales of bigfoot in Oregon at the end of the 1800s:

> On March 31, 1897, the *Burns Times-Herald* reported that "[a] trapper by the name of Powell who has been hunting and trapping the Malheur River south of the Agency Valley this winter reports seeing a very strange animal roaming around in those parts. The Advocate says it is a biped of giant stature, being at least seven feet high, having long and massive arms that reach to its knees, while the whole body is covered with curly, glossy hair.
>
> The last report of the nineteenth century involves two prospectors named Bensen and Robbins. While scouting the headwaters of the Sixes River in 1899, they met a yellow-haired "devil" which stood six feet six inches tall. The beast hurled some of their camping gear over a cliff, then fled under fire from the prospector's rifles.

This last story apparently comes from bigfoot researcher John Green. Back then bigfoot was called "wild man," "devil," and "beast." This one had yellow hair—or was it yellowish-white? It seems that this was an older, white-haired bigfoot. Or are their albinos in bigfoot world?

Another early report of a white-haired bigfoot is from 1903 in northern Arizona. Wikipedia and *Weird Arizona*[59] mention this report of bigfoot in Arizona when it was still a territory:

> The oldest known documented sighting of the Mogollon Monster was reported in a 1903 edition of *The Arizona Republican* in which I.W. Stevens described a creature seen near the Grand Canyon as having "long white hair and matted beard that reached to his knees. It wore no clothing, and upon his talon-like fingers were claws at least two inches long." Upon further inspection he noted,

"a coat of gray hair nearly covered his body, with here and there a spot of dirty skin showing." He later stated that after he discovered the creature drinking the blood of two cougars, it threatened him with a club, and "screamed the wildest, most unearthly screech."

Stevens may have been on the north rim of the Grand Canyon, which is a huge forested wilderness with only some campgrounds, even to this day. This is also the area that Teddy Roosevelt heard his famous bigfoot story.

Stevens described the creature's hands saying "upon his talon-like fingers were claws at least two inches long." When an older bigfoot allows its fingernails to grow they become twisted and long, like talons. It seems that the younger bigfoot do not let their nails grow so long.

Upon further inspection Stevens noted, "a coat of gray hair nearly covered his body, with here and there a spot of dirty skin showing." So here we see that he is an old bigfoot with white or gray hair with the occasional spot of dry, dirty skin showing like the creature had mange or a skin rash and hair loss.

Stevens later stated that after he discovered the creature drinking the blood of two cougars, it threatened him with a club, and "screamed the wildest, most unearthly screech." Wow, did he kill two cougars with his club? That is something. Bigfoot is sometimes seen carrying a club or a branch from a tree. That he screams the most unearthly screech is well known now, as is his tree knocking.

We have here what seems to be the classic old white-haired bigfoot. That Stevens was able to get such a long and close look at this old bigfoot is fairly remarkable, and of course Stevens would have been armed with a rifle and other guns, so he did not have the fear that most people would have today when encountering a bigfoot. He did not know what he was seeing—a devil, a beast or a wild man—but it was

something that he would never forget.

Michael Newton also tells two curious tales in his book, the first of which has an apparent bigfoot wearing overalls and the second concerning a white-haired bigfoot. The first story is from 1945:

> A witness, "Kathleen," and her husband were driving south of Roseburg when they saw "a huge man" sprawled in the highway. Clad in coveralls, the figure lay "draped from the yellow divider line well onto the shoulder, covering at least ten feet" of pavement. Kathleen noted that "it didn't move, but I could see its huge eyes, and its head was on its elbow, like it was resting."
>
> Driving cautiously around the figure, they proceeded on their way and kept the incident secret for years afterward. When interviewed in the 1980s, Kathleen "couldn't even recall if it was hairy or not, but the memory of the huge eyes and feet stuck" with her.[25]

Newton also mentions that in 1959 a startled trucker saw "a tall, white creature that resembled a gorilla" jogging at 35 miles per hour near Millersburg, Oregon. Millersburg is about halfway between Portland and Eugene, just south of Salem. This area is more built up today than it was back in 1959 and has the Interstate running through it.

Still, these granddad bigfoot—we sort of have to imagine that they are all male bigfoot—are cast aside and forced out of their clan. They move closer to human civilization where it is easier to get a meal.

The Old White Bigfoot in California

Elwood Baumann tells the story of a logger near Willow Creek, California in 1952.[5] Willow Creek is east of Arcata on the California coast. Just north of Willow Creek is the Hoopa Indian Reservation that is known for its many bigfoot sightings.

The logger's name was "Bill" but he had two friends named Lee Vlery and Josh Russel and together they were to go north from Willow Creek on California 96 to the logging outpost of Orleans.

Here they were to start preliminary work on a logging operation. Roads, men and heavy equipment were coming to this remote part of extreme northern California.

Bill learned that Lee Vlery had gotten a ride north on California 63, which was still a muddy mountain road at the time, to the logging outpost called Happy Camp. Josh told Bill that Lee needed him to pick him up at Happy Camp, over an hour away, because he had no other way to get back to Orleans.

Bill left in his four-wheel-drive to get Lee at Happy Camp but unfortunately it began raining heavily, turning the road to mud in many spots. He made the journey anyway but found that Lee had gotten a lift back to Orleans with another logger. They must have passed each other along the way, as he had passed several trucks.

Bill began the return trip to Orleans but was soon flagged down by a man with a flashlight. He told him that road was now washed out in a certain spot—the road he had just come on. Bill was then told that he could take an alternative road that went via Bear Valley and Eel River. This road came out at Bluff Creek a few miles south of Orleans. He could then get home.

After about 20 miles down the muddy, rainy dirt road Bill suddenly saw a tall creature with shaggy bluish grey hair standing on the side of the road. It vanished into the forest and Bill decided to shrug it off as some sort of weird event that he didn't want to think about. Was it a gorilla or an ogre or what?

Suddenly his truck went into a violent skid with no warning. Bill fought to gain control of the truck as to one side of the muddy road was a canyon and it would mean certain death if he flew off the road. He got the truck under control and saw the strange white-haired face in the rearview mirror. He kept driving trying to doubt what he was seeing. Was an ogre trying to push him off the road into the canyon? Best to not think about that. How could it be?

Bill went another quarter of a mile but stopped because a small six-inch sapling had fallen across the road. He got out of the truck to move the sapling but as he began to move it he heard the thudding sound of footsteps coming toward him. He knew it was the monster he had seen before, and it loudly stomped around in the forest surrounding him, and Bill could see its face. Its mouth was open in a big snarl and he could see that its eyeteeth were

283

much longer than a human's.

The head was set squarely on the shoulders of the animal with shorter hair on the head than what was on the body. It was only about 6 feet tall, but powerfully built, so Bill was extremely frightened. The creature snarled and circled Bill, and then suddenly walked away—and then came running back toward him when he made a move for his truck.

Bill saw his chance and darted for the truck, just getting inside and slamming the door as the white-haired creature grabbed for the window. He furiously started the truck and drove through the sapling blocking the road and tore down the road back to Orleans.

Bigfoot's legal troubles.

In the morning he had literally forgotten the incident but was then told by his friend Lee Vlery that while they were driving back to Orleans during the rainy night a large hairy creature had tried to push their truck off the road. He added that there was something strange going on around Bluff Creek.

Indeed, we have what is now known to be a bigfoot hotspot and this incident is particularly interesting. The bigfoot (if it was even the same one) was consciously trying to push these trucks off the road and into canyons or steep valleys. This is also an incident involving a grey or silver-haired (white-haired) bigfoot.

We tend to assume that these are older bigfoot whose hair has gone grey or white in old age. What are these grey and white-haired bigfoot up to?

A Strange Bluish-White Bigfoot

In early August of 1960, well-known Canadian outdoorsman and hunter John Bringsli reported that he had driven up a deserted logging road at Lemmon Creek near Nelson, British Columbia to pick huckleberries when he met a bluish-gray bigfoot. Bringsli said:

I had just stopped my 1931 coupe on a deserted logging road and walked about 100 yards into the bush. I was picking huckleberries. I had just started to pick berries and was moving slowly through the bush. I had only been there about 15 minutes. For no particular reason, I glanced up and that is when I saw this great beast. It was standing about 50 feet away from me on a slight rise in the ground, staring at me.

The sight of the animal paralyzed me. It was 7 to 8 feet tall with long legs and short powerful arms with hair covering its body. The first thing I thought was …what a strange looking bear.

It had very wide shoulders and a flat face with ears flat against the side of its head. It looked more like a big hairy ape.

It just stood there staring at me. Arms of the animal were bent slightly, and most astounding was that it had hands… not claws. It was about 8 a.m. and I could see it very clearly. The most peculiar thing about it was the strange bluish-gray tinge of color of its long hair. It had no neck. Its apelike head appeared to be fastened directly to its shoulders.[7]

When the bigfoot began to move toward him Bringsli ran back to his vehicle and tore out of the area. He returned the next day with some friends and they found footprints that were about 17 inches long.[7]

Bringsli's observation of "short, powerful arms" seems at odds with the typical bigfoot description of having long arms. Perhaps the fact that they were "bent" made them seem to be shorter. Bringsli does not mention a strong odor.

Two years later the *Oregon Journal* reported in 1962 a story entitled "Monster Sightings Rekindle Interest in Mt. St. Helens Hairy Giant Saga." The article said that three persons driving along a remote mountain road east of the Cascade wilderness area said that they saw a 10-foot, white, hairy figure moving rapidly along the roadside. The white-haired sasquatch was caught in the headlights as their car passed, but they were too frightened to turn around to investigate. They apparently reported their sighting to the police.

The *Oregon Journal* also said that a Portland woman and her husband fishing on the Lewis River south of Mt. St. Helens saw a huge beige figure, "bigger than any human," along the bank of the river. As they watched the tall creature, it "moved into a thicket with a lumbering gait."[3]

The article also mentioned that the Clallam Indian tribe of Washington State had traditions of hairy giants on Mt. St. Helens. These hairy giants are called the Selahtik, and are believed to be a tribe of "renegade marauder-like people, who lived like animals in the caves and lava tunnels in the high Cascades."[3]

White-Haired Bigfoot Sightings of 1966

In the summer and fall of 1966 there were several different sightings of what would seem to be older white-haired bigfoot that had perhaps been cast out from their tribe and were now dumpster diving. Near Richland, Washington a group of teenagers described a series of encounters they claimed happened with an 8-foot-tall bigfoot with whitish-gray hair and red eyes in the summer of 1966.

These teenagers claimed that they drove around at night all summer looking for the white-haired bigfoot. As in some sort of Hollywood movie these vigilante teenagers—armed with .270 caliber rifles and such—decided to spend their summer shooting at this elderly bigfoot.

The teenagers, Greg Pointer, Roger True, and Tom Thompson all testified, and took lie detector tests, that they had fired at the white-haired bigfoot on several occasions, often at an old gravel pit that they knew was a good place to find the creature. Roger True claimed that he hit the 8-foot-tall bigfoot with at least three bullets from a .270 caliber rifle but it did not knock him down; Tom Thompson claimed that he

The "Tent Flap" photo, circa 2015.

286

fired a shotgun 10 yards from the bigfoot but it hardly flinched. Other teenagers claimed that the bigfoot threw rocks at their car and as it came onto the road they tried to run it down, but it dodged to the side and left scratches on the top of the car.[3]

It is always interesting to study cases where hunters—or in this case, excitable teenage boys with guns and little sense—are suddenly in a position to fire their weapons at bigfoot and unload two or three shots at the bulky, hairy animal. Bigfoot is a thick-skinned and thick-boned hominid that can take a great deal of abuse—including bullets fired into its body.

All large animals can take all sorts of metal bullets penetrating their skin and only bullets to vital organs like the heart, brain or lungs can really bring down a large animal. Similarly the force of a shotgun blast at 10 yards (30 feet) might bring down a duck or a pheasant, but it will not bring down—or even significantly slow—a bigfoot. In fact, no quantity of shotgun blasts, unless at pointblank range, would kill bigfoot.

The only known (and essentially rumored) stories of bigfoot being killed say that he is shot in the head, and for those sharpshooters who know what they are doing, they have shot bigfoot in one of his eyes with a high-powered rifle. This is what happened in the case of the Minnesota Iceman, to be discussed later, a frozen bigfoot that had apparently been shot through its left eye. Otherwise bigfoot just has such thick, matted hair and skin, plus bulk, that it seems any bullet would barely penetrate the skin.

If it did penetrate the skin, it would have to hit a vital organ to cause any damage, and even then bigfoot is likely to stagger away into the forest with some life in him for a few hours. There are many reports of bigfoot that are missing toes, apparently lame or disfigured in the foot for some reason, or (and on top of) having an arm that is broken and useless. These reports are possibly the result of the creature taking some bullets or shotgun blasts in these described encounters. Older bullets in past centuries were often homemade or from older boxes of bullets that had also gotten damp. The firepower of these yesteryear bullets was much weaker than the modern bullets of the same caliber, and any high-powered rifle bullet would probably bring down bigfoot pretty quick.

Another incident involving firearms and a white-haired

bigfoot occurred in the fall of 1966 in Lower Bank, New Jersey. An unnamed couple living in the area saw a face peer in the window of their house—a window that was over 7 feet high. Outside they found five-toed tracks that were 17 inches long. Curious about the bigfoot, they started leaving scraps of vegetables outside and they were being eaten.

Then one night the couple did not leave any vegetable scraps out, and in the middle of the

False news about bigfoot abounds.

night they heard a loud banging outside of the house. The husband decided to arm himself and go outside to see what was causing the noise. What he found was a gray-haired bigfoot throwing their garbage can against the wall of the house repeatedly. He fired a shot into the air to frighten the bigfoot, but the old bigfoot just stood there. The man then fired directly at the chest of the bigfoot and shot it. At this point the bigfoot turned and ran off. He certainly wasn't killed by the shot, but he did not return to the house again.[3] This bigfoot seems to be the classic white-haired bigfoot who is old and cast out of his tribe. He ventures close to civilization in order to find easy food and ultimately become a garbage can and dumpster diver.

The White-Haired Bigfoot Cometh

In the spring of 1969 a sailor with three friends said that after they were parked near Marietta, Washington, their headlights lit up a white-haired bigfoot with long arms. It jumped up and then ran into the woods. Probably another older bigfoot, now dumpster living on the edges of civilization.[3]

288

On July 12, 1969, a man named Charles Jackson was in his backyard with his six-year-old son, Kevin, in a forested area on Cherokee Road near Oroville, California, burning rabbit entrails in a pit. This activity attracted a female bigfoot with long grey hair and large breasts. She was about 8-feet tall with no hair on her face, breasts or palms. Jackson later said that the bigfoot seemed curious as to what he was doing, staring at him with a puzzled look. One might think that the smell of roasted rabbit entrails, rabbits being probably a standard food for bigfoot, had attracted her.

Jackson's immediate reaction was to grab his son and run inside the house. His three normally fierce dogs were all cowering beneath the furniture. This is the typical reaction dogs have to bigfoot. One wonders if dogs have an innate fear of bigfoot in their DNA or whether the smell puts them off, or if previous contact with bigfoot (unknown to their owners) might have occurred.

After they felt it was safe to leave the house, the Jackson family left their cowering dogs behind and drove to the police station in Oroville to tell the cops what was going on around their house. Yes, throughout the years police departments—and the FBI—have been called in on bigfoot reports and missing person reports that may involve bigfoot. Generally the police take these reports seriously and professionally, but there is often little they can do. The police went to the Jackson home, with the Jacksons, the next morning, as the Jackson's refused to return to their home that night. The police could not find any tracks on the hard ground around the Jackson home and some sort of vague report was filed. Later that same month a neighbor who lived on the same road also saw bigfoot and then heard strange screaming in the night.[3]

Throughout the summer and fall of 1969 were the famous Fort Worth, Texas sightings in which a white-haired bigfoot cavorted through a local nature reserve, which was often packed with cars as the beast moved up and down a bluff during evening hours. At one point, the bigfoot apparently became annoyed at the onlookers and it picked up a spare tire and hurled it 500 feet towards the spectators. They all quickly got into their cars for protection.

The bigfoot was said to be 7-feet tall, was covered in white hair and weighed about 300 pounds. The local dress shop owner,

289

A drawing of a bigfoot wearing clothing.

Allen Plaster, took a photo of the back of the white-haired bigfoot and a local author named Sallie Ann Clarke said she saw it tearing down a barbed wire fence, rather than jumping over it.

In one frightening encounter, on November 7, 1969, a local named Charles Buchanan was sleeping in a sleeping bag in the back of his pickup truck along the lakeside in Fort Worth when he was awoken at 2 am being pulled out of the pickup truck and onto the ground, while still in his sleeping bag. Buchanan said the smell of the beast was overpowering; he said he picked up a bag of leftover chicken and thrust it into the bigfoot's face. The bigfoot clenched the bag in its teeth and then shuffled into the water and "swam powerfully toward Greer Island."[3]

On the evening of September 27, 1973 two girls were waiting for a lift in rural Westmoreland County, Pennsylvania when they saw a white, hairy bigfoot with red eyes standing in the nearby woods, apparently watching them. The girls were also surprised to see that it was carrying a luminous sphere in its hand. The girls rushed to their nearby home and told their father, who went into the woods for an hour and then told the girls to stay out of the woods. Later it was reported that some sort of UFO was seen in the area, hovering over the forest with a powerful searchlight coming to the ground from the object.[3]

Michael Newton[25] mentions some cases in Oregon during the spring, summer and fall of 1977 that involve white-haired bigfoot. Newton says that there was a sighting of an 8-foot albino bigfoot crossing Canaan Road near Deer Island in April of 1977. And there were more sightings that summer. Is it an albino or just a white-haired sasquatch? Those with red eyes might well be albinos.

In early September of 1977 there was a sighting of an 8-foot biped near Halfway, Oregon. The witness described the fur on the creature as being a "reddish color with spots of silver or white hair pretty much all over. Then on September 27 on Highway 66 near Ashland, a John Martin saw a 7-foot bigfoot crossing the road. Then a few days later on October 1, two men, Gary Benson and Ronald Kershey, encountered a 7-foot silver-haired bigfoot. When the bigfoot seemingly attacked them they fired shots at the creature which fled. They were not injured.[25]

Things picked up again for white-haired bigfoot in Oregon

and Newton says that in June, 1994, an 8-foot bigfoot ran through a camp on the Bee Ranch and four albino bigfoot were seen making whistling sounds on the Tualatin River. Then in July a grey sasquatch was seen near the Bee Ranch (now apparently the Flying Bee Ranch near Salem).

Then in July 1995, a man named Sean Kehr encountered an albino bigfoot near Willamette, Oregon and a "large white creature" was seen at West Lynn, south of Portland. Then on September 18, 1995 a woman named Barbie Kaneaster encountered a limping albino bigfoot near the vague description of "the Clackamas River" which runs into Portland from the east.[25]

Newton mentions encounters with a few white-haired bigfoot in Washington State including involving a dozen hikers led by Paul McGuire on Mount St. Helens in the summer of 1955 or 1956. They said they met a biped covered with "longish dirty-white hair." Then in the summer of 1966 an eleven-man group of hunters fired shots at an 8-foot bigfoot with whitish-grey hair outside of Richland, a suburb of Kennewick, Washington. Then three boys saw a "white demon" near Sawyer, just south of Yakima, Washington and the same thing apparently chased a youth outside of Yakima a few days later.[25]

In May 1970, two women, Becky Figg and Rosemary Tucker, saw a silver-haired bigfoot near Copalis Crossing. They described it as at least 7-feet tall. Copalis Crossing is on the Olympic Peninsula near Copalis Beach. On August 2 of that year, a man named Ronald Zimmerman claimed he watched a white-haired bigfoot with a "very large stomach" at Boston Basin.

In March 1987 a 9-foot albino bigfoot with "angel hair" was seen near Twisp, Washington. Twisp is very northerly in Washington, near the Canadian border, and surrounded by the North Cascades National Park. In late summer of 1988 a limping, blue-eyed albino sasquatch appeared near Aberdeen, on Washington's coast. On October 30, 1989 Lance Axtell and his friend Richard saw a smoky-grey 8-foot bigfoot at Stossel Creek. Stossel Creek is east of Seattle near the town of Duval.[25]

In September 1996 at Dryad, southwest of Tacoma, Ruth Steele encountered a 7-foot tall bigfoot covered in "grey, white, and sometimes black fur" near the town. Two "trailer people" saw a white sasquatch on Highway 101 above Moclips, Washington, north of Copalis Beach.

Newton says that on October 12, 2003 a bigfoot covered in "thick silver hair" interrupted a picnic at Sullivan Lake, north of Spokane near the Canadian border. Finally, he tells us about a January 2009 sighting by a hunter who claimed that he had seen "a very large white hairy creature" but did not disclose the location.[25]

So we can see from these great reports chronicled by Michael Newton that there are bigfoot "albinos" out there, but also white-haired bigfoot that also have patchy fur, possibly with some dark fur in there, and also sometimes bare skin as if the bigfoot has mange or some other skin/fur problem. This is common in older animals, especially those that are not eating a healthy diet.

It is difficult to say what is a healthy diet for bigfoot, but we know that they eat a lot of salmon and other fish in the Pacific Northwest. Other bigfoot farther inland may be more hungry and the old, white-haired bigfoot are possibly outcasts who must go closer to civilization to get a decent meal.

Kentucky White-Haired Bigfoot

According to the Bigfoot Research Organization (bfro.net) there were several sightings in Kentucky in 1980, including the reporting of a tall, white-haired apelike creature on October 7 near the town of Mayslick in Mason County.

According to the BFRO report, the witness, known as "C.F.," was watching television with his family when he heard a loud noise on the front porch. C.F. said that he heard his son's pet rooster squawking so he peered out the front door, where he saw a white, hairy creature with pink eyes. He said that the creature must have weighed about 400 pounds and was about seven feet tall. It was holding the rooster by the neck and then threw it against the side of the house. The white-haired bigfoot then proceeded around the back of the house to a vacant lot. C.F. says he grabbed his .22 pistol and followed the apeman. He fired at the creature twice, as it ran out of sight. BFRO says that there was a small article concerning the incident in the *Cincinnati Enquirer*.

The same white-haired bigfoot (or could it have been a different one?) was seen the next month, on November 5, 1980, also in

Mason County. According to the BFRO report, which was taken from a police report and information given by a reporter named Doug McGill from the local radio station WFTM, an Alabama truck driver identified as "N.C." said that he was hauling steel west on U.S. Route 68 when he saw a figure on the opposite side of the highway. He slowed his vehicle and turned on his high beams thinking that it was a hitchhiker.

When he approached the figure, he was shocked to see a six- to seven-foot-tall "apelike" creature with white hair. After his encounter, he contacted some locals on C.B. channel 22 to see if there was a circus or zoo in the area. He thought that possibly an ape had escaped. When police were called to investigate, they took N.C.'s statement and filed a report. He stated to police that he had never been to this area before and knew nothing about alleged bigfoot reports in the area.

The white-haired bigfoot that was seen at this time seems quite kingly as he stands by the highway watching the cars and trucks go by. "What's it all about?" he may wonder as he stares at the big rigs with their lights and honking horns.

In his book *Strange Indiana Monsters*[41] Michael Newton mentions a number of interesting bigfoot cases, and some involve white-haired bigfoot. Newton says that in October of 1981 in the southern Indiana county of Knox there were several reports of a strange creature around the White River.

Terry and Mary Harper of the area reported that an unknown prowler had attacked their home on South 15th Street in Vincennes, Indiana. The Harpers claimed that the unseen attacker, presumed to be a bigfoot, ripped and gnawed their aluminum siding, tearing off part of the back door's metal trim. The creature left bloodstains, teeth marks, and two-inch tufts of white hair at the scene.

The bigfoot was thought to have done about $500 worth of damage to the house. Meanwhile the local sheriff's deputies told the Harpers that the blood was not human, but attempted no further investigation. The Harpers concluded that a white-haired bigfoot had attacked their house but they could not figure out why.

One might think that this old, white-haired bigfoot had been looking through their garbage for the last few nights and was disappointed in what he found that night. Did he fly into a rage because of lack of food and the fact that he was an old, probably crippled, bigfoot who had been cast out of his clan? He now resided on the edge of the human world, dumpster diving as best he could.

Newton also mentions an incident in the winter of 1992 in Bartholomew County with a motorist and a white-haired bigfoot. The unnamed motorist was driving west of Columbus in Bartholomew County, Indiana when a "white and furry" bigfoot crossed the road in front of his car.[41]

Newton also mentions that a mother and daughter were driving in Floyd County, Indiana in November 1996 and saw an apelike creature sitting on a roadside log near Edwardsville. This may have been the same bigfoot or another one completely. The color of the fur was not specified but typically younger bigfoot have brown or reddish-brown hair.

Why Did the White-Haired Bigfoot Cross the Road?

In August of 1982 the San Jose *Mercury* reported that two boys and a girl were driving home in the Del Monte Forest near Pacific Grove, California at 1:35 in the morning when a 7-foot-tall "gorilla-type" creature crossed the 20-foot-wide road known as Buena Vista Street "in three steps."[3]

They described the creature as having a bald head, but otherwise being covered with long white hair that reached to its waist. It moved "bent over with a shamble." One has to wonder if the creatures might have been hit by a truck or something? These white-haired dumpster divers might be living too close to the highways and byways of civilization. We should also note here how the bigfoot was described as bald on the top of its head. Like humans, it seems, some older male bigfoot go bald.

A report submitted to the Bigfoot Research Organization was about an incident in July of 2005 that occurred at the Lo Lo Mai Springs Campground by Page Springs, Arizona which is near the New Age mecca of Sedona. Said the report about a grey-haired bigfoot:

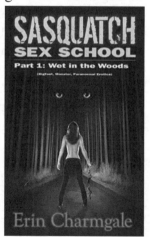

Kinky sex with bigfoot.

I was in Page Springs Arizona on Oak Creek in July 2005 with my kids, camping, and my daughter and I saw something. I saw it twice. Also, a friend of mine and I had some bad feelings in a particular area there. He was camping further down the creek. What I saw was odd. It was grey, 4'-5' tall, slender, fast moving, able to hide, and made a screeching noise twice, once when I think it hit something while moving and again, far away when tons of dogs were barking. Could hear stones clicking, walking and breathing nearby after I went into my tent for the night. Our peaceful camping trip turned into us being frightened.

As mentioned in Chapter 3, on the night of April 24, 2021 a 20-year-old woman walked out of the Warehouse 24-Hour Gym in Richland, Oregon around midnight, her workout complete. She turned to the right and headed to her car in the well-lit parking lot. There were no other vehicles in the lot on that side of the building, constructed and opened in 2018.

The woman heard a twig snap. She looked and saw a creature, seven or eight feet tall and covered in grey fur, racing back into the woods about 30 yards away. It was far too large, likely several hundred pounds, and moved too quickly to be a man, she believed. Shaken and in tears, she called her parents from a nearby restaurant, asking them to come and drive her home.

Yes, here we have the standard scenario of the old, white-haired bigfoot: an old bigfoot limps into town wanting to do some dumpster diving when he happens to see a young woman on her own. He stares at her briefly and wonders if he can abduct her. Instead she sees him and the bigfoot runs away. The woman is now in tears from bigfoot shock and has to call her parents to come and drive her home.

Yeah, meeting the hairy creature at night is bad enough, but when you meet a granddaddy bigfoot who hasn't bathed in years or trimmed his talon-like nails, you might have the shock of your life.

Chapter 11

Can You Prosecute
The Boogeyman?

The open road where the hopeless come
To see if hope still runs
One by one they bring their broke down loads
And leave them where the hobo dreams are stowed
—John Hiatt, *The Open Road*

Can you prosecute the boogeyman? Here we have crimes being committed. Children are kidnapped and sometimes killed. Female adults are assaulted and killed. Male adults are murdered and thrown off cliffs. Who is committing these crimes? Can they be prosecuted? What do the Crime Scene Investigators (CSI) conclude as they look at these horrendous crimes?

Well, they officially conclude that these people have succumbed to hyperthermia and the general exhaustion that comes from being lost in the woods. In the case of those people who have apparently launched off of a cliff or into a steep area of granite rocks and scree the answer is that they were killed in the fall that broke their spine or otherwise crushed and pulverized them.

For a forensic examiner to see someone who has head trauma, broken bones, a fractured spine and has been thrown off a cliff there is the difficulty of determining whether these injuries occurred before the tragic fall or after it. It is natural to assume that the injuries happened during the fall. But, is it possible that the injuries and death occurred before the victim or victims were then flung off of a cliff or into a steep area of rock scree? I would say that that is the case in many of the incidents that I have profiled here.

For the forensic examiner it makes perfect sense that these death-causing injuries were from the fall off of a cliff or steep area. But the question of how these people got to these cliffs or steep areas is unanswered.

So, we have here the conundrum of people falling or being flung off cliffs and other precarious places that have no business being there. Often the authorities are baffled as to how the victims came to be at the spots where they were ultimately discovered, perhaps years after they disappeared.

Therefore, the Park Service and FBI might have realized that there is a serious problem here and it involves bigfoot. Yes, bigfoot, sasquatch, skunk apes and the like. In fact, it would seem that the FBI would have a veritable X-Files squad that was looking into these bizarre deaths and disappearances that are happening across the USA and Canada. Or is the FBI choosing to ignore this uncomfortable theory? What can they do, bring in some suspects for questioning?

The Boogeyman Cometh

In an earlier chapter we discussed the Mayat Datat of the Yakut Indians of central California. The Yakut considered the Mayat Datat to be a bigfoot boogeyman who would steal children:

> Big Foot was a creature that was like a great big giant with long, shaggy hair. His long shaggy hair made him look like a big animal. He was good in a way, because he ate the animals that might harm people. He kept the Grizzly Bear, Mountain Lion, Wolf, and other larger animals away. During hot summer nights all the animals would come out together down from the hills to drink out of the Tule River. Big Foot liked to catch animals down by the river. He would eat them up bones and all.
>
> It was pleasant and cool down by the river on hot summer nights. That is when grown ups liked to take a swim. Even though people feared that Big Foot, the hairy man, might come to the river, people still liked to take a swim at night.
>
> Parents always warned their children, "Don't go near

the river at night. You may run into Big Foot."

Now Big Foot usually eats animals, but parents said, "If he can't find any animals and he is very hungry, he will eat you. Big Foot, the hairy man, doesn't leave a speck or trace. He eats you up bones and all. We won't know where you have gone or what has happened to you."

Some people say Big Foot, the hairy man, still roams around the hills near Tule River. He comes along the trail at night and scares a lot of people. When you hear him you know it is something very big because he makes a big sound, not a little sound.

Children are cautioned not to make fun of his picture on the painted rock or play around that place because he would hear you and come after you. Parents warned their children, "You are going to meet him on the road if you stay out too late at night." The children have learned always to come home early.

It is clear that bigfoot is what we call the boogeyman: someone who comes and steals children—in the day or night! He is to be feared and respected. It is unwise to make friends with the boogeyman.

Beginning in July of 1974 a woman from Watova settlement near Nowata, in northeast Oklahoma, began seeing a brown-haired bigfoot around the house she shared with her husband. Nowata was originally part of the Cherokee Nation reservation. Mrs. Margie Lee would spot the 6-foot-tall bigfoot, which she considered a young male, around the settlement and she noted that the bigfoot was interested in homes where women lived and completely ignored houses where single men lived. She and her husband, John Lee, theorized that the young male was seeking a mate. Indeed, it has been shown that bigfoot takes more interest in homes with women in them and seems to have a desire to mate with these women.

Margie and John became rather fond of their neighborhood bigfoot and even played a little game with him. They discovered that the bigfoot would put a feed pail in the doorway of the barn, blocking the door. So they began hiding the feed pail every day somewhere around barn and the bigfoot would sniff it out every night and place it in the barn doorway. The only time Margie ever heard the bigfoot make a sound was once when it seemed to be laughing. Eventually it became a nuisance, breaking chicken wire windows in the barn and stealing chickens from their neighbor.

Two sheriff's deputies, Gilbert Gilmore and Buck Field, encountered the bigfoot one night late in the summer of 1974 and opened fire on it. It was in the headlights of their patrol car and they both opened up on the bigfoot which ran off into the woods, seemingly unhurt. The next morning Margie said she was taking a shower when she heard a big thump on the wall outside the shower. She dashed to the window to see if she would see bigfoot but he was already gone and that was his last farewell to Margie. He was not seen in the area again.[3]

The next year in Noxie, Oklahoma, only a few miles north of Nowata, a farmer named Kenneth Tosh heard a scratching sound coming from a derelict house near his own home. He called a friend and they approached the empty residence around 8 pm where they came within 10 feet of a 7- to 8-foot-tall bigfoot. It was completely covered in long hair except for the nose and eyes. The men fired pistols at the bigfoot which ran off, apparently unharmed. During that year over 20 people reported seeing or hearing the Noxie bigfoot.[3] Was it the same lonely bigfoot seen at Nowata the year before?

A frightening child-snatch incident happened in Flintsville, Tennessee on April 26, 1976 after a number of bigfoot reports had been made around the town in the preceding days. This included a report of a bigfoot grabbing the aerial of a woman's car and jumping onto its roof. On April 26, Mrs. Jennie Robertson was in her house while her 4-year-old son Gary was playing outside in the evening when she heard her son cry out. She rushed out and said she saw:

> ...this huge figure coming around the corner of the house. It was 7 or 8 feet tall and seemed to be all covered with hair. It reached out its long, hairy arm toward Gary and came within a few inches of him before I could grab him and pull him back inside.

Mr. Robertson ran to the door when he realized something was happening and glimpsed a big black shape disappearing into the woods. Six men then tracked the bigfoot and got near enough to fire guns at it. It threw big rocks at them and ran into the bush. The next day they returned to the scene and found 16-inch-long footprints as well as hair and blood.[3]

The Disturbing Case of Jared Atadero

On October 2, 1999, three-year-old Jaryd Atadero, his 6-year-old sister Josallyn, and 11 adults were hiking the Big South Trail near Rocky Mountain National Park in the Arapaho and Roosevelt National Forest near Fort Collins in northern Colorado. While the group was hiking, Jaryd ran ahead, no more than 100 feet in front of the group and stopped to talk with some fishermen. Following this brief meeting, Jaryd continued down the trail ahead of the group. This would be the last time anyone saw the young Jaryd. In the following days, a massive search and rescue operation failed to turn up any evidence of the three-year-old boy.

The Big South Trail is an 11-mile trail located at 8,440 feet in the rugged Comanche Peak Wilderness (part of the Arapaho and Roosevelt National Forest) eventually crossing into Rocky Mountain National Park. It is a 1,131 square mile forest, established on July 1, 1908 by Theodore Roosevelt. It was originally part of the Medicine Bow Forest Reserve, and was originally named the Colorado National Forest in 1910, but was renamed by President Herbert Hoover to honor President Theodore Roosevelt in 1932. The highest point in the park is Greys Peak (14,278 feet) and it has three other "fourteener" peaks. There are also twelve other peaks over 13,000 feet in the large forest.

The saga of Jaryd Atadero begins on October 2, 1999 when Allyn Atadero (Jaryd's father) and his two children were staying at the Poudre River Resort which was owned by Allyn and his brother Arlyn.

In the fall of 1999, a Christian singles group was staying at the lodge, helping Allyn prepare for winter in exchange for lodging.

The group decided they wanted to go to the trout farm, the fishery right around the corner, maybe about a mile and a half or two miles from the resort itself. At about 10 am Jaryd, his 6-year-old sister, Josallyn, and 11 members of the Christian Singles Network left the Poudre River Resort for a hike on the Big South Trail.

They started to separate or spread out as they walked, some people being faster and some slower. One adult, with Jaryd's sister and Jaryd, seemed to be out ahead of everybody else. At around 11:30 am, Jaryd was ahead of the group and stopped to talk to two fishermen. It was reported that Jaryd asked the fishermen if there were any bears around. The men returned to fishing, believing that Jaryd would soon be met by the group. They are the last known people to have seen Jaryd alive. Jaryd went farther up the trail and disappeared.

At approximately 12:15 pm the hiking group realized that Jaryd was missing and the group began searching for him for about an hour. Some members returned to the Poudre River Lodge to alert Allyn, who drove to the trail and searched for another hour.

Some members of the 11-person hiking party reported hearing a scream, according to the investigation report. Jaryd's sister Josallyn told Allyn she did, too. "I asked her, 'What kind of scream was it?'; like somebody getting attacked or somebody playing with someone," he said. "She said it sounded like a playful scream like someone was going up to tag him."

That afternoon an emergency pager alert was sent to Larimer County Emergency Services Specialist Bill Nelson. By 6:30 pm search personnel reached lower Big South Trailhead. Around 65 SAR members were deployed at this point to find Jaryd. By 8:00 pm searchers from the lower and upper trailhead met between Campsites 7 and 8 without finding a sign of Jaryd. Search plans were expanded and more resources were ordered, including a helicopter planned to arrive at first light.

The overnight search team members were told to be extremely vigilant at dawn as family members had told searchers that Jaryd got up at dawn. A dive team was employed for Big South River.

At that same time an Air Force helicopter (Huey UH-1N) from F.E. Warren Air Force base in Cheyenne, Wyoming made its first flight over the area and then headed to the Fort Collins-Loveland Municipal Airport to refuel.

When it returned to the area at 3:30 pm the helicopter struggled with the fuel load and mountain conditions and stalled out. The helicopter fell 100 feet and crashed onto the Big South Trail. Aboard were four members of the Air Force and Mark Sheets, a Loveland resident and Larimer County Search and Rescue member.

Sheets was the only crew member not in a seat; he was on the floor with the door open. He saw the rotors hit the tops of trees and pieces of helicopter spray into the forest. He tried to shut the door, but a severed tree limb came through and struck the Air Force doctor on board, fracturing the doctor's eye socket. The Air Force crew was able to get out of the helicopter, Sheets said, but he was trapped.

Nearby search and rescue members ran to the downed helicopter, kicked in a window and managed to pull the unconscious Sheets out. All five aboard were transported from the crash site, three via air ambulance and two via ground ambulance. All five survived the crash but two had significant injuries.

The search went on until October 8. More than 200 trained searchers, a dozen dog teams, professional trackers, a dive team and a plane had searched for Jaryd without finding any solid clues. On that day the search for Jaryd was suspended and the family notified.

The helicopter crash added to the stress of a search that grew even more frustrating as the national media took notice. TV trucks and newspaper reporters began to swarm the remote site after the grand jury in another chilling child case—the death of JonBenet Ramsey in Boulder—postponed its announcement of whether it would hand down indictments.

As many as 17 TV satellite trucks lined up along Colorado Highway 14 with anchors walking around asking anyone for information. Psychics professed to know where searchers could find Jaryd. A barefoot man with a mule showed up at the search site, ready to track the boy down. A Native American came to perform a ritual, asking the mountain to give up the boy.

Four years went by and then on June 5, 2003 two hikers named Rob Osbourne and Gareth Watts arrived on the scene. They liked to pick an area and go on hikes together. On this day they chose to explore Poudre Canyon and went for a hike along Big South Trail for the first time. They scrambled off the trail into a rock field and then decided to scramble about 2,000 feet up to a ridge.

They knew about Jaryd and talked about him sometimes, and then they suddenly saw some clothing and a small shoe and knew that they had found him. They then found the other shoe, a brown fleece jacket and blue sweatpants turned inside out. One pant leg was mostly scattered by birds using the material in their nests.

The two hikers took photos and some of the articles of clothing they found to the Larimer County Sheriff's Office. Photos were emailed to Allyn Atadero in Littleton and he confirmed the clothing and shoes were Jaryd's.

The next day, it took searchers about an hour to reach the site near Campsite 2, where they found the remaining clothing scattered across a 25-foot area. Some of the items were sheltered from the elements and some were exposed. While the cloth jacket had what appeared to be puncture marks and the pants were tattered, the nylon shoes had little weathering.

Then on June 14 a party consisting of Larimer County Sheriff's Office members, Larimer County Search and Rescue, Colorado Division of Wildlife and NecroSearch met at Big South Trailhead to begin the search for the remains of Jaryd. Later, Allyn Atadero and personnel from the local Child Protection Network joined the group.

The searchers hiked in approximately 1.5 miles and made the 500-foot vertical climb up to the site where hikers found the clothing.

The team found a skull fragment in a crevice and a tooth on a log spanning the crevice, above the skull fragment. This site was about 180 feet north and about 20 feet higher in elevation than the clothing site. Later that day Allyn, the searchers and others met with the media at the trailhead and announced what they had found.

Everyone was baffled by the discovery. It was said that this area had been searched by earlier teams with dogs in 1999. There were many mysteries surrounding the disappearance and death of Jaryd, and the discovery of his clothing and remains only added more weirdness to the whole story.

A survival expert named Les Stroud said, "I think whatever's happening is beyond our understanding. In a lot of these cases, Search & Rescue, or the volunteer searching people have already gone over certain areas, not once, not twice, but even dozens of times. And then the child is found there a few years later."

When experienced hikers were asked if the boy could have walked to this spot on his own they said that they could not see him doing this as it is very steep and rough terrain. But the story gets even stranger.

Law enforcement felt early on that this case may have been an animal encounter, possibly with a cougar. It was speculated that if a mountain lion grabbed Jaryd it would have killed him with a bite to the neck and then taken him someplace and buried him. With all of the activity going on looking for Jaryd, the cougar left the area but came back later to his kill.

When asked about this theory Allyn Atadero said, "I hear constantly about a mountain lion. Yet, when they tested Jaryd's clothing, there was no mountain lion hairs, no DNA, no blood, nothing on his clothing. The clothing was sent to the CBI. The clothing was tested by the CBI. No mountain lion hairs, no blood, nothing on any of the articles of clothing."

He said that experts had told him that Jaryd's jacket would have been shredded if he had been attacked by a mountain lion and the jacket was fine. He said that the shoes would be scuffed up if he had been dragged up the side of the mountain. His pants were found in good condition with only rodent and bird marks from the animals using it for nesting material.

Allyn said that in one of the reports, a person said the reason they didn't find any DNA or blood or anything on Jaryd's clothing was because either he or something removed his clothing before he was attacked.

Allyn also asked why Jaryd's remains were found 500 feet up the side of the cliff. He pointed out that Jaryd's pants were found inside out. Allyn says that he and his family feel strongly that there is someone out there who knows a little bit more than everyone else does.

Jaryd's disappearance has yielded no official conclusion from law enforcement. Statistically, the probability of being attacked by a cougar is very low. There have only been 14 reported fatal mountain lion attacks in the US and Canada since 1915.

Unfortunately, Jaryd's case does fit that of the standard bigfoot abduction. The sad scenario goes something like this: a young child is with a group of hikers and he gets separated briefly from the main group. Often these children are so young that they are not afraid of others and are very playful. In some cases they seem to play a game of hide and seek with a bigfoot, perhaps a young bigfoot and even a female. This can go on for some time with the bigfoot hiding in the forest but peaking out at the young child from time to time and letting itself be seen.

In some cases, such as Jaryd's, the child asks someone else, "Are there bears around here?" These young children know what a bear is, but they do not know what a bigfoot is. Sadly, this game of hide and seek ends at a time when the child is alone—even briefly. The boy or girl is whisked away with a sudden scream and carried swiftly from the trail. The bigfoot takes the child, probably still alive, to a cave in a boulder field somewhere and examines him. They child may have been crying and will be exhausted. At some point the child will fall asleep.

The bigfoot begins to examine the small child, curious about the shoes and clothing. The shoes are taken off and looked at in wonder. The jacket is removed and even the pants, which are turned inside out. At this point, it would seem, the child is either returned alive to an area near where they were abducted, or the child dies. This can be from starvation, exposure to the cold, strangulation or other means.

If a child, or adult for that matter, dies in the cave of a bigfoot I think that it is likely to remain there for some time. The bigfoot may move around seasonally and return to this cave at some point and then decide to take the skeleton, shoes and clothes back to the vicinity of where the attack happened—but not the exact place. The spot where Jaryd's remains were found is not where the bigfoot cave would be located either. That cave would be somewhere else, probably quite distant and at a lower elevation.

It is troubling and sad that families sometimes go through this terrible personal hell of a child going on an innocent hike with family and friends and suddenly vanishing into the forest as if the mountain had swallowed them up. Maybe the Native American ritual is what was needed to bring Jaryd Atadero back from the twilight zone.

The Disappearance and Death of James McGrogan 2014

A more recent death and disappearance is that of James McGrogan in 2014. According to reports, James "Jim" McGrogan disappeared March 14, 2014 near Vail, Colorado in the White River National Forest. His body was eventually found weeks later on April 3, missing his boots and other articles of his clothing. His disappearance and death remain a mystery.

The 39-year-old Dr. McGrogan, was visiting Vail, a small town at the base of Vail Mountain and the center of the huge ski resort. McGrogan had recently returned to Indiana from Wisconsin to work in the emergency room of St. Joseph Regional Medical Center in Mishawaka.

On the morning of March 14, at about 8:30 am, Jim and three hiking companions left on the 9-mile hike to the Eiseman Hut and beyond to Camp Hale. The camp is a collection of huts deep in the mountains that serve as temporary shelters for hikers or campers. The site was originally built in the 1940s as the home of the 10th Mountain Division of the Army and was a mountain warfare training area.

At the time there was still a lot of snow in the area from the winter—several feet deep in some areas. Although the Eiseman Hut was only four miles from the group's starting point and right near US Interstate 70, the hike itself was up a meandering 9-mile trail through steep and treacherous wooded terrain, and the hut is not considered easy to reach. This is one of the reasons the hut is such a popular target for hikers.

Although it was to be a challenging hike, McGrogan and company were experienced with the outdoors and well prepared. Like the other hikers he was with, McGrogan carried a cell phone, basic medical supplies, a sleeping bag, an avalanche beacon, a GPS, warm clothing, and plenty of food and water.

At about 10 am, with the hikers still about five miles from the hut, the group of four stopped to rest. According to his companions, Jim decided to hike on ahead of the party, and they expected to catch up with him along the way. After Jim left the others behind to hike on alone he vanished. When the rest of the group reached the Eiseman Hut it was late afternoon and there was no sign at all of Dr. McGrogan; he was never seen alive again.

By 5:30 pm that day the hikers had notified the Vale Department of Public Safety and subsequently, the Eagle Valley Sheriff's Department. A rescue operation was started over an 18 square mile area.

McGrogan was well equipped so the authorities were not too concerned. He had food, water, and warm clothing. The doctor was also carrying a split snowboard (a snowboard that divides lengthwise) and other equipment from the outfitter Confluence Kayaks in Denver. He was also wearing special boots that went with the board. McGrogan's cell phone pinged once on the day he went missing but after that, it went silent.

Over the next three days, teams of searchers on foot and on snowmobiles searched for McGrogan. Three helicopters from the National Guard's High Altitude Aviation Training Site (HAATS), based in nearby Gypsum, Colorado, searched the area from the air. But by March 18th, bad weather forced the search to be suspended.

There were further searches and crews spent a combined 1,000 hours searching for McGrogan. Then, 20 days after his disappearance, McGrogan's body was found by a group of backcountry skiers about 4-1/2 miles from the trail on April 3, 2014, near the Booth Falls area, quite a distance to the east of the Eiseman Hut. The reporting party told authorities that he and two others were skiing the Booth Falls area when they located the dead body in an icefall below Booth Falls laying on top of an ice sheet (an icefall is a frozen waterfall which flows down a steep slope).

McGrogan was found wearing his helmet, no coat, no gloves, and very strangely, with no boots. In his backpack his cell phone was discovered and in this area there appeared to be active cellular reception. Jim's snowboard was also found nearby but his boots were never located. His gloves and coat were never found either.

On April 7, 2014, the Eagle County Coroner said that Dr.

James McGrogan died of multiple injuries, including head trauma and trauma to the left side of his chest and a broken femur. His death was ruled an accident.

This is a pretty strange story. It seems that McGrogan was crushed to death and then thrown over the icefall. However the mainstream theory is that he hiked nearly 14 miles across the backcountry in deep snow—up to 8 feet in some cases—and somehow lost his boots, gloves and jacket; some doctors suggest that people who are succumbing to hypothermia begin to undress for some reason. But does this make sense? Why didn't he use his cell phone or GPS tracker, both of which were fully functional?

It seems that Dr. McGrogan made a fatal mistake that day by walking on ahead of his group. As a lone hiker on a remote snow-packed trail he apparently met a very powerful being that bashed in his head, crushed his chest and broke his leg. That powerful being was probably an eight-foot tall bigfoot, likely a male. McGrogan may have struggled against the hairy giant but it would probably not last long. He was then carried away off the trail and deep into the snowy woods. Here his jacket, gloves and boots were removed. His cell phone worked but there was no one to make a call.

After a couple of weeks as a dead body in the cave of a bigfoot, McGrogan was taken some distance away, back towards where

A photo from *The Planet of the Apes.*

he had been killed, and thrown onto the ice slab at the icefall. McGrogan did not get there by himself. He was carried there and purposely dropped at that spot.

It is a sad and mysterious story. One realizes that if he had just stayed with his companions he would have survived that day instead of becoming a casualty at one of America's national parks. Perhaps even now that murderous bigfoot is sitting in his cave looking at McGrogan's boots in fascination. Missing people in national parks and wilderness areas that are eventually found are often missing their boots or hiking shoes. It seems that bigfoot has a fascination for shoes. Perhaps it is because he has such large feet and could never get his foot into one of these boots that he is fascinated with them. If there is a bigfoot museum out there somewhere I would guess that it is full of shoes.

Did McGrogan meet up with a bigfoot that wounded him with a blow to the head and then squeezed him to death in his powerful arms? There would be no bullet holes or puncture wounds. Was McGrogan even in the area when it was searched in the days after his disappearance? Probably not. He was probably dead in some other area, carried through the rugged mountain area to a cave. After some weeks the body begins to smell and bigfoot does not seem to eat people. These creatures do not use fire either. They are more curious about people and their clothing and protective of their

A chart of the rise of man—but is he actually getting shorter?

dwindling domain. It seems that women and children are often kidnapped alive by a bigfoot but men are more typically killed in the instant they encounter bigfoot. Children are sometimes found alive a few days after disappearing. Other times they are found dead or never found at all.

The area that McGrogan was discovered in was probably already searched some six months before, but his body simply wasn't there. It was probably placed there in the weeks after the search and was there for some weeks. Had he actually left the trail to meet his fate or did his encounter happen as he suddenly turned a corner and found himself face to face with a bigfoot? We will probably never know.

The Disappearance and Death of Kiah Wallace

Even more recently we have the mysterious disappearance and death of Kiah Wallace who vanished on a solo hike. On June 18, 2021 tourists found the body of Kiah Wallace below a popular hiking trail at Rocky Mountain National Park in northern Colorado. Wallace was a 33-year-old woman from Arvada, Colorado who enjoyed hiking. The *Idaho Statesman* ran this story on June 21, 2021:

> Rocky Mountain National Park visitors found the body of a 33-year-old woman below a popular hiking trail, The Loch.
>
> Visitors at Rocky Mountain National Park discovered a body last week below a popular hiking trail, rangers said. Tourists at the national park told rangers they found a woman's body below The Loch, a popular hiking destination within the park. The body was found in drainage below The Loch on Friday, park officials said. Weather prevented rangers from retrieving the body until Sunday.
>
> "Park rangers attempted to reach the location on Friday night, but lightning storms and darkness hampered those efforts," park officials said in a news release. "On Saturday, June 19, Rocky Mountain National Park Search and Rescue Team members were again hampered by

weather while conducting field operations." A search and rescue team of 28 people pulled the body from below the Loch Vale Trail on Sunday.

"The woman's body was extricated up 60 feet through steep, rocky, hazardous terrain to the Loch Vale Trail and then wheeled out by litter to the Glacier Gorge Trailhead," rangers said. Her body was taken to the Larimer County Coroner/Medical Examiner's Office. Park officials didn't release her name, and the incident is under investigation.

The name of the woman was withheld for weeks when an update was given on July 13 by Denver7 news:

The Larimer County Coroner's Office has identified the decedent as Kiah R. Wallace, 33, of Arvada. The manner and cause of death are pending investigation.

Original story:

The body of a 33-year-old Arvada woman was recovered Sunday [June 21] in Rocky Mountain National Park after being discovered Friday [June 18], the National Park Service reported.

Park visitors reported to rangers on Friday they had discovered the body below the outtake of The Loch within the national park west of Fort Collins, the park service said in a news release.

Weather, including lightning storms, and darkness hampered the Search and Rescue Team's recovery efforts on Friday night and Saturday, the NPS said.

The woman's body was recovered Sunday with the help of 38 park Search and Rescue Team members, 28 of whom were in the field. Rescuers traveled up 60 feet through "steep, rocky, hazardous terrain to the Loch Vale Trail and then wheeled out by litter to the Glacier Gorge Trailhead," according to the news release.

Very little has been reported on this case and it took them three weeks to report the name of the woman, even though she was identified right away when the authorities said that she was 33 years old.

We have never been told when the woman actually entered the park or what her plans may have been. Essentially all we are being told is that rescuers traveled up 60 feet through "steep, rocky, hazardous terrain to the Loch Vale Trail."

Apparently Wallace was found in steep hazardous terrain away from the trail. What was she doing there? How did she die? The manner of death is under investigation the last report says, and nothing else has ever been reported. It would seem that there is something mysterious about this case and that the authorities are withholding some information from the public.

Did Wallace fall off a cliff and die? Was she a victim of murder? Did she suddenly meet a bigfoot on the trail who murdered her and abducted her? We do not know how long she had been missing. Had the bigfoot tossed the dead body into the steep and hazardous terrain where she was found? How else would she have gotten there? Was she missing her boots or jacket?

These are all questions that we would like to have answered but probably never will. Kiah Wallace is another of those Colorado mysteries that we will probably never solve. Hiking in mountainous areas by oneself is dangerous and if one should fall or be attacked there is no one there to help. Once again we learn the dangers of hiking alone.

Some Very Strange Tales from Oregon

Researcher Michael Newton tells a very bizarre story in his book *Strange Monsters of the Pacific Northwest*.[25] This book has tons of interesting stories and several chapters are about bigfoot.

Newton tells us this story which was first published on the front page of the early Oregon newspaper, the *Salem Oregon Statesman* in 1857. Newton is taking the story from the 1949 book, *Farthest Frontier: The Pacific Northwest* by Sidney Warren (MacMillan, New York)[26]. I have obtained this book and it has extra information that is not in Newton's book. Newton tells us the story begins with a man and a boy who are camping on the South Umpqua River, near Roseburg, Oregon. The man and boy started out in quest of some lost cattle and when night came they settled down to sleep. Then the boy heard a "loud plaintive cry" which awoke him around midnight. He jumped to his feet without waking his companion and walked a few yards toward the noise. Says the article:

> He observed an object approaching him that appeared like a man about twelve or fifteen feet high... with glowing eyes, which had the appearance of equal balls of fire. The monster drew near to the boy... and seizing him by the arm dragged him forcibly away towards the mountains... with velocity that seemed to our hero like flying.
>
> They had traveled in this manner for perhaps an hour, when the monster sunk upon the earth apparently exhausted. Our hero then became aware that this creature was indeed a wild man, whose body was completely covered with wild shaggy brown hair, about four inches in length; some of his teeth protruded from his mouth like tuskes [sic], his hands were armed with formidable claws instead of fingers, but his feet, singular to relate, appeared natural, being clothed whit moccasins similar to that worn

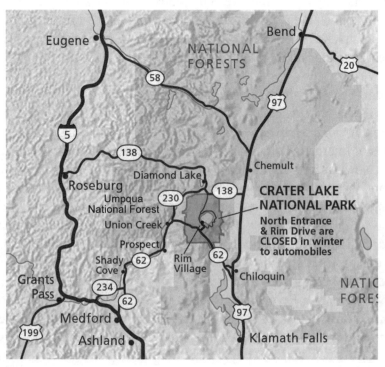

by Indians.

Our hero had scarcely made these observations when the "wild man" suddenly started onward as before, never for a moment relaxing his grip on the boy's arm… They had not proceeded far before they entered an almost impenetrable thicket of logs and undergrowth, when the "wild man" stopped, reclined upon a log, and gave one shriek, terrific and prolonged… immediately after which the earth opened at their feet, as if a trap door, ingeniously contrived, had just been raised. Entering at once this subterranean abode by a ladder rudely constructed of hazel brush, they proceeded downward, perhaps 150 or 200 feet, when they reached the bottom of a vast cave, which was brilliantly illumined with a peculiar phosphorescent light, and water trickled from the sides of the cave in minute jets…

As our hero closely observed the interior of this awful cave, the "wild man" left him… Presently the huge monster returned by a side door, leading gently by the hand a young and delicate female of almost miraculous grace and beauty, who had doubtless been immured in this dreadful dungeon for years… The young lady fell upon her knees, and in some unknown language… seemed to plead for the privilege of remaining forever in the cave… This singular conduct caused our hero to imagine that the "wild man" conscience stricken, had resolved to set at liberty his lovely victim, by placing her in charge of our hero, whom he had evidently captured for that purpose. As this thought passed through [his] mind his ears were greeted with the strains of the most unearthly music…

The "wild man" wept piteously… and sobbing like a child, his eyes moist with grief, he raised her very carefully from her recumbent posture, and led her gently away as they had come.

A moment afterwards, the damsel returned alone, and advanced toward our hero with lady-like modesty and grace, placed in his hands a beautifully embossed card, upon which appeared the following words, traced in the most exquisite hand evidently the lady's own, "Boy, depart hence, forthwith, or remain and be devoured." Our hero looked up but the lady had vanished... He acted at once upon the hint... and commenced retracing his steps towards the "ladder of hazel brush" which he shortly reached and commenced the ascent. Upon arriving at the top, his horror may be imagined when he found the aperture closed! The cold sweat stood on his brow, his frame quivered with mental agony when, ...he bethought himself of small barlow knife ...with which he instantly commenced picking the earth... After laboring in this manner he was rejoiced to see daylight through the earth, and he was not much longer in working a hole large enough through which to he was enabled to crawl.

According to Sidney Warren in *Farthest Frontier: The Pacific Northwest*[26] the final part of the story goes as follows:

The adventure ends with our hero wandering around for a day and a night until he met a small party of miners, prospecting on the headwaters of the South Umpqua River, to whom he told his story. They listened in silence, apparently not believing a word, but they were unable to account for his presence in that desolate region and, after feeding him, directed him home. He related his tale to his father who called in the neighbors and the circuit preacher. "At first they smiled, then doubted, then believed; and the whole neighborhood are now prepared to make affidavit to the principal facts. The boy is a mild, modest, moral boy ...his parents are moral and religious people, and it is hoped that out of respect to their feelings, the story will not be disbelieved as a general thing, although many parts are truly wonderfull.[26]

Warren makes no comment on this story, but immediately begins telling other odd tales from the early days of Oregon and Idaho. But how fanciful is this story? Is it all made up? It doesn't seem so.

While many newspapers in the Old West did fabricate some stories when there was little news to actually report, this story, in the light of 150 years of bigfoot activity that have been chronicled since it was published, has some frightening implications that seem to be true. Let us deconstruct this amazing tale.

We first have the tall bigfoot grabbing the boy by his arm and dragging him through the forest at great speed. He then stops to rest. The boy sees that he has shaggy brown hair all over its body and formidable claws, plus moccasins on his feet. As for the claws, it would seem that these are just the long, overgrown fingernails of the bigfoot. That the bigfoot was wearing moccasins seems doubtful. However, some bigfoot have been seen with partial clothing and carrying clubs, so it is possible that this bigfoot did have some sort of crude moccasins on his feet, possibly to imitate humans. He also has tusks, which some bigfoot have shown. Some researchers believe that bigfoot have tusks that can retreat into the mouth or protrude from the mouth at will.

The pair continued to an impenetrable thicket where the wild man stopped, and "reclined upon a log, and gave one shriek, terrific and prolonged… immediately after which the earth opened at their feet, as if a trap door, ingeniously contrived, had just been raised. Entering at once this subterranean abode by a ladder rudely constructed of hazel brush, they proceeded downward, perhaps 150 or 200 feet, when they reached the bottom of a vast cave, which was brilliantly illumined with a peculiar phosphorescent light, and water trickled from the sides of the cave in minute jets…"

This seems incredible, this description of a bigfoot's cave. There is a trap door and then a ladder of hazel brush leading down 150 feet or more to the bottom of the cave which water was trickling down the walls and a "peculiar phosphorescent light."

Hazel brush is a species of hazel, which genus produces edible hazel nuts and can grow about 90 feet tall. Some caves can have a phosphorescent light and certainly water trickling down the walls.

But the most disturbing part of the story is the woman who has been a captive in this bigfoot's remarkable cave. The bigfoot leads "gently by the hand a young and delicate female of almost miraculous grace and beauty, who had doubtless been immured in this dreadful dungeon for years... The young lady fell upon her knees, and in some unknown language... seemed to plead for the privilege of remaining forever in the cave..."

This is truly frightening as it suggests that this woman, apparently naked, has been kept for many years in this cave, perhaps abducted as a child. She may be a local Indian girl, or possibly even from an early pioneer family. The bigfoot apparently wants to give her to the boy so that she may return to the civilized world and live a "normal" life. But the woman does not want to leave. She knows little about the outside world and is frightened to leave this incredible cave and the sad life that she has lived. Her life in the cave would be eating raw meat, roots and berries. She knows nothing else it would seem.

And what is the language she is speaking? Is it a whistle and click language? Some have described bigfoot talk as like little children talking and laughing. Often there are whistle sounds as well a soft chattering like small children.

That the woman warns the boy to leave or he will be devoured by giving him a handwritten card seems to be a fanciful addition to the story. More likely she told him in sign language to leave and that his life was in danger. He may have had sex with this woman, as that seemed to be part of what the bigfoot monster wanted. If this is the case, he may not have wanted to tell that part of the story and therefore made up the story of the woman giving him the card and disappearing. We must remember that this story has gone from the boy's own words, to the miners and family, and then to some newspaper editor who typeset the incredible tale.

The boy's escape is probably much as he tells it, and he is lucky to have gotten out of this dreadful cave deep in the mountains.

Where is all of this supposedly taking place? The South Umpqua River begins in the middle of Umpqua National Forest. The headwaters of the South Umpqua River, where the boy meets the miners after escaping from the cave, are in a very wild National Forest to this day, with the closest towns being Roseburg,

318

Dixonville and Glide, Oregon. To the east is the famous Crater Lake.

With what we know now about bigfoot—his habit of stealing small children and of abducting adult women—this 1857 story seems oddly prescient (showing knowledge of events before they take place). We have a twelve-foot-tall bigfoot, over a hundred years before the term was created, a hidden cave, and a captive woman. The eyes of the bigfoot essentially glowed, and this has been said many times by witnesses. Many animals have eyes that glow in the light, such as the eyes of cats and rabbits.

Bigfoot seems to have a sexy side.

Do we have an older bigfoot who has inherited this awesome cave and its occupants? Was there also a bigfoot family that was occupying this cave? In the 150 years since this story was told have other people been abducted to this cave? Is this the terrible fate that meets those who have disappeared in the mountains of Oregon and Idaho—and elsewhere? Then there is the bigfoot crying when the woman will not go with the boy—is somebody making all this up? Is some Edgar Allen Poe wannabe writing fantasy for the *Oregon Statesman* newspaper? The paper maintains that it is a true story.

Perhaps that is all we should say about this incredible and disturbing story. We can see how bigfoot is indeed the boogeyman. He is someone who steals children and abducts lone hikers in the woods—especially women.

Will such a monster as bigfoot ever stand trial for their many crimes of abduction and murder? It is impossible to bring any of these perpetrators to justice—because they simply do not exist!

A Strange High Pitched Noise

Janet and Colin Bord[3] tell the story of a woman briefly abducted by a female bigfoot in the Clackamas area of Oregon, southeast of

319

Portland, in 1959. The Mount Hood National Forest lies to east and is a vast wilderness area. A "Mrs. Carol," an employee of Oregon City's *Enterprise Courier* newspaper had this curious experience:

> En route to interview a paper carrier in Estacada, she stopped to relieve herself in roadside shrubbery. While thus engaged, she heard "a very high-pitched tone," lost consciousness, and woke to find herself tucked underneath a hairy biped's arm, being carried through the forest like a rag doll.
>
> The beast—"a young female"—with small breasts and a full-body coat of light brown hair—eventually dropped her, leaving the witness bruised but otherwise unarmed. Before the creature departed, Mrs. Carol—a self-described sensitive "able to commune with animals by picking up their vibrations"—allegedly engaged in conversation with her abductor, learning that the beast liked peaches. Later, Mrs. Carol returned to the site and left a basketful of peaches, which soon disappeared.[3]

There are a few interesting things here. First is the high-pitched tone she heard, the second is that it was a female bigfoot that abducted her, and third is the love of peaches. It is well documented that bigfoot like to hang around peach and apple orchards. Neither are native to North America.

In many ways Mrs. Carol was fortunate, as she probably would not have survived long in bigfoot captivity. Was she being abducted to bring to a male bigfoot? Was she possibly being abducted to bring to a captive male human? This is a scary thought.

But probably the most important thing is that "very high-pitched tone," and the woman's loss of consciousness. This may be important in the many abductions of children—and of adults.

Is this what happens to children and some adults? The bigfoot makes "a very high-pitched tone," and the victim loses consciousness? It has been constantly noted that bigfoot makes whistling sounds and other high-pitched tones. His speech—if that is what it is—is described as something like children chattering and laughing. That bigfoot is able to make some kind of hypnotic high-pitched tone would make a lot of sense. It would explain why bigfoot is said to have a "psychic" component and can literally put a victim in an unconscious hypnotic state.

Bigfoot has celebrity status.

This remarkable conclusion helps us understand how small children can be grabbed by a bigfoot and not cry out—and they are not hurt in any way. This is because the bigfoot is using this high-pitched tone to send the child into unconsciousness. This high-pitched tone is used on adults as well and might be the reason why some victims—like Dale Stehling—do not cry out or scream. They are stunned and disoriented by the high-pitched tone and even lose consciousness. This is no problem for a bigfoot, who scoops the person up in their powerful arms.

How many people, you may wonder, have been walking down the hiking trail alone only to suddenly fall into unconsciousness and then awaken to their horror in a bigfoot's cave? It is a frightening thought.

Primo bigfoot investigator Michael Newton has some interesting bigfoot encounters that make us think of the boogeyman. Bigfoot has been shot at many times and even hit by a truck or two. Newton says that in 1982 a man named Joe Cary claimed he struck an 8-foot bigfoot with his truck outside of Chemult, near Crater Lake, Oregon; "J.W." described a road-killed bigfoot being spirited away by Forest Service officers at Frog Camp; and three hunters known only as "Crouse, Crowe and Lyons" allegedly shot a sasquatch near Yankton, Oregon, north of Portland, and then lost it despite a clear trail of blood and 14-inch footprints.[25]

Newton also says that when Mount St. Helens in southern Washington State exploded on May 18, 1980, it killed 57 people while destroying 250 homes, 47 bridges, 185 miles of highway, and 15 miles of railway. It spilled lava over 230 square miles. He says that Fred Bradshaw's father claimed that National Guard trucks removed "a group of bodies" from Green Mountain while researcher Joe Beelart says that the U.S. Army Corps of Engineers found two dead bigfoot on Cowlitz River and airlifted them to an

321

unknown location.

Newton also reports that two hikers that were fleeing from the eruption saw a bigfoot on Mount St. Helens, and another hiker, "Paul H.," watched "a muddy orange colored monkey" that looked like an orangutan drinking from a stream near Augspurger Mountain, south of Mount St. Helens.[25]

He says that on October 31 (Halloween), 1998, a mushroom hunter said that a bigfoot jumped up from a pit and attacked him near Coquille, Oregon.

He also ends his chapter on bigfoot with an unusual roundup of "unverified" Oregon stories. Among these are:

Datus Perry's assertion that a female creature wearing "a cape of deer skin" near Lava Butte seemed physically attracted to him.

Jim and Pat Stepp's claim that a sasquatch peered into their boat, near Yale.

George Stoican's meeting with an 8-foot creature on a ferry dock at Sequim.

"Mildred" saw five or six bipedal creatures gathered on a hillside near her home, at Moses Lake.

Witnesses ducked stones hurled by a sasquatch at Collins Hot Springs and Swift Reservoir.

A hiker at untraceable "Black Pass" reported a beast making sounds "like a radio playing and an opera singer warming up..."

An elderly man's report of bigfoot "romping with a dog" on the beach at Oysterville.

Another senior citizen's description of a sasquatch clubbing salmon on the White River.

A hairy biped's pursuit of a woman and her sons near Forks.

Another beast that stoned and chased loggers near Mckenna.

A hunter's claim that sasquatch stole his kill near Bonneville.

A report that Lewis County's sheriff fired on bigfoot near Winlock in October 2009.

The story of a Powers family that sheltered a crippled sasquatch; and a "Bigfoot family surrounding soldiers" on Mount Rainier.

The most bizarre stories begin with Ray Wallace's claim that an unnamed hunter had shot a bigfoot near Amboy, offering its corpse for sale with a $100,000 price tag; and two reports of hairy bipeds killed by cars came from Snoqualmie Pass and Yale (where the Forest Service helicopter carried the body away).[25]

What we get from these stories is the allegation that the Forest Service is perfectly aware of bigfoot and that they have recovered some dead bodies of these powerful and awesome creatures. How many bigfoot have been taken out by chopper by the Army or the National Forest Service?

The notion that the National Forest Service and the US Army have the bodies of dead bigfoot is an interesting one. What would happen to these bodies? It seems likely that the Army would demand to possess any bigfoot bodies that were found and demand silence from those who knew about the case. It would literally be Top Secret. While a few FBI officials might be informed, the Army would probably not inform the FBI if they could avoid it. Keep this stuff hush, hush.

With the bigfoot bodies in their possession the US Army would probably keep them preserved in a freezer. With the advanced science that we have today they would probably be studying the DNA and other biological components of the creature. They may even attempt to clone a bigfoot. The possibilities are endless.

Perhaps a cloned bigfoot could be trained and used by the military on Mars or other planets? What would Elon Musk do with a cloned bigfoot? Don't ask.

But back to the boogeyman. Our sasquatch denizens are dodging trucks out on the road. They are stealing clothes and boots. They are stealing children. They are

Bigfoot sex bundle.

murdering adults. Sometimes they are seen wearing these clothes or somehow fashioning a crude tunic. Plus they have their special club with all the spikey bits that tear people to shreds.

They are hairy and often smelly. They can be the size of an adult human or twice the size of a man—or more. No matter what their size or what they are wearing, they are very strong and they can take a lot of abuse themselves, from bullets or from cars.

They are the boogeyman, bigfoot, sasquatch—the wild man you need to watch for. Because, even though you do not see him, he may be watching you.

THE BIGFOOT FILES
BIBLIOGRAPHY

You end up sittin' on a sand bar
Down to a handful of treasures
'Nother shot of gold won't get you very far
When you got forever
—Joe Walsh, *Second Hand Store*

1. *Bigfoot Nation*, David Hatcher Childress, 2018, Adventures Unlimited, Kempton, IL.
2. *On the Track of Unknown Animals*, Bernard Heuvelmans, 1955, MIT Press, Cambridge, MA.
3. *The Bigfoot Casebook*, Janet & Colin Bord, 1982, Granada, London.
4. *The Bigfoot Casebook, Updated*, Janet & Colin Bord, 2006, Pine Winds Press, OR.
5. *Bigfoot: America's Abominable Snowman*, Elwood Baumann, 1975, Franklin Watts, NYC.
6. *There are Giants in the Earth*, Michael Grumley, 1974, Doubleday & Co., Garden City, NY.
7. *Sasquatch in British Columbia*, Christopher L. Murphy, 2012, Hancock House, Surrey, BC.
8. *Who's Watching You?*, Linda Coil Suchy, 2009, Hancock House, Surrey, BC.
9. *Abominable Snowmen: Legend Come to Life*, Ivan T. Sanderson, 1961, Chilton Book Co., NYC. Reprinted 2006, Adventures Unlimited Press, Kempton, IL.
10. *The Bigfoot Book*, Nick Redfern, 2016, Visible Ink, Detroit, MI.
11. *Chasing American Monsters*, Jason Offut, 2019, Schiffer Publishing, Atlglen, PA.
12. *Raincoast Sasquatch*, J. Robert Alley, 2003, Hancock

House, Surrey, BC.

13. *Still Living?,* Myra Shackley, 1983, Thames & Hudson, London.

14. *Things and More Things*, Ivan T. Sanderson, 1970, reprinted 2007 by Adventures Unlimited Press.

15. *Bigfoot: The Yeti & Sasquatch in Myth & Reality*, John Napier, 1973, E.P. Dutton, NYC.

16. *Do Abominable Snowmen of North America Really Exist?,* Roger Patterson, 1966, Franklin Press, Yakima, WA.

17. *The Bigfoot Files*, Peter Guttilla, 2003, Timeless Voyager Press, Santa Barbara, CA.

18. *The Field Guide to Bigfoot, Yeti, and Other Mystery Primates Worldwide*, Loren Coleman and Patrick Huyghe, 2006, Anomalist Books, NYC.

19. *The Hoopa Project*, David Paulides, 2008, Hancock House, Surrey, BC.

20. *Wood Knocks: Volume One*, David Weatherly, 2016, Leprechaun Press, Prescott, AZ.

21. *Wood Knocks: Volume Two*, David Weatherly, 2017, Leprechaun Press, Prescott, AZ.

22. *Wood Knocks: Volume Three*, David Weatherly, 2018, Leprechaun Press, Prescott, AZ.

23. *Wood Knocks: Volume Four*, David Weatherly, 2020, Leprechaun Press, Prescott, AZ.

24. *Wood Knocks: Volume Five*, David Weatherly, 2021, Leprechaun Press, Prescott, AZ.

25. *Strange Monsters of the Pacific Northwest*, Michael Newton, 2010, Schiffer Books, Atglen, PA.

26. *Farthest Frontier: The Pacific Northwest*, Sidney Warren. 1949, MacMillan, NYC.

27. *Meet the Sasquatch*, Christopher Murphy, 2004, Hancock House, Surrey, BC.

28. *Yetis, Sasquatch and Hairy Giants*, David Hatcher Childress, 2010, Adventures Unlimited, Kempton, IL.

29. *Sasquatch: The Apes among Us*, John Green, 1978, Hancock House, Surrey, BC.

30. *Weird America*, Jim Brandon, 1978, Plume, NYC.

31. *Sasquatch/Bigfoot,* Don Hunter with René Dahinden, 1993,

Firefly Books, Buffalo, NY.

32. *Sasquatch: Legend Meets Science*, Jeff Meldrum, 2006, Forge Books, NYC.

33. "Gigantopithecus," E.L. Simons & P.E. Ettel, *Scientific American,* January 1970.

34. *The Mysterious Monsters*, Robert & Frances Guenette, Sun Classic, Los Angeles, CA.

35. *The Beast of Boggy Creek*, Lyle Blackburn, 2012, Anomalist Books, NYC.

36. *The Mogollon Monster, Arizona's Bigfoot*, Susan Farnsworth, 1996 (republished 2010), Southwest Publications, Mesa, AZ.

37. *More Mogollon Monster, Arizona's Bigfoot*, Susan Farnsworth and Mitchell Waite, 2011, Southwest Publications, Mesa, AZ.

38. *Bigfoot Encounters in Ohio: Quest for the Grassman*, Christopher Murphy, Joedy Cook and George Clappison, 2006, Hancock House, Surrey, BC.

39. *Bigfoot in Maine*, Michelle Soulierte, 2021, Llewellyn, Woodbury, MN.

40. *Lower Alabama Bigfoot,* Ashley R. McPhaul, 2021, Authorhouse, Bloomington, IN.

41. *Strange Indiana Monsters*, Michael Newton, 2006, Schiffer Publishing, Atglen, PA.

42. *My Quest for the Yeti*, Reinhold Messner, 1998 (Austria), 2001, St. Martin's Press, NYC.

43. *Strange Abominable Snowmen*, Warren Smith, 1970, Popular Library, NYC.

44. *The Historical Bigfoot*, Chad Arment, 2006, Coachwhip Publications, Darke County, OH.

45. *Big Footprints*, Grover S. Krantz, 1992, Johnson Books, Boulder, CO.

46. *Cryptozoology: Science & Speculation*, Chad Arment, 2004, Coachwhip Publications, Darke County, OH.

47. *Legend Tripping*, Robert Robinson, 2016, Adventures Unlimited, Kempton, IL.

48. *Monsters Caught on Film*, Dr. Melvin Willin, 2010, David and Charles, Devon, UK.

49. *Lower Alabama Bigfoot*, Ashley McPahaul, 2021, Author House, Bloomington, IN.
50. *Sasquatch: True-Life Encounters with Legendary Ape-Men*, Rupert Matthews, 2008, Arcturus Publishing, London.
51. *In Search of Giants*, Thomas N. Steenburg, 2000, Hancock House, Surrey, BC.
52. *Sasquatch Research in America*, Frank D. Sobczak, 2011, Self Published, NC.
53. *Yeti: The Ecology of a Mystery,* Daniel C. Taylor, 2017, Oxford Press, New Delhi.
54. *Encounters with Bigfoot*, John Green, 1980, Hancock House, Surrey, BC.
55. *On the Track of the Sasquatch*, John Green, 1980, Hancock House, Surrey, BC.
56. *Sasquatch/Bigfoot,* Thomas N. Steenburg, 1990, Hancock House, Surrey, BC.
57. *Tom Slick & the Search for the Yeti*, Loren Coleman, 1989, Faber & Faber, Boston, MA.
58. *Mysterious California*, Mike Marinacci, 1988, Pan Pipes Press, Los Angeles, CA.
59. *Weird Arizona*, Wesley Treat, Mark Moran, Mark Sceurman, ed., 2007, Sterling Publishing, NYC.
60. *Weird Florida*, Michael Newton, 2007, Sterling Publishing, NYC.
61. *Bigfoot Memoirs*, Stan Johnson, 1996, Wild Flower Press, Newberg, OR.
62. *Missing 411: Western United States & Canada, David Paulides, 2012, Create Space.*
63. *Missing 411: Eastern United States, David Paulides, 2012, Create Space.*
64. *Missing 411: North America & Beyond, David Paulides, 2013, Create Space.*
65. *Missing 411: The Devil's in the Detail, David Paulides, 2014, Create Space.*
66. *Missing 411: Hunters, David Paulides, 2015, Create Space.*
67. *Missing 411: Off the Grid, David Paulides, 2017, Create Space.*

328

GIANTS ON RECORD
By Jim Vieira and Hugh Newman
Over a 200-year period thousands of newspaper reports, town and county histories, letters, photos, diaries, and scientific journals have documented the existence of an ancient race of giants in North America. Extremely large skeletons ranging from 7 feet up to a staggering 18 feet tall have been reportedly uncovered in prehistoric mounds, burial chambers, caves, geometric earthworks, and ancient battlefields. Strange anatomic anomalies such as double rows of teeth, horned skulls, massive jaws that fit over a modern face, and elongated skulls have also been reported. Color Section.
420 pages. 6x9 Paperback. Illustrated. $19.95. Code: GOR

COVERT WARS & BREAKAWAY CIVILIZATIONS
By Joseph P. Farrell
Farrell delves into the creation of breakaway civilizations by the Nazis in South America and other parts of the world. He discusses the advanced technology that they took with them at the end of the war and the psychological war that they waged for decades on America and NATO. He investigates the secret space programs currently sponsored by the breakaway civilizations and the current militaries in control of planet Earth. Plenty of astounding accounts, documents and speculation on the incredible alternative history of hidden conflicts and secret space programs that began when World War II officially "ended."
292 Pages. 6x9 Paperback. Illustrated. $19.95. Code: BCCW

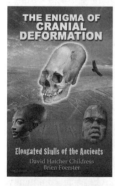

THE ENIGMA OF CRANIAL DEFORMATION
Elongated Skulls of the Ancients
By David Hatcher Childress and Brien Foerster
In a book filled with over a hundred astonishing photos and a color photo section, Childress and Foerster take us to Peru, Bolivia, Egypt, Malta, China, Mexico and other places in search of strange elongated skulls and other cranial deformation. The puzzle of why diverse ancient people—even on remote Pacific Islands—would use head-binding to create elongated heads is mystifying. Where did they even get this idea? Did some people naturally look this way—with long narrow heads? Were they some alien race? Were they an elite race that roamed the entire planet? Why do anthropologists rarely talk about cranial deformation and know so little about it? Color Section.
250 Pages. 6x9 Paperback. Illustrated. $19.95. Code: ECD

ARK OF GOD
The Incredible Power of the Ark of the Covenant
By David Hatcher Childress
Childress takes us on an incredible journey in search of the truth about (and science behind) the fantastic biblical artifact known as the Ark of the Covenant. This object made by Moses at Mount Sinai—part wooden-metal box and part golden statue—had the power to create "lightning" to kill people, and also to fly and lead people through the wilderness. The Ark of the Covenant suddenly disappears from the Bible record and what happened to it is not mentioned. Was it hidden in the underground passages of King Solomon's temple and later discovered by the Knights Templar? Was it taken through Egypt to Ethiopia as many Coptic Christians believe? Childress looks into hidden history, astonishing ancient technology, and a 3,000-year-old mystery that continues to fascinate millions of people today. Color section.
420 Pages. 6x9 Paperback. Illustrated. $22.00 Code: AOG

ANDROMEDA: THE SECRET FILES
The Flying Submarines of the SS
By David Hatcher Childress

Childress brings us the amazing story of the German Andromeda craft, designed and built during WWII. Along with flying discs, the Germans were making long, cylindrical airships that are commonly called motherships—large craft that house several smaller disc craft. It was not until 1989 that a German researcher named Ralf Ettl, living in London, received an anonymous packet of photographs and documents concerning the planning and development of at least three types of unusual craft—including the Andromeda. Chapters include: Gravity's Rainbow; The Motherships; The MJ-12, UFOs and the Korean War; The Strange Case of Reinhold Schmidt; Secret Cities of the Winged Serpent; The Green Fireballs; Submarines That Can Fly; The Breakaway Civilization; more. Includes a 16-page color section.
382 Pages. 6x9 Paperback. Illustrated. $22.00 Code: ASF

GODS AND SPACEMEN THROUGHOUT HISTORY
Did Ancient Aliens Visit Earth in the Past?
By W. Raymond Drake

From prehistory, flying saucers have been seen in our skies. As mankind sends probes beyond the fringes of our galaxy, we must ask ourselves: "Has all this happened before? Could extraterrestrials have landed on Earth centuries ago?" Drake spent many years digging through huge archives of material, looking for supposed anomalies that could support his scenarios of space aliens impacting human history. Chapters include: Spacemen; The Golden Age; Sons of the Gods; Lemuria; Atlantis; Ancient America; Aztecs and Incas; India; Tibet; China; Japan; Egypt; The Great Pyramid; Babylon; Israel; Greece; Italy; Ancient Rome; Scandinavia; Britain; Saxon Times; Norman Times; The Middle Ages; The Age of Reason; Today; Tomorrow; more.
280 Pages. 6x9 Paperback. Illustrated. $18.95. Code: GSTH

PYTHAGORAS OF SAMOS
First Philosopher and Magician of Numbers
By Nigel Graddon

This comprehensive account comprises both the historical and metaphysical aspects of Pythagoras' philosophy and teachings. In Part 1, the work draws on all known biographical sources as well as key extracts from the esoteric record to paint a fascinating picture of the Master's amazing life and work. Topics covered include the unique circumstances of Pythagoras' birth, his forty-year period of initiations into all the world's ancient mysteries, his remarkable meeting with a physician from the mysterious Etruscan community, Part 2 comprises, for the first time in a publicly available work, a metaphysical interpretation of Pythagoras' Science of Numbers.
294 Pages. 6x9 Paperback. Illustrated. $18.95. Code: PYOS

VIMANA:
Flying Machines of the Ancients
by David Hatcher Childress

According to early Sanskrit texts the ancients had several types of airships called vimanas. Like aircraft of today, vimanas were used to fly through the air from city to city; to conduct aerial surveys of uncharted lands; and as delivery vehicles for awesome weapons. David Hatcher Childress, popular *Lost Cities* author, takes us on an astounding investigation into tales of ancient flying machines. In his new book, packed with photos and diagrams, he consults ancient texts and modern stories and presents astounding evidence that aircraft, similar to the ones we use today, were used thousands of years ago in India, Sumeria, China and other countries. Includes a 24-page color section.
408 Pages. 6x9 Paperback. Illustrated. $22.95. Code: VMA

THE LOST WORLD OF CHAM
The Trans-Pacific Voyages of the Champa
By David Hatcher Childress

The mysterious Cham, or Champa, peoples of Southeast Asia formed a megalith-building, seagoing empire that extended into Indonesia, Tonga, and beyond—a transoceanic power that reached Mexico and South America. The Champa maintained many ports in what is today Vietnam, Cambodia, and Indonesia and their ships plied the Indian Ocean and the Pacific, bringing Chinese, African and Indian traders to far off lands, including Olmec ports on the Pacific Coast of Central America. Topics include: Cham and Khem: Egyptian Influence on Cham; The Search for Metals; The Basalt City of Nan Madol; Elephants and Buddhists in North America; The Cham and Lake Titicaca; Easter Island and the Cham; the Magical Technology of the Cham; tons more. 24-page color section.
328 Pages. 6x9 Paperback. Illustrated. $22.00 Code: LPWC

ADVENTURES OF A HASHISH SMUGGLER
by Henri de Monfreid

Nobleman, writer, adventurer and inspiration for the swashbuckling gun runner in the *Adventures of Tintin*, Henri de Monfreid lived by his own account "a rich, restless, magnificent life" as one of the great travelers of his or any age. The son of a French artist who knew Paul Gaugin as a child, de Monfreid sought his fortune by becoming a collector and merchant of the fabled Persian Gulf pearls. He was then drawn into the shadowy world of arms trading, slavery, smuggling and drugs. Infamous as well as famous, his name is inextricably linked to the Red Sea and the raffish ports between Suez and Aden in the early years of the twentieth century. De Monfreid (1879 to 1974) had a long life of many adventures around the Horn of Africa where he dodged pirates as well as the authorities.
284 Pages. 6x9 Paperback. $16.95. Illustrated. Code AHS

NORTH CAUCASUS DOLMENS
In Search of Wonders
By Boris Loza, Ph.D.

Join Boris Loza as he travels to his ancestral homeland to uncover and explore dolmens firsthand. Throughout this journey, you will discover the often hidden, and surprisingly forbidden, perspective about the mysterious dolmens: their ancient powers of fertility, healing and spiritual connection. Chapters include: Ancient Mystic Megaliths; Who Built the Dolmens?; Why the Dolmens were Built; Asian Connection; Indian Connection; Greek Connection; Olmec and Maya Connection; Sun Worshippers; Dolmens and Archeoastronomy; Location of Dolmen Quarries; Hidden Power of Dolmens; and much more! Tons of Illustrations! A fascinating book of little-seen megaliths. Color section.
252 Pages. 5x9 Paperback. Illustrated. $24.00. Code NCD

GIANTS: MEN OF RENOWN
By Denver Michaels

Michaels runs down the many stories of giants around the world and testifies to the reality of their existence in the past. Chapters and subchapters on: Giants in the Bible; Texts; Tales from the Maya; Stories from the South Pacific; Giants of Ancient America; The Stonish Giants; Mescalero Tales; The Nahullo; Mastodons, Mammoths & Mound Builders; Pawnee Giants; The Si-Te-Cah; Tsul 'Kalu; The Titans & Olympians; The Hyperboreans; European Myths; The Giants of Britain & Ireland; Norse Giants; Myths from the Indian Subcontinent; Daityas, Rakshasas, & More; Jainism: Giants & Inconceivable Lifespans; The Conquistadors Meet the Sons of Anak; Cliff-Dwelling Giants; The Giants of the Channel Islands; Strange Tablets & Other Artifacts; more. Tons of illustrations with an 8-page color section.
320 Pages. 6x9 Paperback. Illustrated. $22.00. Code: GMOR

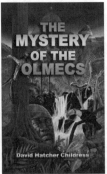

THE MYSTERY OF THE OLMECS
by David Hatcher Childress

The Olmecs were not acknowledged to have existed as a civilization until an international archeological meeting in Mexico City in 1942. Now, the Olmecs are slowly being recognized as the Mother Culture of Mesoamerica, having invented writing, the ball game and the "Mayan" Calendar. But who were the Olmecs? Where did they come from? What happened to them? How sophisticated was their culture? Why are many Olmec statues and figurines seemingly of foreign peoples such as Africans, Europeans and Chinese? Is there a link with Atlantis? In this heavily illustrated book, join Childress in search of the lost cities of the Olmecs! Chapters include: The Mystery of Quizuo; The Mystery of Transoceanic Trade; The Mystery of Cranial Deformation; more.

296 Pages. 6x9 Paperback. Illustrated. Bibliography. Color Section. $20.00. Code: MOLM

ABOMINABLE SNOWMEN: LEGEND COME TO LIFE
The Story of Sub-Humans on Six Continents from the Early Ice Age Until Today
by Ivan T. Sanderson

Do "Abominable Snowmen" exist? Prepare yourself for a shock. In the opinion of one of the world's leading naturalists, not one, but possibly four kinds, still walk the earth! Do they really live on the fringes of the towering Himalayas and the edge of myth-haunted Tibet? From how many areas in the world have factual reports of wild, strange, hairy men emanated? Reports of strange apemen have come in from every continent, except Antarctica.

525 pages. 6x9 Paperback. Illustrated. Bibliography. Index. $16.95. Code: ABML

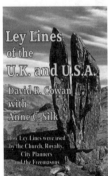

LEY LINES OF THE UK AND USA
By David R. Cowan with Anne Silk

Chapters include: Megalithic Engineering; Burial Grounds across Scotland; Following a Straight Ley Line to its Source; Saint Columba and Iona; The Royal Triangle of Great Britain; The Strange Behavior of Ley Lines; The Dance of the Dragon; Ley Lines in the USA; The Secret Knowledge of the Freemasons; Spirit Paths; The Occult Knowledge of the Nazis; How to Use Divining Rods; The Amazing Power of the Maze; more. Tons of illustrations, all in color!

184 Pages. 7x9 Paperback. All Color. Profusely Illustrated. Index. $24.00. Code: LLUK

THE CHILDREN OF MU
By James Churchward

According to Churchward, the lost Pacific continent of Mu was the site of the Garden of Eden and the home of 64,000,000 inhabitants known as the Naacals. In this, his second book, first published in 1931, Churchward tells the story of the colonial expansion of Mu and the influence of the highly developed Mu culture on the rest of the world. Her first colonies were in North America and the Orient, while other colonies had been started in India, Egypt and Yucatan. Chapters include: The Origin of Man; The Eastern Lines; Ancient North America; Stone Tablets from the Valley of Mexico; South America; Atlantis; Western Europe; The Greeks; Egypt; The Western Lines; India; Southern India; The Great Uighur Empire; Babylonia; Intimate Hours with the Rishi; more. A fascinating book on the diffusion of mankind around the world—originating in a now lost continent in the Pacific! Tons of illustrations!

270 Pages. 6x9 Paperback. Illustrated. $19.95. Code: COMU

ANCIENT ALIENS ON THE MOON
By Mike Bara
What did NASA find in their explorations of the solar system that they may have kept from the general public? How ancient really are these ruins on the Moon? Using official NASA and Russian photos of the Moon, Bara looks at vast cityscapes and domes in the Sinus Medii region as well as glass domes in the Crisium region. Bara also takes a detailed look at the mission of Apollo 17 and the case that this was a salvage mission, primarily concerned with investigating an opening into a massive hexagonal ruin near the landing site. Chapters include: The History of Lunar Anomalies; The Early 20th Century; Sinus Medii; To the Moon Alice!; Mare Crisium; Yes, Virginia, We Really Went to the Moon; Apollo 17; more. Tons of photos of the Moon examined for possible structures and other anomalies.
248 Pages. 6x9 Paperback. Illustrated.. $19.95. Code: AAOM

ANCIENT ALIENS ON MARS
By Mike Bara
Bara brings us this lavishly illustrated volume on alien structures on Mars. Was there once a vast, technologically advanced civilization on Mars, and did it leave evidence of its existence behind for humans to find eons later? Did these advanced extraterrestrial visitors vanish in a solar system wide cataclysm of their own making, only to make their way to Earth and start anew? Was Mars once as lush and green as the Earth, and teeming with life? Chapters include: War of the Worlds; The Mars Tidal Model; The Death of Mars; Cydonia and the Face on Mars; The Monuments of Mars; The Search for Life on Mars; The True Colors of Mars and The Pathfinder Sphinx; more. Color section.
252 Pages. 6x9 Paperback. Illustrated. $19.95. Code: AMAR

ANCIENT ALIENS ON MARS II
By Mike Bara
Using data acquired from sophisticated new scientific instruments like the Mars Odyssey THEMIS infrared imager, Bara shows that the region of Cydonia overlays a vast underground city full of enormous structures and devices that may still be operating. He peels back the layers of mystery to show images of tunnel systems, temples and ruins, and exposes the sophisticated NASA conspiracy designed to hide them. Bara also tackles the enigma of Mars' hollowed out moon Phobos, and exposes evidence that it is artificial. Long-held myths about Mars, including claims that it is protected by a sophisticated UFO defense system, are examined. Data from the Mars rovers Spirit, Opportunity and Curiosity are examined; everything from fossilized plants to mechanical debris is exposed in images taken directly from NASA's own archives.
294 Pages. 6x9 Paperback. Illustrated. $19.95. Code: AAM2

ANCIENT TECHNOLOGY IN PERU & BOLIVIA
By David Hatcher Childress
Childress speculates on the existence of a sunken city in Lake Titicaca and reveals new evidence that the Sumerians may have arrived in South America 4,000 years ago. He demonstrates that the use of "keystone cuts" with metal clamps poured into them to secure megalithic construction was an advanced technology used all over the world, from the Andes to Egypt, Greece and Southeast Asia. He maintains that only power tools could have made the intricate articulation and drill holes found in extremely hard granite and basalt blocks in Bolivia and Peru, and that the megalith builders had to have had advanced methods for moving and stacking gigantic blocks of stone, some weighing over 100 tons.
340 Pages. 6x9 Paperback. Illustrated.. $19.95 Code: ATP

HAUNEBU: THE SECRET FILES
The Greatest UFO Secret of All Time
By David Hatcher Childress

Childress brings us the incredible tale of the German flying disk known as the Haunebu. Although rumors of German flying disks have been around since the late years of WWII it was not until 1989 when a German researcher named Ralf Ettl living in London received an anonymous packet of photographs and documents concerning the planning and development of at least three types of unusual craft. Chapters include: A Saucer Full of Secrets; WWII as an Oil War; A Saucer Called Vril; Secret Cities of the Black Sun; The Strange World of Miguel Serrano; Set the Controls for the Heart of the Sun; Dark Side of the Moon: more. Includes a 16-page color section. Over 120 photographs and diagrams.
352 Pages. 6x9 Paperback. Illustrated. $22.00 Code: HBU

ANTARCTICA AND THE SECRET SPACE PROGRAM
Hatcher Childress

David Childress, popular author and star of the History Channel's show *Ancient Aliens*, brings us the incredible tale of Nazi submarines and secret weapons in Antarctica and elsewhere. He then examines Operation High-Jump with Admiral Richard Byrd in 1947 and the battle that he apparently had in Antarctica with flying saucers. Through "Operation Paperclip," the Nazis infiltrated aerospace companies, banking, media, and the US government, including NASA and the CIA after WWII. Does the US Navy have a secret space program that includes huge ships and hundreds of astronauts?
392 Pages. 6x9 Paperback. Illustrated. $22.00 Code: ASSP

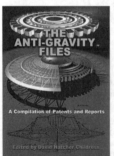

THE ANTI-GRAVITY FILES
A Compilation of Patents and Reports
Edited by David Hatcher Childress

With plenty of technical drawings and explanations, this book reveals suppressed technology that will change the world in ways we can only dream of. Chapters include: A Brief History of Anti-Gravity Patents; The Motionless Electromagnet Generator Patent; Mercury Anti-Gravity Gyros; The Tesla Pyramid Engine; Anti-Gravity Propulsion Dynamics; The Machines in Flight; More Anti-Gravity Patents; Death Rays Anyone?; The Unified Field Theory of Gravity; and tons more. Heavily illustrated. 4-page color section.
216 pages. 8x10 Paperback. Illustrated. $22.00. Code: AGF

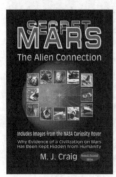

SECRET MARS: The Alien Connection
By M. J. Craig

While scientists spend billions of dollars confirming that microbes live in the Martian soil, people sitting at home on their computers studying the Mars images are making far more astounding discoveries... they have found the possible archaeological remains of an extraterrestrial civilization. Hard to believe? Well, this challenging book invites you to take a look at the astounding pictures yourself and make up your own mind. *Secret Mars* presents over 160 incredible images taken by American and European spacecraft that reveal possible evidence of a civilization that once lived, and may still live, on the planet Mars... powerful evidence that scientists are ignoring! A visual and fascinating book!
352 Pages. 6x9 Paperback. Illustrated. $19.95. Code: SMAR

BIGFOOT NATION
A History of Sasquatch in North America
By David Hatcher Childress

Childress takes a deep look at Bigfoot Nation—the real world of bigfoot around us in the United States and Canada. Whether real or imagined, that bigfoot has made his way into the American psyche cannot be denied. He appears in television commercials, movies, and on roadside billboards. Bigfoot is everywhere, with actors portraying him in variously believable performances and it has become the popular notion that bigfoot is both dangerous and horny. Indeed, bigfoot is out there stalking lovers' lanes and is even more lonely than those frightened teenagers that he sometimes interrupts. Bigfoot, tall and strong as he is, makes a poor leading man in the movies with his awkward personality and typically anti-social behavior. Includes 16-pages of color photos that document Bigfoot Nation!
320 Pages. 6x9 Paperback. Illustrated. $22.00. Code: BGN

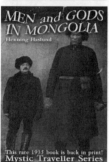

MEN & GODS IN MONGOLIA
by Henning Haslund

Haslund takes us to the lost city of Karakota in the Gobi desert. We meet the Bodgo Gegen, a god-king in Mongolia similar to the Dalai Lama of Tibet. We meet Dambin Jansang, the dreaded warlord of the "Black Gobi." Haslund and companions journey across the Gobi desert by camel caravan; are kidnapped and held for ransom; witness initiation into Shamanic societies; meet reincarnated warlords; and experience the violent birth of "modern" Mongolia.
358 Pages. 6x9 Paperback. Illustrated. $18.95. Code: MGM

PROJECT MK-ULTRA
AND MIND CONTROL TECHNOLOGY
By Axel Balthazar

This book is a compilation of the government's documentation on MK-Ultra, the CIA's mind control experimentation on unwitting human subjects, as well as over 150 patents pertaining to artificial telepathy (voice-to-skull technology), behavior modification through radio frequencies, directed energy weapons, electronic monitoring, implantable nanotechnology, brain wave manipulation, nervous system manipulation, neuroweapons, psychological warfare, satellite terrorism, subliminal messaging, and more. A must-have reference guide for targeted individuals and anyone interested in the subject of mind control technology.
384 pages. 7x10 Paperback. Illustrated. $19.95. Code: PMK

LIQUID CONSPIRACY 2:
The CIA, MI6 & Big Pharma's War on Psychedelics
By Xaviant Haze

Underground author Xaviant Haze looks into the CIA and its use of LSD as a mind control drug; at one point every CIA officer had to take the drug and endure mind control tests and interrogations to see if the drug worked as a "truth serum." Chapters include: The Pioneers of Psychedelia; The United Kingdom Mellows Out: The MI5, MDMA and LSD; Taking it to the Streets: LSD becomes Acid; Great Works of Art Inspired and Influenced by Acid; Scapolamine: The CIA's Ultimate Truth Serum; Mind Control, the Death of Music and the Meltdown of the Masses; Big Pharma's War on Psychedelics; The Healing Powers of Psychedelic Medicine; tons more.
240 pages. 6x9 Paperback. Illustrated. $19.95. Code: LQC2

ORDER FORM

One Adventure Place
P.O. Box 74
Kempton, Illinois 60946
United States of America
Tel.: 815-253-6390 • Fax: 815-253-6300
Email: auphq@frontiernet.net
http://www.adventuresunlimitedpress.com

ORDERING INSTRUCTIONS

✓ Remit by USD$ Check, Money Order or Credit Card

✓ Visa, Master Card, Discover & AmEx Accepted

✓ Paypal Payments Can Be Made To:

    info@wexclub.com

✓ Prices May Change Without Notice

✓ 10% Discount for 3 or More Items

SHIPPING CHARGES

United States

✓ POSTAL BOOK RATE

✓ Postal Book Rate { $4.50 First Item / 50¢ Each Additional Item

✓ Priority Mail { $7.00 First Item / $2.00 Each Additional Item

✓ UPS { $9.00 First Item (Minimum 5 Books) / $1.50 Each Additional Item

NOTE: UPS Delivery Available to Mainland USA Only

Canada

✓ Postal Air Mail { $19.00 First Item / $3.00 Each Additional Item

✓ Personal Checks or Bank Drafts MUST BE

US$ and Drawn on a US Bank

✓ Canadian Postal Money Orders OK

✓ Payment MUST BE US$

All Other Countries

✓ Sorry, No Surface Delivery!

✓ Postal Air Mail { $19.00 First Item / $7.00 Each Additional Item

✓ Checks and Money Orders MUST BE US$
and Drawn on a US Bank or branch.

✓ Paypal Payments Can Be Made in US$ To:
info@wexclub.com

SPECIAL NOTES

✓ RETAILERS: Standard Discounts Available

✓ BACKORDERS: We Backorder all Out-of-Stock Items Unless Otherwise Requested

✓ PRO FORMA INVOICES: Available on Request

✓ DVD Return Policy: Replace defective DVDs only

ORDER ONLINE AT: www.adventuresunlimitedpress.com

**10% Discount When You Order
3 or More Items!**

Please check: ✓

☐ This is my first order   ☐ I have ordered before

Name			
Address			
City			
State/Province		Postal Code	
Country			
Phone: Day		Evening	
Fax		Email	

Item Code	Item Description	Qty	Total

Please check: ✓

Subtotal ▶	
Less Discount-10% for 3 or more items ▶	
☐ Postal-Surface Balance ▶	
☐ Postal-Air Mail Illinois Residents 6.25% Sales Tax ▶	
(Priority in USA) Previous Credit ▶	
☐ UPS Shipping ▶	
(Mainland USA only) Total (check/MO in USD$ only) ▶	

☐ Visa/MasterCard/Discover/American Express

Card Number:

Expiration Date: Security Code:

✓ SEND A CATALOG TO A FRIEND: